T0283985

Lucio Urtubia

TO ROB
A BANK
IS AN
HONOR

Lucio Urtubia

TO ROB
A BANK
IS AN
HONOR

TRANSLATED BY PAUL SHARKEY
FOREWORD BY PHILIP RUFF

To Rob a Bank is an Honor

© 2024 Lucio Urtubia
Translation © 2024 Paul Sharkey
Introduction © 2024 Philip Ruff
Prologue © Francisco Rodriguez de Lecea
This edition 2024 © AK Press
ISBN: 978-1-84935-578-0 (paper)
ISBN: 978-1-84935-579-7 (e-book)
Library of Congress Control Number: 2024939491

AK Press
370 Ryan Ave. #100
Chico, CA 95973
www.akpress.org
akpress@akpress.org

AK Press
33 Tower St.
Edinburgh EH6 7BN
Scotland
www.akuk.com
akuk@akpress.org

The above addresses would be delighted to provide you with the latest AK Press distribution catalog, which features books, pamphlets, zines, and stylish apparel published
and/or distributed by AK Press. Alternatively, visit our websites for the complete
catalog, latest news, and secure ordering.

Originally published as *La revolución por el tejado* (2008) by Txalaparta, this edition was
published by permission

Cover design by Crisis
Cover photo supplied by Txalaparta

Printed in the USA on acid-free paper

CONTENTS

Foreword

LUCIO URTUBIA JIMÉNEZ

Basque anarchist and bricklayer. Born February 18, 1931, in Cascante, Navarra–died July 18, 2020, in Paris, France.

Lucio, the biographical film about Lucio Urtubia, turned the man into a legend, a sort of anarchist Robin Hood, but until the age of fifty, Lucio spent most of his time trying to keep out of the spotlight.[1] The spectacular conclusion to his life of crime in 1981, with the Citibank forgery trial, was a pyrrhic victory for the prosecution, but—against all odds—Lucio was the real winner.

Lucio was many things to many people. Radical theatre director Albert Boadella, whose dramatic escape from under the noses of the Spanish police in 1977 was organized by Lucio, dubbed him "a Quixote who tilted, not at windmills, but at real giants." French counter-terrorist cop Paul Barril cast Lucio as a dangerous criminal mastermind who pulled the strings of a vast international anarchist conspiracy. And the examining magistrate who presided over the Citibank case, Louis Joinet, had Lucio over for dinner—twice! To Stuart Christie, Lucio was "a man of generous spirit who valued freedom and justice above all else, even above his own life."

Growing up in the brutal poverty of Franco's Spain, Lucio was instinctively drawn towards the twin-flames of rebellion and crime, which became the leitmotif of his life and propelled him into the ranks of the anti-Franco resistance. At the age of seventeen, he became a smuggler. Conscripted into the army, he wrangled himself a cushy job in the canteen and began selling off the contents of the army stores on the black market of Logrono. Fortuitously he was on leave in August 1954 when his thievery was discovered. He promptly deserted and moved to Paris to live with his sister.

---

1   *Lucio*, directed by Aitor Arregi and Jose Mari Goenaga (Spain: Irusoin, 2007).

1

Lucio found work as a bricklayer, and one day he fell into conversation with a Catalan workmate. While discussing politics, Lucio said he considered himself a "Communist," because the Communists were against Franco. His friend laughed and told him, "You are an anarchist!" The Catalan gave Lucio a copy of *Solidaridad Obrera* and later introduced him to the CNT local in Paris. Lucio never actually joined the CNT, but he was accepted into Juventudes Libertarias (FIJL, the Libertarian Youth).

By his own account, the turning point in Lucio's life came in late 1958, when he was asked to look after the famous expropriator Francisco Sabaté, El Quico. Lucio says Sabaté stayed with him for several weeks; that he persuaded Sabaté to surrender to the French police to avoid extradition to Spain; and that before going to prison Sabaté gave him his guns to take care of (a pistol and a Thompson sub-machine gun). The story goes that Lucio put the guns to good use by taking part in several robberies before Sabaté left France. In the film *Lucio* he says the experience was not what he imagined it would be, and that every time he pointed a gun at a bank employee, he wanted to wet himself: "I wasn't made to rob banks. We did it because there was no other bloody option. It was the only means the anarchists had." The money from the robberies went to the anti-Franco resistance inside Spain.

Alas, oral history doesn't always match the facts. Things get changed in the telling over time. Dates and sequences of events fall out of kilter. And Lucio never let the facts get in the way of a good story. Francisco Sabaté was actually arrested in Céret in the south of France, on November 12, 1957, and served six months in prison in Perpignan and Montpellier. A Spanish request for extradition was refused by the French government and Sabaté was released from prison on May 12, 1958. Germinal Garcia was a militant of the FIJL and CNT in Paris during 1950s and 1960s, and his apartment was often a safe haven for Sabaté. In the film *Lucio*, Germinal is skeptical about Lucio's claims: "Who knows, with Francisco Sabaté, there was a question mark . . ." Any association between Francisco Sabaté and Lucio ended abruptly on January 5, 1960, when Sabaté and four comrades walked into an ambush on the Spanish border and were all killed. The manner of their deaths, the result of betrayal, had a strong effect on Lucio, who from then on trusted nobody and based his future activities on a strict need-to-know basis.

Carried away by the overthrow of the Cuban dictator Batista, Lucio and several other Spanish anarchists approached the Cuban embassy in Paris seeking material support for the anti-Franco resistance in Spain, all to no avail. Fidel Castro, whom Lucio subsequently lambasted as the "devil incarnate," was more interested in cultivating diplomatic relations with the fascist Caudillo. Lucio's meeting with Che Guevara in 1962, to propose a grand scheme to devalue the American dollar by flooding the world with forged US currency, is dismissed as pure fantasy by Germinal Garcia, "I don't believe it at all!" But the reality was closer to a scene from *Minder*, with Lucio in Arthur Daley-mode pitching his plan to Che during a brief stop-over at Orley airport. Che was not enthusiastic, and Lucio found him "cold." He was later informed that the Cuban government had rejected his proposal.

Lucio found love in Paris in the middle of a riot in May 1968, when he met his French wife, Anne. Their romance produced a daughter, Juliette, on whom Lucio doted. Anne and Lucio set up a print shop to produce anarchist posters and pamphlets, and they surreptitiously brought together a team of people with more specialist skills to produce fake Spanish ID cards and passports, drawing upon the expertise of Laureano Cerrada (who was shot dead in Paris by a Spanish police agent on October 18, 1976). The forging operation blossomed to include documents of other countries, which Lucio supplied to revolutionaries or sold to criminal customers as circumstances decreed. Through all this, Lucio was scrupulous in keeping up his day job as a bricklayer (it was good cover if anyone asked how he supported his family); leaving for work early every morning and spending his evenings at the print shop.

By the 1970s a new generation of resistance had emerged in Spain. The Iberian Liberation Movement (MIL, 1971–1974) was a coalition of anarchists and council communists, which had grown out of the strike movement in the Spanish car industry. Their Autonomous Combat Groups (GAC) robbed banks to finance anti-Franco propaganda, operating with swashbuckling audacity. On one occasion, after the police confiscated a MIL printing press, the MIL simply marched into the police station and took the press back again at gunpoint. On September 22, 1973, MIL activist Salvador Puig Antich was arrested in Barcelona after a shoot-out with police in which one of the cops was killed. Despite widespread international protest Puig Antich was sentenced to death and garrotted at dawn on March

2, 1974. On May 3, 1974, the Groups of International Revolutionary Action (GARI), formed in solidarity with the MIL, kidnapped the Paris representative of the Banco Bilbao, Balthasar Suarez. The kidnappers demanded the release of a hundred political prisoners in Spain (under the Franco government's own laws) and the repayment of part of the CNT funds seized by Franco. Suarez was released unharmed twenty days later, after payment of an undisclosed sum. The moment Suarez was freed, French police arrested nine anarchists in Paris, including Lucio and Anne. All were eventually released on conditional liberty pending trial.

Octavio Alberola was arrested in possession of the ransom money, which sparked bitter recriminations. Lucio had repeatedly warned Octavio to stick to being a spokesperson and not to get directly involved, and he blamed the arrests on Octavio's high profile and the surveillance it naturally attracted. That triggered a series of accusations and counter accusations focused on some of Lucio's less salubrious connections. The argument resulted in a lot of bad blood that never really went away. By the time the Suarez case finally came to court in 1980, Franco had been dead for five years and the moral stature of the kidnapping as an act of antifascist resistance had attracted a lot of public sympathy, even in high places in the French government. After a ten-day trial all the accused were acquitted for lack of evidence.

Lucio was back to his old tricks even before the Suarez case was over, forging documents and accumulating weapons. In 1977, Lucio had the bright idea to create fictitious identities for workers who didn't exist, and his team forged "paychecks" for these people, which were promptly taken to a bank and exchanged for cash. His next idea was to copy genuine books of $100 traveler's checks, but to change the serial numbers so they would not appear on any lost-or-stolen lists. Checks with the identical serial numbers could then be presented simultaneously at multiple banks and all be cashed without arousing suspicion. The crime would only become apparent after the checks had passed through the clearing process. Citibank was chosen as the target because their checks could be cashed all over the world. The operation eventually encompassed revolutionary groups and "ordinary decent criminals" all over Europe, the United States, and Latin America. Citibank lost millions of dollars, their share-price plunged, and in the end, they were forced to ban all checks above the value of $10.

The Citibank fraud went wonderfully until July 1980, when Lucio met an American called Tony Sarro, who said he knew someone who would buy the checks off him for 30 percent of their value. The prospect of easy pickings got the better of Lucio's natural caution. When the day came to do the deal, Lucio met Tony at a table outside the famous café Les Deux Magots in the Saint-Germain-des-Prés area of Paris. As soon as Lucio sat down, cops appeared from all directions, and he was led away in handcuffs. Tony was an agent working for the French police. Lucio was released pending trial, but in July 1981 he received a summons to appear in another court case. A man had been arrested with false documents that he claimed had been given to him by Lucio. Enraged, Lucio wrote a long letter to the judge, refusing to attend and explaining his reasons for declining the invitation. He promptly disappeared and went on the run, with false ID papers in the name of "Fermin Gil Munarriz." On October 9, 1981, he was finally arrested on the street.

"A bricklayer may only be a bricklayer," Lucio says in the film, "but he can have friends in high places." Roland Dumas, a former French Foreign Minister, agreed to defend Lucio in the Citibank trial. When he appeared in court Lucio was released by the judge on conditional liberty. Between the first and second hearing, Citibank got a phone call from an advisor of the French Prime Minster. The French government had reached the conclusion that a trial was "detrimental to France," and Citibank was told to negotiate a deal directly with Lucio for the surrender of the printing plates and remaining checks, and to drop all charges against him, in return for his promise to stop the forgery operation. With typical chutzpah Lucio demanded of Citibank that they also pay him to stop, otherwise the fraud would continue even if he went back to prison. Citibank agreed to everything.

A lawyer delivered the plates and checks to Citibank officials in a Paris hotel room, and was handed a case containing a large sum of cash. Lucio received a derisory six months in prison for forgery. Citibank dropped all other charges. Lucio went back to bricklaying.

In 1996, Lucio renovated a derelict building on Rue des Cascades in the Belleville area of Paris and opened it up as Espace Louise Michel (named in honor of the famous Paris Communard and anarchist), to serve as a cultural space for anarchists and anti-establishment projects. In 2007 he came to London for the screening of the film *Lucio* at the Anarchist Bookfair.

Lucio Urtubia was a rare individual who lived life according to his own rules and defied authority at every opportunity. Lucio's memoir, *To Rob a Bank is an Honor*, is a good yarn. Not all his exploits were exactly as he portrayed them, but he did make an immense contribution to the Spanish resistance and to the ongoing cause of anarchism. In a reflective moment during an interview for *Vice*, Lucio told Alex Orma, "I used to spend a lot of time with Jean-Marc Rouillan, who was responsible for the French revolutionary group Direct Action. He has spent 28 years in jail. We're very good friends and I'm very fond of him, but I'm fed up with all his 'armed struggle' nonsense. We don't need anyone to lecture us on what we must or mustn't do. When the time comes, everyone will act as they see fit. These days, we must be intelligent above all else . . . I don't regret anything at all. If I had to start my life all over again, I would do everything the same way. One thing I am particularly proud of is standing up to a judge and saying, 'Yes, Sir, I'm an anarchist because I believe in anarchy.'"[2]

History should mark his passing kindly.

Philip Ruff

Anarchist historian Philip Ruff was an active member of the Black Flag group and Anarchist Black Cross during the 1970s and 1980s. He was first introduced to Lucio Urtubia and his wife Anne at their home in Paris in 1975, and last spoke to Lucio in London in 2007. Philip is the author of *A Towering Flame: The Life & Times of the Elusive Latvian Anarchist Peter the Painter* (London: Breviary Stuff, 2019). This foreword is adapted from Philip's obituary of Lucio, first published by Freedom Press, August 11, 2020.

---

2   Alex Orma, "Life Advice from Spain's Real Life Robin Hood," *Vice*, May 28, 2014, https://www.vice.com/en/article/xd38dn/an-interview-with-the-anarchist-Lucio-Urtubia-Jimenez#.

Prologue

LUCIO'S SECRET

by Francisco Rodriguez de Lecea

I never met Lucio Urtubia in the flesh until January 9, 2007. That was the day he stepped off the Paris train in Barcelona at eight o'clock in the morning and called me from the station. "What's your address?" he asked. "I'll grab a taxi and pop over; we'll be on your doorstep in ten minutes."

He didn't even know where I lived. He knew me only as the translator of his biography, published in 2001 by Ediciones B; he had got my number from the publishers and phoned me a couple of times to alert me to some minor errors in the French edition. He came away with the impression that I was a real pro, and I that Lucio was not a man to beat about the bush when it came to getting what he wanted.

The moment I set eyes on him I recognized him straight away from the unmistakable stocky physique: and the beret, the grey jumper and the corduroys were giveaways too. The only difference from the picture of him I had in my head was his height; he was somewhat shorter than me whereas I had been convinced that I was about to come face to face with a giant.

We dropped into a coffee shop for breakfast, and he placed a bulky package in my hands: books, magazines, photocopied articles, photos, and a 264-page manuscript written in tiny letters in ballpoint pen with hardly any margins, unpunctuated and unparagraphed, devoid of syntax and with addenda on the back of many pages. Lucio asked me if I could take charge of the text and knock it into shape.

"I'm no writer," he explained simply.

"What's it about?" I asked him and he made a vague gesture.

"My life, my way of thinking, the lives of others. Everything, really."

I read the opening sentence: "I shall do all in my power to convey and explain my life . . . " Slowly, I leafed through the text: Lucio had written it

7

the way he talks, complete with repetitions and continually digressing to chase up an idea or somebody whose path crossed with his along the way; some of the words were actually in the French; he had "*entreprise*" instead of *empresa*, or "*cour*" instead of *tribunal*. But I was also struck by a number of stunningly blunt expressions as if carved from granite. This was a style worth the effort of trying to retain.

I had other work on my plate, but it never even entered my mind to tell him that there was no way I could take all this on. Sometimes people hit it off almost automatically and a twenty-four day is enough for many of things, if the right effort is put into them. We never mentioned anything about contracts or costs, let alone terms. There was only one condition: the time frame. Four or five months, perhaps more, for I might need to beef up certain sections and incorporate further episodes. Lucio raised no objection to any of it. "You're the expert," he said.

I had planned a trip to Paris with Carmen, my wife, to mark our wedding anniversary. I called Lucio to tell him that I would use this opportunity to put a list of queries and suggestions to him and hand over a hundred pages of the book already knocked into shape.

"I'll let you know where we're staying just as soon as I can. We're on the look-out for a cheap apartment."

"What do you mean, 'apartment'?" he replied. "There's more than enough room here. Come to my place and we can sort ourselves out."

Which is how easy things can be where Lucio is concerned. Carmen and I were his guests on the top floor of the Espace Louise Michel, and we found that Lucio's home is always open to all-comers, that the locals drop in at all hours to say hello, without a second thought. One day there was a meeting to do with the prisoners, as advertised with posters in the streets of the neighborhood, and the hall at the Espace filled with people. They screened a filmed interview with a female Action Directe activist who had been released on health grounds and who was to pass away shortly afterward. At that meeting we made the acquaintance of Héliette Besse, fairy godmother to the Action Directe prisoners, a woman whose utter selflessness is stunning. She doesn't give a damn about her clothes, coiffure, or appearance; she lives life through twinkling eyes awash with compassion and through her humble and direct talking.

Right there in the Rue des Cascades and in neighboring streets we had occasion to glimpse the gangs of teenagers that Lucio describes in his book, leaning with their backs against the walls, smoking and, as often as not, spitting on the ground; every one of them wore a "hoodie" and had his hands thrust into his jacket pockets. Whenever we passed them, they would call out, "OK, *Lucho*?" And Lucio would grunt an answer, "OK."

On the Thursday night Lucio took us out to dinner in a bistro near the Belleville gardens. We were not yet inside when the owner and the cook came racing out into the street to welcome him. As we were eating, a huge performer, Riton-la-Manivelle, was setting up at the back of the room with a mini organ. He distributed songbooks containing some lyrics and then launched into an endless repertoire . . . Piaf, Ferré, Brel, Brassens, Mouloudji, Gainsbourg, "Le Chant des partisans" and "L'Affiche rouge," cranking the handle of the organ and singing bawdy songs and anthems to encourage us to dance. We customers mingled as if we had known one another all our lives. Lucio was singing along in his booming voice, and Carmen and I did likewise with the ones we knew. It was a long and animated evening and as we left, drinking in the panoramic view of Paris from the heights of Belleville, Lucio and I competed as we duetted on a half-remembered Italian anarchist song about Caserio, the guy who stabbed the French president Carnot in Lyon. To Lucio, songs are always rather special; he says so repeatedly in his book, beginning with the ones he used to sing with the family out in the open air outside their home in Cascante during summer nights back in the 1940s.

Carmen and I visited Cascante in early May 2007, by which point the revamping of the book was well advanced. We had both spent many hours on the task and we used to allude to it with one of Lucio's sayings: "It's not work, it's pleasure." In Cascante we met Lucio's three sisters—Satur, Ángeles, and Pili—some cousins, neighbors, friends, and acquaintances. We chatted and, above all, listened to tales of the old days and the civil war. Without rancor, as Lucio preaches: but without forgetting.

And there was time for a few surprises: I shall not mention the biggest of them, as it is not my place so to do, but I was taken aback to see my maternal surname over a very interesting cultural club in town . . . Lecea, or Leitsea ("The Cave").

And as luck would have it, outside the gates of the priceless Cistercian monastery in Tulebras, three kilometers from Cascante, we bumped into Eulalia Echauz, the great eighty-five-year-old poetess, who was kind enough and in good enough form to recite some of her poetry for us.

There was also time to discuss the outcome of the second round of the French presidential elections which had just taken place. Little did we suspect that Bernard Kouchner, fulsomely praised in a number of places in the book, would, within days, become, objectively speaking, a minister for the right, in a personal decision that was greeted by Lucio with stoicism ("Closeness to power always corrupts") and with splendid, fiery indignation by Anne Urtubia, a diehard '68er (by which I mean that the spirit of May '68 lives in her still).

From Cascante, we took a trip over to Valcarlos; we strolled through the Pekotxea *barrio* and took photos outside what had once been the home of Lucio's older brother, Alfonso, and we skipped across the border at Arnegi via one of the bridges spanning the river Gave. These days the customs post is all boarded up and unmanned, but you can still get a sense of what it must have been in days gone by; a spot with its back turned to two countries, a no-man's-land, a regular mitral valve sluicing the rich blood of contraband from auricle to ventricle and back again. The younger Lucio's starry eyes must have drunk in all the stark contrasts there of an Eden-like landscape torn in tow by a fiction, a frontier, something invisible and untouchable, but which has a telling effect on a community that still communicates in Basque but which is governed by different laws and learns Spanish or French at school, depending on whether it is on this side or the other of the invisible line. A fiction that can pit rifle-carrying youngsters from one side against rifle-carrying youngsters from the other, in the service of faraway and incomprehensible interests. A fiction that, to someone, can represent a very real danger or a haven, the law or outlawry, life or death.

To the young Lucio, Valcarlos was a school filled with practical examples and personal guides to behavior. One of his favorite sayings is, "I believe in nothing, but I believe in everything," may owe its birth to careful observation of life in that microcosm.

The reader is free to make of this uncategorisable book what he will: very free-flowing memoirs, a novel that Baroja would have entitled "*Urtubia the Adventurer*," or even a highly unconventional self-help manual. It is also the impassioned inside story of an unequal war waged by a genuine modern-day Robin Hood from the Sherwood Forest of Lucio's thousand safehouses and hideouts around Paris as he robs the rich and helps the needy: in the latter case the story comes to an exemplary conclusion, with a solemn peace treaty, the sort signed between great powers.

But above all else, what must be seen in these pages is a living document that turns the historical spotlight on to a specific time and place and recounts a singular life story which is at the same time—as all human lives are—the story of lots of lives.

"I am no more than anybody else," Lucio says several times in the book. True, he is not, but his presence and the shadow he cast down through the years with his extraordinary activities have enthralled friend and foe alike. Let me just cite three telling examples: theater director Albert Boadella said that Lucio "is a Quixote that tilted, not at windmills, but at real giants"; gendarme Captain Paul Barril describes him as a sort of Count of Montecristo; and magistrate Louis Joinet scandalized Barril by being even more fulsome in his praises "Lucio represents everything I would love to have been."

Not that any of these statements should be taken literally without further ado. To take the last one first, Joinet's intention no doubt was to say that he would love to have been a peasant, deserter, smuggler, bricklayer, bank-robber, counterfeiter, or all these things together. I shall explain anon what it appears to me he was trying to convey with those words, if I have construed them correctly.

To Barril, Lucio was the brains pulling the strings of a criminal organization with international ramifications; like Montecristo, the hero of Alexandre Dumas's novel, Lucio had access to infinite wealth for his purposes, to the fabled "Lucio's treasure," the "CNT war chest," made up of gold, strong currencies, and prime works of art. With other activists drawn from several countries, he set about promoting and funding terrorism and agitation against the established order around the globe. Barril does not believe in Lucio's cement-stained hands and reckons that his humble demeanor in front of the judges and prosecution counsel was as phony as the clumsy French in which he spoke: all this he views as simply "a clever disguise." Barril speaks about Lucio with fear and respect, as if he were one of the biggest and most dangerous criminals he has encountered during his career: yet he has it seriously wrong when he puts a figure on the activities of Lucio's gang and the funding to which it had access and we are entitled to suspect that for him to make such play of the strength of his foe, his real purpose might be to hype his own merits.

Albert Boadella's comparison of Lucio and Don Quixote is so spot on, so suggestive that it has been taken up by dozens of reporters and sprinkled through their interviews or reviews of Bernard Thomas's book about Lucio. But the comparison is as polished as it is bereft of substance. When all is said and done, Don Quixote was a nutcase and a loner, refused to see that the golden age of his dreams was no longer with us and failed; whereas Lucio was never crazy, never alone, was able to tailor his actions to whatever the technological society required, and was a success, for a time at any rate.

Which brings me back to Louis Joinet's opinion, because, as I see it, it encapsulates Lucio's secret, the key to the fascination he holds for those who know him. These days Joinet is first advocate-general with the Court of Cassation and a man who wears the toga of France's No 2 magistrate with a personal humility, freedom of thought and sense of humor that are beyond compare. An anecdote will suffice to describe him, and the reader will find this inside the book: he was the man who invited Lucio to dine with him, first in Matignon, the prime ministerial residence, and later at the Elysee, the presidential palace; and he did so out of friendship, but also as a personal reminder of on whose behalf he wields his power and in whose service those who rule should be.

What is it that is missing from the life of Louis Joinet, the complete, acknowledged public figure, and which he finds in the life of Lucio Urtubia? Freedom, I think. Freedom is a word often bandied around in today's world, but nearly always misused. There are those who invoke freedom just to sink into drug addiction, those who invoke religious freedom to stake a claim to privilege for a single religion. Lucio has a lofty, militant, demanding conception of freedom: in order to defend the chance to be free one has to be prepared to lose one's freedom, it says somewhere in the book. To Lucio, freedom is the blunt refusal to obey some arbitrary authority, to earn one's independence through the harsh practice of one's trade, being mindful of solidarity with the dispossessed, and being open-handed in giving and taking the wealth that life places in our hands. In short, to quote from the anarchist dictionary, managing one's own life. Without fail, without complacency, without condescension, and without compromise.

Such inner freedom is not easily earned, but Lucio has pulled it off. Step by step, this book explains how he did it. So let me bid you welcome, dear reader, to the life of Lucio and to his secret. Welcome to utopia.

INTRODUCTION

My life, many lives

I shall do all in my power to convey and explain my life, a long life, filled with other lives that I have shared with many other people. The entire process has, bit by bit, made me what I humbly am: a man who is happy but discontent.

These many lives of mine are awash with adventures and a great number of jobs and physical and mental exertions that have given me a profound appreciation of small pleasures and major ones, and equipped me to recognize how profoundly valuable they are in our lives.

And this is what brings me to analyze my performance throughout my life, most especially my deeds, some of them impromptu and others deliberate. Why impromptu? Because they occur quite unexpectedly, and when performed, bring equally unexpected outcomes; acts of lunacy, miracles, and utopias, all readily explicable, but very definite and very real.

I bear no ill will for the arrests and imprisonments I have had to endure since I was a boy, and I usually tell myself that these mishaps too have played their part in making me what I am. If I had any hate inside me, I wouldn't be able to live with myself. My foundations are planted in experience, as well as in everything that is and has been around me: what lives alongside us and keeps us alive.

The value of utopia

We are like a petrol-driven engine: the petrol runs out and we grind to a halt. Utopia is vital to us, these days more than ever. If we are to move forward, we have to discard everything that makes us "settle" for what we already are, and we must seek out what is different, that which is not the same. Everything that is the same is just more of the same. It is boring to live without searching for the new and the different; there is no value to one's plans. Some may like to live this way, but not me.

That sort of life is like the life what we see in the movies; at first it looks like a life, but it isn't. We must look beyond the movies for the truth.

At first sight, utopian truth looks unbelievable, but it exists and is achievable. But how are we going to convince those who are blind and will not see? And how stunningly beautiful will it be for one whose eyes have been sightless for many years.

Part of intelligence is patience, and we have to have it and we have to exercise it, even to mark time. Running will not get you where you're going any faster, and if you stop, you will never get there. If you don't walk you will not get there at all. But sometimes you get there, even without breaking into a run. Nothing can be taken as ordained, and nothing is certain. That's how life is; you should never stop moving. If you do, it is all over.

Everything we do in life is necessary and is part of a gear mechanism that keeps us rolling onwards, ever onwards. When are we right? If not today, tomorrow. We can never be a hundred per cent right, and that is something we should always keep in mind.

Lucky to be poor

I tell myself that it was a blessing that I was born poor. Where would I have ended up if things been otherwise? What would become of my freedom and the freedom of others? I affirm my freedom, I believe in my freedom, because it involves a struggle to move beyond the self. Everything is struggle and without it one gets nowhere. Pity those who have are born with money, for there is nothing left for them to do, nothing to discover. Those who have "made it" have nothing to prove and are already "there," which is their misfortune. Whereas those of us who are eager to move on and discover fresh horizons find ourselves obliged to search within for something we didn't know was there—strength, the urge to move on, to pick ourselves up or to start all over again. We must crave and suffer, or resign ourselves to pressing on without really being.

My good fortune and my wealth reside in what I have lacked, in this enduring eagerness to "make it," or quite simply the appetite for life. But there is a price to be paid for life. Where should we get what we need to pay the price of existence? I say it is from within ourselves, from our conviction and determination. Someone bereft of the requisite self-belief and faith in the possibility of his moving on and making progress in life, without ever allowing it to overwhelm him, is nothing.

Living alongside everybody else

I urge my friends and family, the members of my own class, to dare to *be* because they have what they need, the essentials moving forward. This potential means nothing if opportunities aren't seized. All the wealth in the world is useless unless put to work. If we mean to be, we will either be, along with everybody else, with the world, or we will not be at all. One cannot exist if a half is missing.

To relent in the common thrust is to show a lack of respect for others. Progress can only come through those who have the wherewithal to devise solutions. You cannot draw upon what you don't have, just as you cannot give what you don't have. Our standards of living have improved greatly, it's true, but at the same time we have had a hand in the sinking of other countries and continents. In the past, this was not something we felt much remorse about. That was the way of the world, and the looting of poorer nations was part of it. It's the rationale of international capitalism, of course, but I think there was another factor that was very significant—the nationalism, or rather, nationalisms, which prompted countries to rouse themselves and move on, albeit by sending others to the bottom.

We all know individuals who are different, who behave decently and of these we say they're a good person. In their case the scale tilts in the direction of the positive and the good. Collectively, the common person sometimes behaves well and in an intelligent way as an individual, but many others do not. In collective affairs, even the person who behaves decently as an individual can throw his weight behind selfish behavior at odds with his own day-to-day conduct. The selfishness of nations is a poisonous idea, backed by people who mean well; but we need to know that we shall only make real progress when we all move on together, the wealthy countries and the poor ones.

My way of thinking

Let me say a little more about how I think. As a libertarian, I believe the idea of *contestation* is necessary if our intelligence is to advance. Libertarian ideas stand for honest knowledge and a behavior free from corruption. That and much more besides. Libertarian thinking is needed, and it is our good fortune that we have it to rely on. We have immense resources we can call upon and we must know how to harness them. Everything depends on how we do so. Possession is indispensable, but there is no point in it unless whatever one has is put to good use, unless we know how to use it.

As an individual, I stand by my own self. When we are part of an organization we change and cease to be what we once were. It would be very interesting to know the reasons why people join certain organizations or parties, religions included. I believe the keynote of existence is doing right by one's neighbor. Such solidarity is excellent for every *individual* because it is also excellent for *everybody*. "Give and ye shall receive": my own experience has confirmed this.

However, it doesn't suit me to belong to what purports to be a serious organization, and it is not for me. Time and again, I have observed that people who do nothing and who give nothing, are at the front of the line when the jobs are being handed out. Particularly in France, history shows us that intelligence is not one of the qualifications required for the presidency.

We are what little we each are, we understand nothing and can explain nothing. All we have is something inside ourselves: let's call it courage or ignorance. It is that something that makes us be and believe in our being. Nothing sits still; the Earth moves on, and individuals and social classes do too. But some move on in the direction of progress and others in the opposite direction, sliding backward.

Contrary to the very widespread dictum, you do not always reap what you sow. First-hand experience has taught me that much, but, ultimately, having had thousands of agents of repression searching for me "by land, sea, and air," to borrow an expression from one very important and well-known police officer, I regard all the exertions and suffering I have experienced to date as worth it. Perhaps my own life can serve as a very modest proof that libertarian ideas live on and are life enhancing.

It may well be that suffering and hard times make us more appreciative of life. The only certainty in life is that we lack what we need. I have known what is to want for food, clothing, and above all schooling, which is vital. We knew that everything we didn't have was out there and that others had access to it. Given that the population of this world is so great, why are we not producing and distributing enough of what we need?

My life does not belong to me alone

I could not have done everything that I did by myself, and I wouldn't want anyone to believe I had. I was never alone; there were always lots of people at my side, working and lending a helping hand. This is why I am so insistent that nothing in my life, nothing of what I have lived through, is mine or my own exclusive property. It is common property, belonging especially to my libertarian friends, to the workers who, through their toil, have acquired the essential know-how needed to create and make. Nothing is exclusively mine; it all belongs to all of us. And as you can see when you read my words, I had very little schooling, which is why I never had the opportunity to learn more or be anything other than what I am. This blind spot may have kept me in the ignorance I needed in order to carry out certain deeds. This is my personal feeling, but I am convinced that the only thing that really keeps us going in life is culture and education, no matter how many objections we might raise about the education given to us. I can own what I did, but I can't defend it. Like many others like me, everything I did sprang from the poverty in which I lived and from the yearning to break free of it. To this day I don't think I ever had any religious beliefs, but I have often asked myself why that is. And nothing and nobody has come up with any answer for me.

If I had been smarter, I wouldn't have thrown myself into the ventures that I have, or those that I've had a hand in. All of this brings to mind the utopian deeds impossible to explain but that have been done and experienced by the poor. Intellectuals very often try to explain away what I call the inexplicable, which makes me think that we actually know very little and that we should not say much unless we are very sure of what we are talking about. Why do I say that? Because intellectuals offer us thousands of different explanations and make mistakes by the thousands. I have read of some important people trying to explain me away and I know they have it wrong: and if any two them offer an explanation, one explanation is different from the other and each explanation carries its own mistakes.

Of my family or friends—some made through my work and others through my day-to-day living—I want to say that they have all been helpful to me and that they have all believed in me. Naturally, they have had their moments of doubt or of being kept in the dark, but that has never stopped them from believing in me.

Life is short, all too short, if you consider how much of it we spend asleep. Today, at the age of seventy-six, I don't envy anybody anything. I want greater justice for all, and greater understanding as well. Know this: if you give, you shall receive. If I had to start my life all over again, I would do pretty much the same as I have done.

So let me try to explain my life, which has been rich in other lives, rich in adventures, hard work, and pleasures. My deeds done successfully, utopian deeds, inexplicable to some extent, sometimes crackpot acts, unbelievable but true: my many arrests and periods behind bars, from boyhood onward, for sometimes trivial matters, and my struggle against all established systems, even should they purport to be socialist.

PART ONE

WHERE I COME FROM AND WHO I AM

My grandparents

My paternal grandfather, Doroteo Urtubia, was a peasant with a powerful physique, and he was a great worker: I will always remember his harvester's hands. He was a faithful Carlist as the saying goes, a Carlist of the purest stripe, and he passed on his Carlist ideas to his three sons, Tomás, Amadeo, and Bautista. Carlism was never revolutionary but it did stand for certain values, among them separation, and indeed independence from Castile. The Urtubias as a family had made a name for themselves centuries ago as champions of Navarra, back in the days when Navarra stretched as far as Bordeaux, Burgos, and Soria. Remember that long before France and Spain existed as nations, there was a kingdom of Navarra, or so the historians tell us.

My grandfather Doroteo was a religious man but no fanatic. He would attend Mass every Sunday and took communion once or twice a year. He had lots of friends, and every Sunday he would lunch with them in the taverns. In those days, virtually all his friends were of the Carlist persuasion. Nobody interfered with anybody else and there was great respect for the Church.

My grandfather's cronies were all working men, some of them smallholders and others day laborers or peasants. No well-to-do farmer ever sat in on their lunches or get-togethers. Respectable people did not mix with working men, with poorer people.

I remember my grandfather Doroteo very well, for when the civil war broke out our entire family moved in with him. He showed that he loved his grandchildren to the point of distraction.

Neither Uncle Tomás nor Uncle Bautista had any children, and our moving in with grandfather engendered some misgivings and annoyance. But it should be remembered that moving in with grandfather may have saved the lives of my father and mother.

Though he wasn't one to meddle in other people's affairs, my grandfather was still a Carlist: my two uncles and my father had once been Carlists too, but they had gone socialist, especially my father, Cascante's deputy mayor, after he was appointed secretary of the UGT union. Uncle Bautista was appointed a corporal of the guard under the republic. Uncle Tomás was always apolitical.

For his part, my maternal grandfather Claudio Martínez was steward to one of the wealthiest families in Cascante in those days, a family with a great holding in lands and houses in the village alone, and a string of mules and horses used for the ploughing and farmwork, plus an olive oil press, or *trujal*, and massive cellars. The owner of all these assets was one Martín Guelbenzu, but my grandfather and my mother's entire family referred to him as *Señor Amo* (Mr. Boss).

Not only was Señor Amo an estate-owner; he stood for election to the *Diputación* on the Liberal ticket. It was commonly believed that Liberal politics were more forward-looking than Carlist politics, but the fact of the matter is that, between them, the two sides owned the bulk of the wealth in the village and all of it was untouchable. The distribution of ownership had been virtually unchanged for several centuries and what few families owned the estates were all, or almost all, intermarried with one another.

Grandfather Claudio used to visit the nearby villages of Corella, Fitero, Cintruénigo, Castejón, and the like by horse and cart, carrying with him cash and a commission to buy up votes for the Liberal candidate, paid for either in cash or in kind, with a sackful of beans, say. For this reason, Grandfather Claudio was often spoken of within my mother's family as being an "honest" man, an example to all.

Grandfather Claudio had two male children plus my mother. Uncle Elías was very rightwing and Uncle Santiago a republican, but they both grew up under the spell of Señor Amo.

In those days, grandparents and grandchildren lived with one another, and our grandparents would pass history on to us. Love was the same as it is these days, but grandparents tended to die at home in the company of their sons and daughters. These days they pass away, dumped by their families in homes and poorhouses. Take it from me, prison is preferable to the poorhouse: I speak from experience.

My mother

I only wish I was a good writer! Maybe then I might set down the praises my mother, Asunción, deserves to have showered upon her. What I am about to say about her in particular is equally applicable to many another woman from those times. They all deserve praise for everything they did for us, in which the social rank, wealth, or poverty of each of them, or their understanding or intelligence, made not one bit of a difference.

What do I remember of my mother? She had been brought up alongside Don Martín Guelbenzu, her Señor Amo, and been taught by my grandparents Claudio and María to respect the established order and, above all, had been trained in household chores, for she could turn her hand to anything: cooking, sewing, laundry, washing-up and cleaning, not to mention that she brought six children into this world and gave them a particularly religious education. My mother learned all this as a very young girl, largely from what very little schooling she received at the convent school.

That's how things were back then. Boys and girls would attend school up until the age of eight or nine. The children of the poor, I mean, of course. Lots of stories were passed down by grandfathers and grandmothers. Our mothers, the women of those times, had the intellect to absorb everything that was passed on to them and the strength and courage to put it into practice: and they also managed to retain their love for their elderly parents. From early girlhood, it fell to them to look after their grandparents.

When I think back about my mother and the womenfolk of those days, I personally feel very small. Physically, I would not be up to all the very demanding work they carried out on a daily basis, and I believe that lots of us would rather kill ourselves than put up with everything our mothers endured. Why we have kept quiet about all this I have no idea, for it brings honor to us. We males may have gained the upper hand, but I do not think it was because of our superior knowledge or intellect but rather by means of brute force, which may have its part to play but should never outweigh the intelligence and fortitude displayed by women, our mothers.

Before the military revolt, there were four of us children: Alfonso, Satur, Lucio (me), and María. My sister Ángeles was born that very year, in 1936, and my sister Pili some years later.

Through her relationship with my father, my mother grew in self-confidence and acquired certain values. My father had ceased to be a Carlist some time before, largely due to his prison experiences. The prisons back then were a school for anarchists and socialists.

When the civil war broke out, my father suffered a setback because he was the deputy mayor, and my mother watched as her mistresses, the daughters of Señor Amo, alongside whom she had been raised, donned the uniform of the Falange overnight, complete with the Sam Brown belt and arrows insignia. It came as a real shock to her to see people she was fond of, people she thought she knew well, suddenly dress in this uniform. She lost control of her tongue and cursed them for so thoughtlessly changing, and the inevitable followed. Someone told her that the Falangists were on the look-out for her; and the fact is that in Cascante, as well as throughout the Ribera de Navarra, women reputed to be republicans had their heads shaved by the Falange and were force-fed castor oil. They were made to file through the center of town like cattle on a drive, until cramps reduced them to emptying their bowels in public view.

They came looking for her several times, but my mother hid herself behind a pig pen and they were never able to find here. At that time she was in the later stages of pregnancy and carrying my sister Ángeles and, when she emerged from her hiding-place, she was very unwell, and her nerves never quite recovered. She had a tremor in her left arm that lasted the rest of her life, and she was unable to carry anything with that arm.

It was at this point that we all moved in with Grandfather Doroteo in our search for greater protection. My mother gave birth to my two younger sisters in that house, and she began looking after our grandparents, Doroteo and María, as well as the ailing Auntie Gala. My grandparents helped as much as they could, but all Auntie ever did was repeat the same prayers in a loud voice for hours on end.

My mother would get up at six o'clock each morning and light a fire with vine shoots to make ready the stewpot, which would bubble away for hours after she dumped whatever she could find to feed the lot of us. She also stitched my sisters' dresses and the boys' (including my father's) pants and shorts. And, the odd time, made us shoes.

Women back then were miracle workers. Our mothers' work was unbelievable and cannot be comprehended or detailed without something being underestimated. I think it will be a long time before we could match those women for their merits and worthiness. We have forgotten, or in many instances never said a word (or nearly so) about the riches they stored up and their daily exertions. Including trekking out to nearby villages in search of a few pounds of beans or potatoes, or whatever they might find to give to their children. They did everything, everything short of begging for charity.

I must mention that in our homeland women also had won the right to the vote in elections beginning in 1933. French women only gained that right in 1945 even though France too had a leftwing Front (better known as the Popular Front). Though the Front was made up of socialists, communists, and radicals, they did little or nothing to help women. Without bragging, there is no denying that here in Spain ideas of liberation were forever in the air, and there were revolutionary movements and, above all, an anarchist organization, the CNT, which was very important. Although we were poor, and in the Ribera de Navarra where it was very conservative and religious, with a few factories, there were lots of people who subscribed to and fought for the great ideas of progress, socialism, and anarchism.

We might say that back then, in a state poorer and less industrialized than France, ideas inherited from France were put into practice. Especially the ideas of revolutionary syndicalism or anarcho-syndicalism.

My father

My father Amadeo Urtubia, a peasant and worker his whole life, was a Carlist up until his time in prison. A working man of very passionate temperament, he was excused from military service because of flat feet. Like poor people in those days did, he attended school and learned to read and write. His life changed when he became an adult.

One May Day, Cascante's Liberals mounted a demonstration. May first, as we know, was the date chosen for the commemoration of the 1886

Chicago martyrs, the anarchists of the day. The International Working-men's Association (IWA) proclaimed the First of May a day of struggle: it had nothing to do with the feast day it has become. The IWA also spread around the world the demand for a maximum eight-hour workday, with a further eight hours given over to education and the remainder to rest. We all know what the United States is like these days, but back then it was a country growing fat off the sweat of poor immigrants arriving half dead from starvation from all parts of the globe and especially from Europe, in search of a new life and greater opportunity.

On that landmark date for workers, my father, not one to embrace anything emanating from outside the borders of Navarra or from outside Carlism, demonstrated against the Liberals by taking up arms: he walked into the church and started shooting at the Liberals who had sought refuge within, and a number of people were wounded. My father was arrested, tried, and jailed, and spent quite some time in Navarrese prisons. By the time he was released, Carlism was a thing of the past for him. The prisons back then were jam-packed with anarchist and socialist prisoners, which is to say, prisoners drawn from the two organizations that have shaped our history. Most especially the anarchists, for how the socialist leaders have conducted themselves from time to time is common knowledge.

My father entered prison a Carlist and emerged a socialist. Prison was the finest revolutionary school in those days. Every revolutionary did a stint inside. On my father's return to Cascante, they elected him local secretary of the Unión General de Trabajadores/Workers' General Union (UGT). That is the way things were in those days: you had to have been in prison before you could be a somebody. Years later, my father was elected deputy mayor on the Socialist Party ticket. The actual mayor was Señor Romano, a good man, but no revolutionary. Years later that very decent man, a republican, was shot by the fascists, with the connivance of the Church.

As deputy mayor, my father's focus was on bringing a drinkable water supply to each and every house in the village: this was later confirmed to me by rightwing people who had jobs in the town hall. He was never able to see his dream achieved. Years later the water reaching the village was still insufficient to meet the demand and a cart and donkey or mule had to be dispatched to Tudela or to Tarazona to get more.

My father was also in charge of dividing up the garden allotments. As far as I understand, these were in the communal hills: allotments of equal size were parceled out to the poorer peasants so that they might work them, alone or jointly—which was a great boon to the poor. My father refused to accept any allocation until everybody else had been sorted out, so that he wound up with the worst parcel of land: the soil was of very poor quality, and nothing could ever be planted or produced.

One very cold winter, the town council held a potato-based meal for the neediest. It was my father who served the plates. My sister Satur wandered over to see what was going on and my father grew edgy at the sight of her. He gave her a little slap and told her to hurry her along, because he thought: "Here I am, the man in charge of distribution. If people see my daughter come up, they'll think she's here in search of food for the house and that I'm out for my own gain." My father had that sort of pride and, like him, I have it in abundance. But the fact is that, even as my father was out distributing food to others, my mother had nothing to put on our table.

Another time, my father had a difference of opinion in the street with some leftist friends who were very worked up about a priest named Don Victoriano, a nasty piece of work. My father came to his defense and said that he was not going to countenance any criminality and that he was ready to die rather than allow certain violent acts. That very same priest, years later, rose early from his bed to scratch my father's name off the list of those marked down to be shot.

My father also protected from arson or vandalism a seventeenth century altarpiece dedicated to the much venerated and revered Saint Bernard of Clairvaux in the church in Tulebras, a small village near Cascante. My father commandeered the portrait and held it for several days under lock and key in the only safe place he could think of: the prison. A few days later, once the danger had passed, he returned the altarpiece to its rightful place, but his action was misconstrued by some religious and rightwing people. It was said that my father had thrown Saint Bernard into jail and for many years, not just my father, but our entire family were looked at askance in Tulebras.

Another controversial intervention came during an altercation between the Civil Guard and a bunch of leftwingers. My father knew no fear and defied the Civil Guards, telling them, "Do to me what you did in Arnedo and Casas Viejas, if you have the balls for it." It seems this made the Civil Guards think twice and the heat was taken out of the situation.

During the war, my grandfather, father, and brother Alfonso (still only a boy at the time) were forced to do hard labor, and back home we had nothing, but that punishment was better than their going to jail or being dispatched to the front.

My father had to go to the front to bring in the harvest under crossfire, smack dab in the middle of the republicans on one side and the Falangists on the other. Back in the village, he was forced for a long time to work unpaid for rightwingers who had sons or relations serving on the front. That situation lasted several years.

That was my father. We all managed to survive our circumstances thanks to the love and the morals our grandparents were able to give us.

Poverty

Poverty is a spur to creativity. When I say poverty, I don't mean the sort of poverty found in, for example, Haiti, where hunger has reduced certain people to eating dirt: poverty that extreme makes it impossible to light the merest spark of life; it is the very negation of life, it is death. Death is anything but creative. The poverty I have in mind is also not the sort of poverty found in this country today where there is social security and work to be had if one is young and fit enough. Our street kids who are between twelve and twenty-five years old are poor, sure, but their poverty is not creative; they are simultaneously protected and trapped, and entrapment is not creative. They survive in the midst of a stifling reality.

Typically, life in the countries we live in today is nothing like life in the past when poverty meant malnutrition, squalor, and sleeplessness. I remember a number of youngsters who died of tuberculosis, a disease that back then wrought havoc, due largely to such dismal living conditions. Not everybody was strong enough to get up and look for what he needed, or make some move to obtain it, by, say, stealing. More and more of our needs went unmet and we lacked the very essentials for survival.

When I say that the poverty I experienced was a blessing to me, don't think that I am defending it; nothing could be further from the truth. But I cannot help noticing that whereas economic impoverishment was a fact, I was also privileged to know the solicitude and bounty of love that prompted my parents to strive and commit everything they had to getting what we needed and passing on all they knew to us.

My body and my nature enabled me to bear the lack of everything and to react and do what was necessary. My siblings didn't do as I did; their ways and lifestyles were always very different from mine. But whenever I had an episode of pleurisy, they all sacrificed a portion of their food so that I would not go hungry. We didn't always have bread on the table, and I still remember bread as the best thing about home, the finest of meals.

Besides food, there were other basic necessities that we found it very hard to come by, like sandals, but as it happened there were a few sandal-makers among my father's friends; or clothes, home-stitched by our mothers. Such shortages spurred us into action and forced us to fend for ourselves and molded us as human beings with ambitions and cravings for social progress. Which is why I persist in the belief that poverty can prove revolutionary, and wealth can lull us to sleep.

My life has also been marked by my ignorance, my lack of learning, my lack of cultivation. Let me say the same as I said about economic poverty; the gaps in my knowledge prompted me to react slickly and spurred me immediately into trying to achieve the difficult and the forbidden. As with poverty, I am not arguing in favor of ignorance and lack of cultivation here, quite the opposite. I never had the good fortune or privilege to be able to study comfortably in appropriate surroundings.

Even though with the passage of time memory usually lets us down, I have never forgotten that I was undernourished and this has forced me to build up my physical strength so that I can tackle hard work without fear—no matter how hard—as well as carry out some none-too-Catholic acts, from which I have always, by some inexplicable freak of luck, emerged unscathed. There were some very dangerous operations or expropriations that took a toll on all of us, and I was at dire risk of costing others their life or liberty. Those were the toughest times in my life, a life shaped by poverty and ignorance.

These days, what I did back then seems like madness to me; not that I renounce anything of my past, let alone how I think about this society, which remains as unfair as it was then. Or even more so.

Born poor, a blessing

As I am always saying, being born poor was a stroke of good luck, a blessing. But that is no reason for me to argue for it; quite the contrary. My whole life long I fought against poverty and carry on fighting it, just as I fight against wealth, or against a form of wealth accumulation that I regard as impoverishing. But I shall never tire of saying that poverty can and ought to be the riches of the poor.

I know what poverty is and I know what I am talking about, although "poverty" is something that eludes us, something indeterminate. Poverty comes in thousands of guises; there is the homeless man who lives life even though he may sleep on the ground. There are others living in better conditions but with many more problems. That's what I call death rather than poverty. As long as there is breath in his body, the poor man is called upon to rise up, being unable to sink any lower. The rich man, if he wishes to rise, will look to his defenses, fearful for his assets, thwarting the rise of the poor man if he needs to. But memory serves and we know that the nucleus that has broken free of this fuzzy logic is very tiny. These days our thoughts are with the countless families that once existed but that no longer do. I always say that Spain's gold and its wealth were what led to its ruination. I mean that, born where I was, I was lucky enough to lose respect for all assets, for private property, the Church and the State. I call this my blessing. The poor man blessed with disrespect cannot ask for anything more.

If I were to be born all over again and had the chance to choose, I would pick the very same life I led, the life I have; that is what I preach to those all around me at every opportunity. You are what you are, even though you might want to be something different.

Ignorance is one of the greatest advantages enjoyed by States, religions, and unscrupulous masters. I still believe in education and in a free culture not imposed by some religion or despot or government, be it fascist or Stalinist, and I shall do all in my power to explain my utopian existence, my unbelievable life. You are fully within your rights to believe it or not. There are no heroes in our midst. Heroes are the creations of Caudillos and all these heads of state. Machiavelli said that all heroes who govern, govern through crime. All who govern are criminals.

No one is any better than anybody else and nobody can negate actions and accomplishments. One can display courage today but be a coward tomorrow. I have known people with courage to spare but who never thought of themselves as being different from anyone else. There are those who look upon George W. Bush as a man of courage and valor. I take an opposing view. Take certain actions and, if they succeed, you are a hero, but if things go wrong, the very same person turns into something else, even though we may know nothing about him, other than the results of his actions. There are times when we lack courage or when we do the wrong thing, and there are times when we behave like idiots, but this is not to say that we *are* idiots, merely that our behavior is idiotic.

In my lifetime I have known lots of people who have gambled their freedom, day in and day out. But they haven't gambled their lives and have taken due precautions and weighed up the risks of their actions. There is the intuitive feeling that nothing bad is going to happen, for we have been through this thing time and again. We feel confident and clever, and death is a matter for other people to worry about, because we have the strength needed to see to our defenses and an intelligent outlook.

Memory

Memory, my memory. I hold on to certain memories as if they were treasures, especially those of my boyhood years. Each of us is what he is, as well as what he has inherited from his surroundings and we each follow the path traced for us by our own people. That is the theory, but it is not the practice. Memory is history, old age, memory is what one retains of life experiences, the warehouse of the intellect. One of the greatest burdens I bear, one that I still carry from when I was a very small boy, is the heavy burden of history. It crushed me, and to this day I have not quite been able to straighten myself up again. I might have been only five years old at the time, but, after carrying that terror around with me for year after year, how could I forget what I went through in 1936, that genocide? How could I forget the fear and panic I experienced year after year, when there was no alternative and no encouragement other than that offered by my nearest and dearest and my friends who shared the fear and the deprivation, ever watchful for the unbelievable, the unexpected, the horror, the criminality, and the injustice.

In my early years, life was all sentiment. Very often quietly fraternizing with the enemy and being obliged to attend certain religious gatherings. Sometimes in order to pull the wool over my adversary's eyes and have him believe that we were all brothers, that all that was behind us now. And sometimes in order to escape fines and sanctions, sometimes for hostility, sometimes for refusing to attend Mass. And then, as I say, there was the day to day smothering sensation, sharing certain moments with my adversaries who were still what they had never ceased being. Some of them had once been but no longer were and had nothing to do with the past. These I regard as "sound."

PART TWO

CASCANTE

I was born on February 18, 1936, in Cascante, a farming village in the Ribera de Navarra, only a few miles from Tudela, the main county town. I can barely remember starting school in a street behind the church, Los Corralazos Street, but I have no real recollection of the woman who looked after us: although I do believe her name was Hermenegilda. The school was only a place where younger children could be dumped. I have no memory of actually doing anything throughout that time.

When we moved in with my grandfather in the Calle de San Francisco, my mother did everything she had to do to get me into a different infant class in the Calle Nueva, which is just about all that I can remember.

Before we moved into the Calle de San Francisco, we lived in El Castillo or in the Calle del Hospital. There, where there are apartments now, lived the Pimpos family, Señora Barillera, and the Perdices sisters. We were all neighbors, but we were much, much more than that: a real family.

The neighbor women would step outside and set up a table with four wicker chairs and play cards, *brisque* or *guiñote*. Those games were played by the whole neighborhood. Most of the local residents were peasants and farm laborers; a few had a tract of land, and others worked the allotments that I spoke of earlier.

The houses were still not plumbed so the women would go down to the river to do the washing-up and clean the clothes. Water was also brought back, and mothers would bathe our bare necks and heads with cold water. There were three or four locations on the Botero and Queiles rivers where the women would set up tables for laundry and washing the dishes.

Most of those women could neither read nor write and they never laid eyes on a newspaper. However, virtually every one of them was familiar with the classics of Spanish drama, thanks to there being frequent performances at the theater or in the public square. Everyday life was tough but there was still the warmth of friendship and neighborliness. People knew each other and talked to one another and played together during the winter and much more so during the summer.

The men lived a life apart. I can remember my father on his way out to pass some time in the tavern, wearing a *boina* (beret) and his sash, which was wrapped around his waist several times and into which he tucked his knife and handkerchief; he also used to tuck a crust of bread into it or, on occasion, a morsel of dried cod or maybe a peach or an apple.

There was a Carlist Club for the Carlists, a Liberal Club for the moderate leftists and above all there was the Casa de La Pelleja, a venue for political meetings and lectures. That was where the members of the UGT and CNT would gather, and I remember going there many times on my father's shoulders or on the shoulders of some of my father's friends.

The two houses

Before we moved in with Grandfather Doroteo and up until the outbreak of the civil war, at the time when my father was deputy mayor, the Calle del Hospital, so-called, was home to us. It was a very small house. Just inside the door was a small room off to the side where my brother Alfonso and I slept. Over to the right there was an adult's room which was my father's, a short hall that incorporated in the pigpen and, right at the end, a covered corral used as a hayloft and which my father would occasionally make available overnight to poor callers to the house. I also remember that, once, when I was five years old and out for a breath of fresh air, I discovered that a number of my father's friends had opted to sleep in the fields between the stacks of cut corn, wheat, and barley, what we used to refer to as *fascales*.

To access the main part of the house there were five steps behind the door: half of the area was taken up by the fireplace and the rest by a tiny kitchen and a single bedroom where my parents and sisters Satur and María slept. The only thing upstairs from there was a small storage space for grain.

We all answered the calls of nature in the corral for we had no flush toilet or *retrete* as it was called back then. We didn't have electricity either, so lighting was by way of an oil lamp, a small container of olive oil with a cotton wick that burned for a long time. Many years later, when I was an inmate in La Santé prison, we used to use the same gadget after lights out; we would put some water into a sawn-off tin can, pour on some olive oil and light the wick.

When the civil war broke out my father stepped down as mayor and the persecution of our family began so we moved in with Grandfather Doroteo on the Calle de San Francisco. That was where my little sisters Ángeles (with whom my mother was pregnant when she had had to hide in the other house), and Marí Nieves Pilar (or Pili) were born. The house was home to Grandfather Doroteo—my paternal grandfather—as well as my maternal grandmother, María, and to Auntie Gala, an invalid who spent all her days and some of her nights praying loudly and getting on all our nerves. The tailor who made my first communion suit, a slightly unbalanced fellow, snapped one day and tried to throw Auntie Gala out of the window.

With so many mouths to be fed, I can't explain by what methods or miracles my mother was able to fill all our bellies at a time when tuberculosis was common among the poor. We had a far from continuous but reasonably regular supply of water at home thanks to the works carried out by the previous left-leaning council. Though that didn't spare us from having to set off for Tarazona in a donkey-drawn cart every two weeks, laden with a five-hundred-liter tank, in search of more water, especially water for drinking and cooking.

The façade of my grandfather's house was not made of dried mud but of packed clay and it was riddled with holes in which sparrows and swallows nested; in the evenings and especially at the crack of dawn the commotion from those birds used to wake us up. The farming family living opposite, very kind and decent people, used to say that it was only the sparrows and swallows that held the front of the house together and that it would otherwise have collapsed. The father of the family next door, Justino Rosell, was another of those who were shot: he was a man rather well up in years and he practiced his religion. His only sin was that he wanted to see more fairness.

The floor, as you stepped inside the house, was also packed earth. At the far end was the stable where grandfather kept three donkeys and across from it there was a very cramped hayshed, a pigpen and, beyond that, a corral where we later kept a few animals. At this point we had no livestock because the fascists had commandeered them all and shipped them to the front lines for the use by Spain's "saviors."

To the right of the front door there was a very dark room where Grandfather Doroteo, my brother Alfonso, and I slept. On the first floor, besides the kitchen and fireplace, there was Auntie Gala's room and a room where my parents slept. My maternal grandmother had rented a room in a house nearby and that's where she slept, usually taking one of my sisters with her when she left each night. Much later, my parents were able to add on two extra rooms plus a small hall, complete with toilet. The toilet was a wooden bench to sit on with a hole in the middle and everything fell into the small stall; constant care being taken to cover the droppings over with dirt. This soil was greatly prized because it was used to fertilize the vegetable patch.

Beside the kitchen, there was a woodshed with two benches that had been arranged with their backs to the kitchen wall to take advantage of the heat. Each bench could hold three or four people: the fireplace was raised about forty cm above the level of the kitchen floor and that platform was used as a seat at the table around which we ate. The women spent much of their time seated, and cooking, and the fire was always lit. At night, red-hot coals were lifted from the fire and placed in a bedpan to warm our beds through the night. Whenever it snowed or when the temperature took a real dip, we stayed in bed longer so as not to waste firewood or food.

The kitchen floor was a bit uneven and was made of plaster and boards, in which the passage of time had left gaps. We all fit around the table as best we could and ate out of the same pot. Our food was virtually always vegetables grown by my father and grandfather and we rarely ever had meat. On those occasions when my mother managed to add a few ounces of meat to the pot (for that was it, two or three ounces of meat between the eleven of us), the scrap vanished from the pot unseen by anyone. I never quite managed to get a seat at the table; I would squat near the door with half of me sticking outside because virtually every day there were visits by people coming to complain about some mishap or other to my parents. They would call out to my father from the street outside and he would toss whatever came first to hand, so I was always ready to run whenever we sat down to eat.

My mother used to really talk up the meals she made to get us to eat them without any complaints. We ate *a lot* of cauliflower, and our first course was a soup of boiled cauliflower; we also had beans (when we could get them) and chickpeas, which we used to call "fast day" (*vigilia*) since a stew made from them represented no breach of the abstinence from meat preached by the Church. My mother prepared her potatoes with hot peppers and a dash of cod, by which I mean *bacalao* (dried cod).

After dinner every night, my little sisters would climb on to the table, and we would all sing or clap while they danced. After the war, in the summertime, the partying spilled out on to the street, as I shall recount later.

School days

My earliest school years were spent in El Claustro, where the Civil Guard stabled their horses and had their barracks. I can still remember them with their capes "*smeared with wax. / They have skulls of lead / which is why they shed no tears.*" From El Claustro I transferred to Doña Josefina Ortiz's school. Boys and girls were in mixed classes at both these schools; and we were all taught to sew and embroider, to read and write, as well as cook. All this was back during the civil war years. There is nothing unpleasant about all these memories; everything was great, which was not the case at other schools. I think those first two schools must have been secular, which is why they were later shut down.

The secular schools were very important, and memories of the Catalan educator Francesco Ferrer y Guardia, shot for promoting that style of education, were alive and well within them. The teachers were all very kind, and all (or almost all) were left-leaning republicans, socialists, or anarchists. Which is why their profession was the hardest hit by repression during and after the war.

After those two schools, I moved on to a school run by the Carmelite Sisters. I had no problems there but little of what they taught me was of any interest to me. The days slipped by, and I was growing up and what I was interested in was games. I was always eager for class to be over so I could get out with my friends. Now I realize that schooling held few charms for me. I learned to serve at Mass and every day I would help serve Mass at eight o'clock in the morning in the convent. The nuns attended to their worship prior to the start of lessons at nine o'clock. Usually, Mass was said by Don

Victoriano, who was a very gruff man, who washed his hands of me many times; the truth is that I used to drink his altar wine and dilute it with water. I could not stand this priest, even though he had protected my father. From time to time, Don Victoriano would be replaced by other priests who were more Falangist or Carlist, but they were more pleasant and would tip me once Mass was over.

School began at nine o'clock but some days after Mass I would head home; other days, I would head straight for school. The first thing we did when we got to school was a prayer. After that they would teach us very cursorily some grammar, geography, or history. We spent much of the morning either saying prayers or learning religious stories and their meanings. In the afternoons, virtually all we did was sacred history and at least two or three times a week somebody would turn up—usually some priest—to talk to us about religion. That was the ethos in which I grew up under the Carmelite Sisters, after having sampled a different type of schooling that, if not the rationalist education on offer elsewhere, had at least not been religious, was without the prayers every hour, and they had taught us more than just religion. They had not been authoritarians and there was love in what they had been doing and above all, the homework had been very diverse. I can remember very little from those times, but I cannot think of anything bad about my first school.

Nuns in those days dressed the way Islamist women do today. When I see Muslim women dressed from neck to toe and with their heads covered, I cannot help but think of the Carmelite Sisters.

One thing that really intrigued me was what these nuns did once the schoolchildren went home. Time and again I hung around to lend Sister Borja a helping hand in the garden or with the animals and when everybody else had gone I delighted in hiding in the bushes to watch the sisters with their wimples removed and bare headed. I felt this was a privilege and it was something that worried me and motivated me. I would spy on them from behind the kitchens and watch them as they cooked and helped each other out. There was one nun, Sister Petra, who would uncover herself and even showed her bare arms. She was very pretty, gorgeous, and I could not see enough of her. I cannot say whether this was a sexual attraction; I don't think so, but the fact is that I was really eager to gaze on her face, her uncovered head, her arms. My thoughts have often turned to Luis Buñuel's

Viridiana when the nun is removing her clothes and her legs are seen, which is rather exciting. Something like that happened to me.

I remember how likeable Mother María was and how she behaved. Whenever I misbehaved, Sister Victoria would throw me out and send me home. At home I said nothing but then along would come Mother María to take me by the hand and shoulder, escorting me through the streets and calling me her friend and bringing me back to class. On many occasions Sister Dominga would belt me and throw me out, and again Mother María would go in search of her friend Lucio and bring me back to school.

So far, I had learnt nothing except an antipathy I developed for the priests, especially those I served at the altar. One of them because he was a nasty piece of work and the rest because they were evil. I knew all about these priests from my parents' friends and from my parents themselves.

From religious school I moved on to a new school. Logically, it should have been more relaxed, more humane, more civil, and should have shown the students greater understanding, especially since the schoolmaster came from Cascante and was from a poor family himself. In Cascante everybody knew everybody else. Well, this was far from the case; things are as they are rather than as we would like them to be. This was the last school I ever attended, and I think I must have been around ten years old. The teacher's name was Don Ángel Arbiol. Physically, he was thin, anything but handsome, a bachelor, and fancy free. Outside school he was forever going around clutching his Bible and every day he would pay a visit to the Virgen del Romero, Cascante's patroness. I think he probably used his time inside the church to think about how he was going to punish us when he got to school. He behaved very badly with most of his students. In the town they called him "*Picha santa*" (Holy Joe) because, although he was a lay teacher, in religious terms he was more of a stickler than the Carmelite Sisters. And even though the sisters had often thrashed me with the belts they wore, but among them was also the very kindly and undemanding Mother María.

Our school, or *Gorria* as we called it, began at nine o'clock in the morning. The front gate was closed once we were all inside with Don Ángel. After we had arrived and blessed ourselves—which we were obliged to do any time we passed any of the churches in town—this man would line us up, standing to attention and with our arms raised in the fascist salute and he would raise the flag and have us sing the Nationalist anthem "*Cara al sol.*"

After that we would say a few prayers. This same nonsense was repeated in the afternoons before we headed home.

I don't believe that these days there are teachers as idiotic as Don Ángel Arbiol: he was a religious fool, an idiot teacher whose behavior did great harm. Our poor imbecilic Don Ángel was very strict and punished us for any silliness. Sometimes, for no or very little reason, he would have us kneel to pray or copy out religious texts or would stop us from going for lunch at noon. Other times, he would punish us by having us hold heavy books with outstretched arms. I won't forget the rulers he brought down on our hands, right on the fingertips, or on our legs or across our backsides. He was, as I say, a bad egg. There might be somebody explaining something or reading something, and this man would creep up stealthily and noiselessly behind them and without saying a word or giving any sort of warning, he would slap them across the head with the knuckles of a closed hand. Who knows how many lumps this wretch gave us?

So much for my schooling. If I crave and show so much respect for education, it is because I missed out. School and family are the two things in which I place the greatest stock in life. Anyway, I have seen for myself how, even among the common people, the most reliable people are the teachers. I'm not saying they can be relied upon 100% but I think theirs would be one of the best professions and without education we will get nowhere. This was the profession that suffered worst in the Civil War because education is the key to progress. In Cascante, there was a teacher named Gorría who raised a whole generation of the most intelligent people, a sort of irreplaceable intellectual elite. Gorría was in the CNT and abided by the principles of Ferrer y Guardia but was forced to flee because they would have shot him on sight.

By the time my school days (or whatever you want to call them) were over, I could just about read and write. Never having learned to do these things any better than that.

Work

I began to work the land along with my father, helping him in whatever way I could or knew how. Farm work was very hard to endure, and also very exacting. Everything was done manually, through sheer strength. The land was largely tilled using a hoe. It was horrible drudgery and took a lot of getting used to. Hoe-work and manual toil were de rigueur in the vineyards and wherever else the plough could not reach.

Come the olive crop, the olives were picked off the ground, one by one. We nearly always worked at this in sub-zero temperatures, malnourished, poorly dressed, freezing in the cold, and on our knees all day long.

Come harvest time, we would rise around four o'clock in the morning if we had a way to travel. During the summertime, there are *fiestas* in all the nearby villages. You'd get back from some village *fiesta* at daybreak and be woken by your father saying, "If you're man enough to go partying, you should be man enough to get up and go to work as well." Half asleep, you'd cling to the tail of the donkey or other beast for three, or two hours or just one hour and then you'd work for all that you're worth, as best you can and as best you know how. At noon you'd head back home covered in dust and thirsty, dead tired, with no thought of anything other than getting some sleep and a drink of cold spring water.

During the grape harvest the work was a lot lighter and less exacting, and the climate was neither too cold nor too warm.

That was what it was like when I started working and learning from my father, my grandfather, and my brother. I think anyone would understand that I was sick of the way things were. I always say that it is not the work that kills, it is the injustices, and we faced plenty of those.

I was still only a boy and, come dusk, nothing and nobody could stop me from joining my friends, all of them very young, for a drink of lemonade, if the chance offered itself, and to sing.

Later my brother Alfonso and I learned a bit about working with brick-layers. We used to get work from a man named Arcos (who had earned himself the nickname "Poison"), and there was another fellow named Baigorri. My father had previously been down to Castile, working on the harvest or as a herdsman.

It was at around this time that I went to work near Pamplona in the El Perdón mountains. I had been hired by somebody from Ablita, and we dug holes for pines to be planted in the mountains. We didn't have beds or huts but slept out of doors, in every sort of weather, on the ground, with only a blanket for cover. Work was from sun-up to sundown and really tough. For food we had a little milky coffee in the mornings, some potatoes with some bits of beef at noon and, for dinner, the same again. Our pay was five pesetas a day, which was very little, but we helped one another out and contributed to the household.

Devilment

Before then, when I was younger, my friends and I got up to some trouble, and from time to time I got caught. In those days there was a tiny church—long gone now—called San Antonio en la Virgen and it was usually locked up. Worshippers would drop small sums of cash, five *centimos* or ten or one *real*, into the alms box there. We used to fish out the coins using a mud-filled hollow reed that they would stick to.

I remember the trucks that came from Valencia were laden with oranges for sale in the square. In order to get there, they had to negotiate the curves in the road at La Victoria and Cuatro Caminos, which forced them to slow down considerably. The oranges came in sort of shopping baskets or wicker panniers and us boys used to seize this chance to climb on to the back of the trucks and offload as much fruit as we could in two minutes.

We also used to raid the rich people's orchards for the finest fruit. And in wintertime we sneaked into certain homes and made off with the honey. Once we tore up the iron pipe that carried water from the station to Pepe el Legiero's garden and sold it off for scrap—we could have derailed the train. The Civil Guard was after us in a number of locations, but they never found us. We even sold off iron from Urzante church. On several occasions I ventured out at night with others to steal olives. All our "swag" was sold off and our customers included some quite respectable people.

I can remember all that, but I don't attach any great significance to it. These days, in the part of Paris where I live, in the 20th arrondissement, there are loads of youngsters every bit as poor as I was; or maybe, in comparative terms, somewhat less poor than we were in my day. In an unguarded moment they too swipe anything they can find. They have robbed me of a load of things. I run a cultural center and don't ask anybody to pay a penny; people can exhibit whatever they like—sculptures, paintings, plays, talks. The door is practically always open but in some unguarded moments they have robbed me of a few radios, cameras, and cash. Just the other day a friend of mine was dozing with the door ajar, and they made off with his bicycle, unbeknownst to him. I get angry but then reflect on my own past and realize these youngsters wouldn't do these things if they had decent families and money in their pockets, but they are very poor and have nothing at all.

Devilment, sometimes to get something to eat, sometimes just to spend time with friends. Once, my friend Luisito el Tortera and I tried to rob his father of a sackful of barley so we could sell it. The grain storage where the barley was kept was on the second floor. Luisito climbed up into the storage area and tied a rope around the sack, but unwittingly, he also got tied up in the rope. I was waiting for him downstairs, and it was a good while before my bound friend was able to be freed.

We had olive oil at home. We used to top up bottles of olive oil with water. Since the water was heavier than the oil, it sank to the bottom, and the oil rose to the top. We were forever up to some mischief. Our mothers told us that we should ask rather than steal. Ask, ask! But our mothers couldn't give us what we asked for because they had nothing. I was arrested several times for matters like these and was taken to the little jail or a room that passed for a jail in Cascante. On other occasions I wound up in the jail in Tudela where they had a gaoler. On still other occasions, with the fines beyond my mother's ability to pay, I was sentenced to plant trees in La Virgen Park. There are still a few acacias there that I planted along with my brother-in-law Juan Cruz.

Life was like that

I remember the war years as a time of terror: I was six or seven years old at the time and, brandishing a wooden rifle I had to drill in the misuse of weapons, what we called training, while my grandfather, father, and brother Alfonso were forced to work for fascists whose sons were away fighting the Republic. Such forced and unpaid labor was not referred to as hard labor but rather as "volunteer work," a curious invention. My parents and family friends avoided talking about the matter when I was within earshot.

By the time the war was over, we were growing out of our childhood, although my youngest sister, Pili, was still quite small. I remember that whenever we went to the mill, we used to trade 140 kilos of wheat for ninety of mixed grains, which was a bit mysterious, because it was said that the Civil Guard and tax officials oversaw things. But it was all a scam: we would toil away, and they would cheat and rob us. It was the same with the olives: no matter what you offered for sale or trade, they would swindle you and we, the poor, were getting progressively poorer. It was the same for many, many farming families. We had a hard time of it, but we soldiered on.

There were several espadrille shops such as La Pataticas, Señora Francisca Crispin's, La Cerberaña, and Jesús Baigorri's place. The latter two were a bit more trusting of my mother because they were republicans, but still, I couldn't change my espadrilles every Sunday. I never wore shoes. Señora Cerberaña, Señora Francisca, and Jesús Baigorri would give my mother credit and all three of them would lend us espadrilles. These borrowed sandals were worn by my father, my brother Alfonso, and me. My brother was fussier and always kept his sandals cleaner than mine. When he wasn't looking, I would steal them or swap mine for his and keep them for the Sunday. On a few occasions he took them off my feet with people watching; they were his and somewhat newer than my own.

On another occasion I snatched the jacket he used to wear to Mass. When he realized, he marched to the church, found me hiding, and took it away from me, leaving me with only a t-shirt, freezing in the cold and exposed to all the world.

I refused to go get bread because my mother had run up a bill in several bakeries and, sometimes, they would refuse me. I would come home bread-less and crying because the woman at the bakery had shamed me in front of everybody: "I won't give you any bread because your mother still owes me." That's how things were; any time my mother bought me clothes it was on credit and since we knew what days payment was due, we would keep watch for the collector and my mother would hide until he had moved on. It was horrible when this situation dragged on for a while, but we kept our sense of fun. On summer nights my father would open the jute curtain that covered the door, bunches of kids would sit around it. He would tell us stories and sing, and we'd sing along. Some things just defy explanation: we were very poor, but my father used to read to us and urge us to read Unamuno and

Cervantes. Those were the toughest times we ever knew, but my parents were at least able to offer us some glimmer of hope.

I don't have bad memories of those times, and these days I tell myself that they were a boon to us, that before one can appreciate the positive one must experience the negative. Those were days when we went without bread. When we did have some my mother would hide it away or keep it under lock and key because I ate more than my siblings and was a big eater. But I remember the love of my nearest and dearest, the happiness, and how delicious what little we did have to eat seemed to us, especially the home-made meals and the paellas shared with my father's friends out in the fields. They were dishes made with cuts of meat that these days would be thrown away, things like the feet, offal, and heads that made them all the tastier.

The death of my father

My father got cancer and ended up in Pamplona hospital. There they were unable to say what was wrong with him, but he suffered mightily. One day he told me that I should ask an uncle for the thousand *duros* he had offered and buy morphine to ease his pain. But my uncle made excuses and never lent us the money. That was the worst of times for the family. My father, driven to distraction, disease-ridden, broken, and in enormous pain said to me, "Son, I wouldn't wish this even on my worst enemy." All my mother could do was put a wet cloth on his forehead and do what she could to ease his pain. Another time, my father, racked and twisted with pain, said, "Son, you're made of the right stuff. If you truly love your father, finish me off."

Having no money and no medicine, I thought about robbing a bank or savings fund. I came close a couple of times . . . Luckily I didn't, as it would have been yet another catastrophe. Rather than solving the problem, I would have been arrested and my life would have ended right then and there. That was back in 1950 when I was nineteen years old. I can't explain why I didn't rob the bank, because I was definitely tempted to.

There is another thing I need to say: I probably am embellishing about what a blessing it was to be poor, but it was because of my poverty that I had no problem losing all respect for the established order, private property, Church, and State.

My father died. He was a good man, an idealist. As an aside, every time I go to see the doctor and he writes me a prescription, I think about the days when my father was ill. No matter what the cost, we must defend Social Security for the sick and the elderly. There is no sadder sight than the suffering of our loved ones and no greater injustice than for a good man to die in horrific pain.

A spirited boy

I was working very hard and I was full of self-importance, full of pride. I had never owned a pair of shoes, nor a pair of white trousers, not even when I made my first communion. Boys used to make their communion in white or blue suits, but, above all, in long pants. I wasn't able to do so. Uncle Elías sent us a good bolt of salvaged cloth for the making of the suit, but it needed tailoring and stitching. My father knew somebody from the tavern who was just out of the mental asylum. He was a tailor by trade and my father took advice from him and he told him that we had received the cloth. He brought the tailor home to have a look at it and to see what could be done. The tailor grabbed the length of cloth and spread it out on the table. He explained how it might make a jacket and some short trousers, but that was all. As payment for his labor, we would take care of his needs for as long as it took to make the suit. He made the jacket in a single day, but the remainder of the suit took him a month. In the end I was able to make my communion at the church alongside the other kids, but in short pants rather than in the trousers the others were wearing.

Despite all this, I grew up proud. I began planting vines and digging ditches. It was the toughest of work; it was physically very demanding and very few people were up to it. Very often, in the winter, once work was over, I would bathe naked in a dam, showing off a bit. I also used to go out wood cutting with El Chache and El Bernardino: axes and adzes were our tools, plus a huge thirty kilo sledgehammer for splitting trunks. Few people could handle it: I used it to open splits in tree trunks. Sometimes I went tending herds in Zudaire near Estella just to bring a little money in for my mother.

I had a sack of gravel that weighed 154 kilos. No one could lift it except me, and I won bets by doing so. And I thought nothing of grappling with either cows or bulls.

Under the sign of Aquarius

I have heard it said many times that February is the best month for friendship, and that Aquarius is the sign closest to humans insofar as it relates to loyalty, closeness, and respect, rather than love. Aquarius is the star sign of deep-seated loyalties, and this is something confirmed to me with lots of evidence by Madame Magdalena from the Rue de Paris in Clichy, a neighbor of mine, when she would "read" my cards. I never believed in tarot, but there was something about that good woman that struck a chord with me.

Magdalena was her clairvoyant name. Her real name was actually Patricia, and I got to know her because, just outside her home, there was a utility room where we would bring our laundry to be washed: shirts, bedsheets, trousers. She would hand me back every article of clothing a couple of days later, washed and ironed. She let it be known to a few of her customers that she came from Seville and was of gypsy stock, but I cannot say how much truth there was in that: she had the gift of the gab, wore her hair very long, and was as pretty as she was religious. Like me, her birthday was in February, and she had made a specialty of the sign of Aquarius, having read loads of books on the subject, and since her conversation was pleasant and intelligent, I enjoyed being in her company. Over time, she got to know me very well. Since we men are quite narcissistic, she knew how to tell me things that flattered me and she pressed me for a thousand details about my life, especially up to the age of twenty-three, at which point I had my first taste of what we might term making or sharing love. Up until that time I had known nothing about that, and since then I can say that my experiences in that area have been quite satisfying and free of frustration, and also free of bombast and exaggeration as well as of rushing around trying to make up for lost time.

In Cascante, we youngsters used to look forward to the month of May dreamily and happily, for it was the month of flowers, the days were lengthening, and the weather milder. In the Del Romero church there were devotions to the Virgin and we young boys would climb up there; the devout would slip inside the church and sing with the choir while those less eager to go inside could hang around outside. Once the singing finished, all of us boys and girls would meet up outside the church and would take a walk together. That was the month when many young people got to know each other and became sweethearts. It was not the custom to hang out in taverns and cafés back then, so we would be out strolling in the open air and chatting away. The chief topic of conversation was the movies showing in the cinema on Sunday because there was no television back then. I can remember a number of those movies, revolting products of the fascist era like *Los últimos de las filipinas*, *Raza*, and performers such as Miguel Ligero, Cantinflas, Alfredo Mayo, and Jorge Negrete, the last of whom was spoken of dismissively by some people on the grounds that he was a Mexican. There was also football talk, we all were fans, but not at the same scale as what goes on these days. Back then we were all fans of Atlético Bilbao, and virtually every member of the Spanish national side was a Basque and the Atlético colors were dearer to us than those of Osasuna from Pamplona. I can still remember the people who played in the Atlético Bilbao colors and on the Spanish national team who were nearly all Atlético players. Navarra has always been a very backward-looking place and we had been so crushed that even for us, when I was a youngster, Vizcaya and Guipúzcoa were— especially in my own eyes—the last word in revolution, although they were anything but, because, for whatever reason, those two provinces were, to us, lands of plenty. Real Sociedad also had a following around there, but above all it was the likes of Zarra, Gainza, and Panizo . . . all that crew. We looked up to them.

When I was young, I used to go down to Tudela to watch the trucks passing through with fish bound for Barcelona. It was one way we had of whiling away the time. In May, we eagerly looked forward to the so-called feast of La Cruceta when we would set off on a pilgrimage into the hills with horse- or donkey-drawn carts decorated however each particular group saw fit, for the blessing of the fields. In the run-up to this feast and for many months prior, we youngsters used to pool our resources, and the money amassed was spent on the feast. On the great day we had breakfast on La Cruceta mountain, and people would sing and dance with their groups. The dancing continued when they arrived back in the village, and later men and women, boys, and girls would dine together. That was why the feast of La Cruceta was so eagerly anticipated, not just on account of the fun of the dance but also because of the mingling of the sexes. We were all shy, that being our way and how we had been raised, so being in the company of girls meant our being on our best behavior, watching our language, and not using swear words. I regard these traditions as part of my heritage and when I compare the dealings between youngsters back then and those of today's youth, there are times when I long for the past.

At *fiesta* times, there was music and dancing in the Avenida cinema and every Sunday there was dancing at Perico Lizarbe's place. Young people from all the neighboring villages—Ablitas, Murchante, Monteagudo, Barillas, or Tulebras—would come. Male and female, we would always walk together to the parties, crossing the fields to get there, but I don't remember ever having taken the roads. Nor can I recall there ever having been any fighting or anything else untoward. There were two cousins from Tulebras, very good-looking girls. One of them, María, was the daughter of the convent gardener. When working in the garden he wore a small bell on his belt to warn the nuns that there was a man nearby. These days Tulebras is famous for the El Cister convent, which has been restored to its former elegance. It was from there that my father had seized the St Bernard altarpiece, which resulted in people saying silly things about him and looking at me askance.

I became very close friends with María and several times, when it was getting late and she had to make her way home in the dark, I escorted her back to Tulebras about three kilometers away. On the outskirts of the village, she would set off by herself and I would head for home. These days whenever I meet someone, we greet one another with a kiss on the cheek and the same for when we part company, but things were not like that back then. Far from it. But one night, after I had walked her home, I gave María a goodbye kiss and I think it was the most nervous kiss of my entire life. It was such a big thing to me that I skipped along the return journey, and I was back in Cascante before I knew it.

That's how I was. A simple goodnight kiss and I was completely over the moon; it was a stroke of luck, an unexpected privilege, and a source of great personal pride. It meant a lot and at the same time it meant nothing, but be that as it may, it was something that has left me with a very warm memory. My fortune or misfortune was that it was a one-off, so I have no more vivid memories of those times.

Cascante had a number of taverns: La Pelleja, which had lost its license, but sold bread and snacks; Señor Sierra's tavern; and Borrega's tavern. All three were left leaning and it was perhaps for that reason they were required to pay a special tax. By contrast, the Bar Nacional was the hang-out for "respectable people." Its owner, Nicolás, was very much into the Falange and had three sons and a daughter, Carmen, who helped at the bar. She was a very striking and unaffected girl, very unlike others of her social class, who were smug and silly. Carmen was dark and very good looking. Working with her father meant that Carmen was well known, and the discretion of her behavior earned her a lot of prestige in the eyes of the young. She had everything one could have wished for in a girl in those days: looks, likability, and lack of pretention.

I wasn't an egotist, but I will say modestly that whenever I saw other young men dressed in white outfits, my inner pride told me: they may be dressed better than me, but I am the better boy. That was my consolation. Also, because of the way I was made and the turn my life had taken, I had lost all fear, most likely due to my ignorance. For whatever reason, the upshot was that an inexplicable situation arose: me, the son of Amadeo Urtubia, an impoverished red, fell most respectfully and fondly in love with Carmen, the wealthy daughter of a leading fascist. It was that simple, that nonsensical. It was an overpowering young love but also an entirely platonic love. As my friend Magdalena always said, Aquarius relates more to friendship than to physical love.

Life and nurture have brought me the love of my nearest and dearest and the hatred of my adversaries. The bar owner, Nicolás, hated me because I loved and admired his daughter Carmen. One day, during the town *fiesta*, I was on the dance floor at the Avenida cinema with my friends, male and female, including Carmen, when Nicolás appeared. In front of everyone, he commanded, "María Carmen, home immediately!" We were stunned: several of us followed them to ensure that he would not slap her in the street with people watching. Carmen went inside and I was left outside with my friends. In just a few minutes she emerged, a pitiful and horrifying sight to behold, and went off to sleep in her grandparents' house.

Two days later, somebody let me know that I could go see Carmen in the home of her aunt and uncle, María and Cándido. So I did. We met there but soon there was a knock at the door, and it was Nicolás. They had me scuttle upstairs into the grain-storage area and hid me there in a pile of barley teeming with those little weevils we used to call *pajarillas*. By the time I emerged I was covered from head to toe in lumps and bites.

This worrisome situation was the final straw and it prompted me to leave town without a penny for the journey. Life was impossible in that sort of atmosphere.

Flight and return

I made up my mind to get far away. I went to Tudela and then on to Bilbao. I didn't have a ticket, so I stowed away on the good ship *Marqués de Comillas* and was found and kicked off. I went to Elizondo where, quite by accident, I bumped into my friend, Celso, who was doing his military service. Then I crossed into France via Ibardin, and Celso helped me make the trip. I arrived in Biarritz and was arrested by the gendarmes who brought me back to Endarlatza. I wound up in the prison in Vera de Bidasoa and, within weeks, was transferred to the prison in Pamplona. There, the Osasuna soccer players kitted me out from head to toe. From Pamplona I made my way back to Cascante dressed like a prince, and every stitch I had on had been lent to me or been given to me as a gift by the Osasuna soccer teammates of my brother-in-law, Juan Cruz, a defender. Including Fandos, Goyo, Armendariz, all those players.

When I arrived in Pamplona, I had been covered in the sort of grime one picks up over a month without washing or showering, for there no such facilities in the prison of Vera de Bidasoa. Neither was there any food made so throughout that entire time I had been living on apples, nothing but apples.

In Pamplona, the Osasuna players sent me food every day from Catachu's in the Calle Linda Txikia where they ate, especially Salvatierra, a brother-in-law of mine from Tudela. I could not believe this new life of mine and could not quite take in what had happened to me in such a short time. From going hungry to sitting down to dishes from a fancy restaurant; I felt blessed.

Nicolás punished his daughter more than just physically; he banished her, so to speak, to Barcelona to stop us from seeing any more of each other. Later, when I was working in Valcarlos with my brother Alfonso, I received an anonymous letter from Barcelona where Carmen was living and working; it said that she had other admirers now and never thought about me. Nonsense, not that it matters, but it injured my pride. Unhappy, I swallowed the bait and was left crushed. Now I can say that ours was a priceless platonic affair and that I have great respect and am on friendly terms with Carmen's children.

After my "break-out," life began afresh for me: some people now referred to me as "*el Francés*" but to others I was "*el Rojo.*" The latter epithet was used by one person who should have been saying something quite different, given that his own father had been shot. The lousy reports that the Civil Guard had about me emanated from that source: and for a time, one of his descendants carried on playing the informer. Friends of mine from Bilbao suggested a few times that I should retaliate, but I was always against that. My life began anew in the town I had wanted to leave behind.

Military contraband

Off I went to do my military service with the Logroño artillery regiment and from there we were sent to a nearby camp for training. I thought it nonsense at the time, and I stick to that view even today. Military service has never been for me. I learned what I needed to learn and later I realized that I had been through a deep depression, even to the extent of being close to suicide. We played quite a lot of sports, and I won a few minor prizes. No sooner was I back in Logroño that I was taken aside by Captain Albéniz who asked me a few things already known to him: my first and last name, the village I came from. He spoke to me man to man and from that day forth I liked and respected him. He asked me what my line of work was, and I told him farm laboring and waiting. He asked me if I would like to run the regimental mess and assigned me there. For a soldier it was the very best of postings: I began buying and selling all sorts of foodstuffs and became friends with some Galicians in charge of the stores that held tons of goods needed by the regiment. Every day we smuggled out supplies hidden in the barrels that were used to carry feed to farm animals and it was all sold to a gentleman in Logroño, with the full knowledge of one of the people in charge of the stores. We split the profits, and I began to send my mother quite a sum of money, which suited her very well, as she'd never had anything before. And I was able to help my friends.

Later they granted me several months' leave and I went to Valcarlos to work with my brother. He was working on the border as a bricklayer by day and by night kept an eye on the Civil Guard. When conditions were favorable, he smuggled goods across the river from the Basque side south of Ipurralde or from Pekotxeta and Arnegi to Valcarlos. Our contraband was alcohol, coffee, and tobacco, spare car tires, and nylon goods, among many other things.

Most of the inhabitants of Valcarlos and Pekotxeta lived by smuggling and made a good living out of it. Smuggling was banned, but that was nonsense. They could bring some cartons of tobacco, or coffee or alcohol over the border if they declared them and paid the fees; that payment was a clear imposition by a few, an exploitation that favored only a privileged minority. I am critical of certain behaviors that breach the law but disregarding this law strikes me not only as moral but as revolutionary. Every day my brother brought in a truckload of goods from Pamplona, unloaded them, and returned with another full load. This was an economic goldmine for my brother's boss as well as for many others, not least the Civil Guard commanders. Customs officials often turned a blind eye and let the smugglers—people with the requisite gumption and physical stamina to carry goods back and forth over long distances—get on with it. Such exhausting journeys were often rounded off with joyful celebrations, feasting and singing.

My brother Alfonso was a very devout Catholic, almost as devout as his female boss, La Cipri, and when we were climbing up toward the Ibañeta pass, we used to make bets with each other: I would try to guess what bend in the road he would be on at a given time and I would say to him "If I'm right, you skip Mass," and he would retort "And if you're wrong, you'll go to Mass."

We had plenty of work but were making a load of money and things began to get easier for my mother. My sisters left to work in Barcelona and later in Paris and with help from all of us my mother was able to pay off all her debts.

The bosses were a bit closefisted; they would let us have food and a bed for the night but we never quite managed to get a drumstick to eat. My brother would say, "Lucio, here we have a breed of chickens with no legs." One day I tossed away some bread, and La Cipri flew into a rage: the bread was a few rolls from Valcarlos that they brought in for breakfast and, once they had gone hard, they used to give them to us. She told us bread was not for throwing away, because that was a sin. Whereupon I replied that we were very poor, but we had at least been taught that what was not good enough for oneself was not good enough for anybody else. Such was the atmosphere in Pekotxeta. One day a friend of mine from Ablitas, José Chueca, adjutant to the colonel, warned me that the regiment was on to what was going on in the stores and that my name had been mentioned. They were on the look-out for a scapegoat. They arrested somebody who had had no connection with it, and they also heaped the blame on me. Thousands upon thousands of pairs of boots, shirts, ropes, and watches were missing from the stores. In short, several million pesetas' worth. True, we had made *some* money, but the entire operation was being run by other people and I do not mean ordinary soldiers. I mean officers.

This was a very serious matter within the army in those days. They were looking for me, meaning to lock me up and they might even have asked for the death sentence, given the scale of the theft. I was supposed to rejoin the regiment and I did not, opting instead to cross the border and take the train to Saint Jean-de-Pied-de-Port, Bayonne, and Paris. And so, I became a deserter and I bet somebody—maybe Captain Albéniz who was later promoted—did his best to help me, because I was never troubled again about the affair or about having deserted.

PART THREE

PARIS

Undocumented

I was desperate to get out, for those were bad times in Navarra. People whose hands were stained with blood and who had done ghastly deeds had not retired and were still in power, whereas we were crushed. People like us, poor leftwing folks were flattened. By that time, I had two sisters in Paris: Satur was in Vaucresson and Ángeles in Saint-Cloud. They immediately looked for work for me. I was working in the parks without papers. We siblings pooled all we earned and got by that way. I could have applied for papers as a refugee but that would have meant lying and neither my sisters nor I were for that. Finally, the mayor of Marnes-la-Coquette sorted me out with papers and gave me work. And so I started work on a site in the building at the junction of the Rue Rambuteau and the Rue Vieille du Temple. And it was there too that I met a crew of Catalan workers, most especially my friend Miguel Curto who was the greatest influence on me. He asked me where I was from, and I replied that I came from Navarra. "You'll be a Carlist then," he teased me. "Oh sure, sure I'm a Carlist. Where I come from, we're all Carlists!"

Miguel believed me and reacted accordingly, and for two full months he refused to speak to me because he didn't trust me. In the end, with the passage of time, the foreman on the site told me that Curto's crew had asked for me, and I sighed with relief and delight.

I began working with the Catalan crew. Breakfast back then consisted of a morsel of something, and we usually had a fifteen-minute break for a snack. The first thing they did to build trust was to pass me a full wine bottle and chat amiably with me. They had all seen from my actions what sort of person I was and what sort of worker.

Every one of those Catalans was a member of the CNT: furthermore, some had served in General Leclerc's division and had taken part in the liberation, not only of Paris but also of many other cities. After a while, they opened up to me. On one occasion I was asked where I stood, ideologically. As usual, I replied bluntly and candidly, "I'm a communist and a deserter." They grinned: under Francoist rule, in those days and as part of the international propaganda drive, the communists got the blame for just about every act of opposition to the regime in Spain. They started to talk to me about the anarchist ideas of the CNT and Libertarian Youth, of the new world they wanted to see, and of their achievements: the abolition of money, the collectivizations, and the responsibilities of workers in Italy and Germany. And they also broached the confusion of the communists and their treachery.

We discussed all this over several days. This was not the sort of propaganda one heard from Spanish national radio or from French national radio, or even from Radio Pyrenees; no, the men telling me these things were workmates of mine who ate and drank with me and who cherished dreams of the changes that were needed. But I could not quite comprehend the treachery of the French Popular Front or the behavior of communists worldwide.

24 Rue de Sainte-Marthe

I had dreamt for years of going to France. In the summer, when my brother was working in Pekotxeta, we used to get a bicycle and ride over to the *fiesta* in the villages of Iparralde. Wages in France were ten times higher. There was no work where we were but there was a lot of misery. In France the shops were bulging with all manner of products, people ate better and could breathe freely. Going to France was a dream of ours back then; nowadays the differences are less pronounced and, as to food, we eat better in Spain than they do in France.

There was a sort of an obsession which is illustrated by this Spanish saying, "The French Pyrenees: seen by many, crossed by few." Concentration camp escapees reaching our home district were spotted at some distance by my father who would always take them aside and, in the shelter of some embankment, they would chat. They came from a slave labor camp, and they were heading for France. In those days I didn't know how atrociously France had treated our republicans and left-wingers, but I thought the fact that these people were heading there was symptomatic of something. This was reinforced a short time later when I went to Valcarlos to work. The only decent living anyone could make was from smuggling. But when you crossed into France via Arnegi and Pekotxeta, everyone was just dropping their bicycles wherever they chose and just left them there, never bothering to chain them up—well, that was real wealth. As far as we were concerned, France was a land of plenty where there was work and wages to be had.

In those days, I made no distinction between Iparralde and France. Pekotxeta was hopeless, but there was one enormous difference. Valcarlos and Arnegi . . . they were both the same country . . . Later I found out differently.

It was in France that my life really started: I had never heard anything about anarchism back home, except one time, out in the fields when my father had suffered some injustice. He said, really resentfully, "If I had another life to live, I'd be an anarchist."

My workmates started to bring me libertarian newspapers such as *CNT* and *Soli* (*Solidaridad Obrera*) and told me that there were French lessons and job training available at the CNT's local at 24, Rue de Sainte Marthe. I was nervous about showing up there and not being an anarchist and I asked them if I could drop in and enroll. My comrades told me I would be made very welcome if I were to say that they had sent me, and so I enrolled for French lessons. Not that I learned much French, for I found the lectures a lot more interesting. It was at the CNT hall that I began to make a lot of new acquaintances; I was left dumbfounded listening to them talk about the collectivizations during the civil war at home and about the war to liberate France, and about anarchy and the *kibbutzim* in Israel. All this was news to me; I knew nothing about any of it. There were some comrades there who taught trades, and teachers, journalists, bricklayers, and people from all sorts of trades rubbed shoulders there without any sort of discrimination. And there was an acting troupe, "Mosaicos Españoles," which staged García Lorca plays.

It was there that I saw Albert Camus, the man who left the deepest impression on me. He showed up one Saturday looking for some books, a very handsome, elegant figure. Another time he came with someone and gave a speech. I also got to hear Lanza del Vasto, Louis Lecoin, André Breton, Daniel Guérin, Gaston Leval, René-Louis Laforgue, and many others whose names escape me now. There, I also saw the greatest singers of the day on stage, people like George Brassens, Léo Ferré, and Mouloudji. I had suddenly stumbled upon what I needed, and what I had there was something I never dreamt I would get. There were talks put on every Friday at eight o'clock and finished at eleven, and then we would move on as a group to the Point du Jour café which was always packed with elderly anarchist and republican refugees. The owner let them stay even when they were not buying; it was his way of paying tribute to Buenaventura Durruti, whom he had met in the flesh.

Fridays were sacrosanct for me. I had neither radio nor television and I knew nothing (or next to nothing) but I was privileged to meet men who would leave their mark on history. Fridays back then were precious to me, my inheritance. What a delight it was to be able to work, earn a living, and learn. Besides, by that time, my mother's problems were over and after listening to some intellectual I used to dream about going back to Cascante to tell them all what I was learning.

Quico Sabaté

One day, my friend and comrade Germinal García, who remains fit and well even today, much to my delight, said to me, "Here, we know you have a studio flat. Any chance you might do us a favor? We need a place for a friend to stop over for a short while." I told him I was up for it if we were talking about a real revolutionary, not some tourist. We sealed the deal and agreed to meet up the next day in Saint-Germain. Germinal was waiting for me there with three other people and we took a cab to the 16th arrondissement. Upon arrival at our destination three of them decided to enter by the main staircase while I went up by the service stairs. I was ahead of Germinal's friend in the half-light and, on reaching the second floor, I heard a strange noise, turned, and saw that the guy had opened a huge knife, a switchblade.

I was shocked but before I could utter a word, he said to me in Catalan, "Listen, kid, don't ever trust anybody."

The others were waiting for us upstairs along with one of their wives. We sat down to a very fine dish of Catalan *pilota* before we headed out for my building, to view my flat. The guy from the staircase and I went up while the others waited downstairs. I said, "Look, I'll leave the key here, on top of the nameplate. Drop in any time you like."

They all left, and I was left with no idea who that guy was or what he'd done. Arriving home after work that Wednesday, I reached for the key above the nameplate where I'd left it, only to find that it wasn't there. I rang the bell, and the guy was inside, rustling up a bit of dinner that he had fetched himself. We chatted and while we were having our dinner I asked, "But who are you?" To which he merely replied, "I am Quico Sabaté."

I was stunned on hearing his name and very nervous too, I can tell you. Quico caught on to this and carried on talking as if nothing had happened. I was dying of embarrassment; in my eyes Quico was a super-man, a sort of a god, something beyond imagining and he just carried on chatting to put me at my ease and reassure me. Which is how we got to know each other. The flat was tiny, just one room plus kitchen and toilet, one big bed and another very tiny steel-framed bunk. We sorted ourselves out as best as we could and for quite some time Quico would drop in as it suited him.

Since he was ultra-cautious, Quico must have had me on "probation" until he could be sure that I was trustworthy. It was a long time before I stopped feeling afraid when I was facing him.

For a time, my friend and comrade Quico Sabaté and I used to visit more and more friends and acquaintances rather than refugee militant comrades. We thought this necessary, in that the former were much less guarded. There was a family living on the Avenue de la Grande Armée in Paris who were friends of mine but not refugees. The wife, who was abso-lutely gorgeous, came from La Ribera in Navarra. Later I learned that her father had been a very kindly republican, but illiterate. No one in his village nor in the surrounding area could say a bad word against him. His sole and gravest shortcoming in those days in the eyes of the Falange and the Church was that he did not attend Mass. Back in those days this was considered a crime, and he was shot as a result, as were thousands of others from the area. The husband of this Navarrese woman was a building worker in Paris and his father had been jailed in Burgos fourteen years earlier for being a member of the CNT trade union. After some time, he was freed on medical grounds, so he wouldn't die in prison.

We used to keep our stash—the loot from expropriations and a huge cache of weapons—in the cellar of the house of these kind friends. I should say that, despite there being huge sums of money stored there, we were fed by these friends and many other families. At the time it didn't seem right to us to squander the money at a restaurant. So, we were very used to eating whatever we could get.

The friend I mentioned died very young, unfortunately, and is buried in Paris. If his wife would like to spend some time in my company, she can give me a call and I'll be delighted to reminisce with her about those times.

Jobs and expropriations

The war in Algeria was on. I had a new employer and was working in Asnières with an Oran-based firm whose staff all spoke Spanish. The real owner was a gentleman by the name of Chevalier who was the mayor of Algiers; he had bought up some mountains in the Marne region where he had stone quarries from which we would receive the building materials for a thousand sites around Paris. For a while, I also worked in a factory in Clichy. Broadening my circle of acquaintances with Quico afforded me a personal security that I had not had before. He was a man on the wanted list and was pursued by the police and the Spanish army. A hero, we might say.

This situation continued for one or two years . . . I was back working in the ramshackle district of Nanterre on a site where we took turns building and demolishing; indescribable. Out of the blue, Quico suggested that we pay a visit to the Grand Hôtel Le Royal Monceau, to the man who had been lawyer to Durruti and Ascaso. Years later that lawyer went on to serve as a minister under General De Gaulle. Never in my life had I witnessed such luxury, with all those waiters, the fine dishes, wine lists, and menus; it was the first time I had set foot in such a place.

Our friend the lawyer spotted us looking rather lost in the corridors and called out "Francisco, Francisco." There was a change of atmosphere and during the meal—not that I had much idea of what was happening—it was agreed between the two of them that Quico would surrender himself to the French authorities. There would be no extradition, but he would serve six months in jail.

Back in those days, the Spanish were very highly regarded because the part that they had played in the Second World War in France had not been forgotten. The communist Henri Rol-Tanguy, one of the heroes of the French resistance, says in his memoirs that at least half of the territory of France was liberated with Spanish refugees playing a crucial part. Prior to that, Spaniards had been sneered at and insulted and treated worse that livestock in French concentration camps like Saint-Cyprien, Argelès, Gurs, and twenty-odd others, not to mention the camps in North Africa such as Bir-Hakeim. But it was those very same Spaniards who made up the vast majority of General Leclerc's Second Division, the liberators of Paris, and the first tanks to enter the French capital bore the names of Brunete, Guadalajara, Teruel, and Belchite. Virtually all the officers and men spoke the language of Cervantes, which was the official, working language of No 9 Company, up to and including its commanding officer, the French Captain Droune. Droune was embarrassed that his men, who had fought so well, were all antimilitarists, but they had been fighting for freedom and in those days, fighting was the only way of obtaining it. As General Leclerc used to say, "A practicing French Catholic myself, I am surrounded by Spanish devils filled with courage."

Leclerc was itching to enter Paris but was forbidden by the American high command. Ignoring this, he ordered Droune to strike out for the capital with his men. Droune replied that that was a breach of orders and might have dire consequences, to which Leclerc replied that stupid orders should never be obeyed: "Forward with No 9 Company!"

The "Ninth" specialized in street fighting and did very important work in the Opéra, Luxembourg, République, and École Militaire districts. The general commanding the Second Division, Giroud, tried to prevent Leclerc's troops from taking part in the victory parade since they had disobeyed orders. "You're under my orders, not those of General De Gaulle!" he stated. But General De Gaulle stepped in, and the Second Division served as escort for Droune's No 9 Company as it paraded down the Champs Elysées behind Droune in his tank, and an escort of three Spaniards brandishing the flag of the Spanish Republic.

It has taken seventy years for France to erect a statue in memory of the Spaniards who stood by Free France. And why that unique, telling, and glorious fact fails to get attention anywhere I still do not understand. Perhaps it's because all those men were freedom-lovers and many of them were anarchists.

Getting back to Quico . . . He was accused to owning two arms dumps that had been found by the gendarmes and I think they also suspected that he had had a hand in a hold-up and some other affair I was never quite able to identify. He turned himself in to the authorities, but before he did, he handed me his submachinegun, a Thompson, and his celebrated switchblade. He went away and returned after eight months. During that time, I was able to "liberate" lots and lots of money from several banks, on my own or with company, not that it matters, and I don't like talking about it. Such expropriations were the only means we revolutionaries had of raising the funds to mount operations. It is not pleasant looking death in the face or risking loss of liberty in such conditions: an expropriation is liable to degenerate into violence and cause loss of life. This had happened in a few instances around that time, though never to me personally. When that happens, nothing good comes of it. It must be said too that, back then, expropriating a bank was relatively straightforward; these days there are security systems which have rendered it all but impossible.

Believing in nothing but believing in everything

One day at a time, I had unwittingly built up a modest arsenal of weapons. Me, who had never had any expertise in weapons. Quico asked me to look after his wife Joaquina Dorado in the event of his extradition. He asked me to take care of everything until he was freed from jail; that was an unbelievable task, just as the results I was able to achieve despite my lack of experience were unbelievable also. Lots of times I said to myself that I was responding to it like my father did, badly, to assert myself. I think it was from there that I drew my rationale of believing in nothing but believing in everything.

What was likely to come of a meeting with Quico and what might pass between us—one of us Catalan and the other Navarrese, one educated and with a record of revolution and the other ignorant of everything? Quico had suffered the loss of two brothers and many of his comrades, whereas I had not. Quico knew the importance of terms such as emancipation, CNT, FAI, anarcho-syndicalism and *garrote vil*, whereas I knew nothing of all that. And yet even so, I was the one to whom Quico entrusted his belongings.

Just what words he used to hold me enthralled I do not know. Or how it came about that I quickly embraced Quico's ideas and arguments. Or what it was that Quico saw in me that made him expend so much time and patience on me. He was a mature man who had looked death in the face many times and his life was tainted with violence; and yet he spent hour after hour in my company, patiently explaining the incomprehensible to me with endless understanding and patience. We might describe this as a miracle or as a paradox. As for me, I usually say that if I espoused Quico's argument it was because he had (and always did have) a practice and an example whereby he held back in nothing, and that included being generous with his money and what he knew.

The money that I was able to "liberate" using Quico's arsenal of weapons never led me astray and didn't turn me into a different person. My interest has always been in the human being, not in the millions earned. Quico's gift to me is what made me who I am. More and more I am convinced that crossing someone's path can be a life-altering experience, changing it for the better or the worse. And the same goes for a conversation, a book or some make-or-break moment.

On money and work

The human being, the individual . . . All of that is what really interests me. So why do people—even friends—utter slurs about each other? Let me tell you a story about money. "El Chato" was a fellow who was implicated in the story of Granados and Delgado and the would-be assassination of Franco. This fellow was traumatized by his experience. He was married to a girl from Cintruénigo. One day he came to see me and asked if I could take him on to work alongside me for three or four months and thereby benefit from his being out of work. "Just what I was looking for," I replied. I hired him; he's an electrician. We were putting the finishing touches on the apartments we were building, doing the painting, and when everything was done, I realized that we had forgotten about the sockets for the television and phone connections. I criticized him. And he tells me that I hadn't told him they needed to be installed. "Do I need to tell you, at your age, that all premises these days have television and phone?" I replied, annoyed.

The fact is that every human being has his own view. He insisted that he was in the right. I lost my temper and told him, "Since you're such a bright spark, why don't you set up a company of your own instead of answering me back the way you do?" He grinned. "Oh, I don't have the money others might to set up a company," he answered. I turned round and replied, "Can you see that guy working over there, Manuel da Silva? He can tell you. My first paycheck to him was written in the belief that I had the money to back it when I did not. I paid him, he cashed the check, and within two days he had a phone call from the bank saying, 'Some boss you have who hasn't two pennies to rub together!' I was penniless, but had I been able to set up a firm or a hundred firms with money stolen from the Americans, that would have been a more honorable course of action." That shocked him.

I have never had any theoretical principles; anything I tell you about how I have lived is fact. I am not one to place any value on this money business. It's important to take care, if there is violence involved, if somebody might be killed. And taking care for the sake of others. Especially when the violence is being used to a good purpose.

Another point I should like to make is that people are very critical of ETA [Euskadi Ta Askatasuna] (be it the *milis* or the *polimilis*) or of Action Directe, the Italians, the Tupamaros, or whoever it may be, even ourselves from the GARI . . . I have never known a single one of them that has lined his own pockets, not one, and I know all those movements. Nobody has made his fortune through them. No one. Neither the *milis* nor the *polimilis*, and we have all had heaps of cash. And among the anarchists it has always been made very clear that theft is a revolutionary act, as long as it is done for a good purpose rather than for personal advantage.

On the other hand, I am a great one to put forward the case for working. Several of my friends take me to task for that. Work and you will be exploited, but it will also bring you a sort of strength and a feeling of hostility towards your enemies. If you do not work but claim welfare or any sort of benefit, you will never be a revolutionary. Welfare and all the benefits available from the State are specifically there to lull people to sleep. If unemployment created revolutionaries, it would long ago have been gotten rid of. Unemployment is what lulls people to sleep.

On one of the charges I was facing, the top-ranking police congratulated me, because stealing a poor old lady's handbag is one thing and robbing one of the world's major banks is quite another. Everybody sees it as an honorable thing, and everybody sees it as a pleasure. And, if they could, they'd keep on doing it.

Clearly, it's one thing to do bad things and another to do good things, but as I see it stealing is rather good, or as the song by my young friends from Oñati says:

> Whenever I go out, I will rob the thief
> the nation's largest bank
> and I will share the money
> to make the revolution

I have worked my whole life. I have no idea what is like to step out with a prostitute or piss my life away with drink, in some night club or such like. My life has been work, and I'm proud of that and would recommend it. Any time the police came looking for me they found me working. Every time. Yet even the police didn't believe that I was a real worker.

What I can say is that everything carries a price. Everything must be paid for. Things do not fall from the skies. And just as I am against capitalism, because, generally speaking, it brutalizes and stupefies and numbs, so I am *for* work and for active poverty. When one is poor and has something to do and fight for, you are not poor. We need to get our heads around this. Creativity emanates from poor people. Who is that has done everything? The poor.

Who devised the First of May? The poor. Who built the United States? The poor. Who are the inventors of everything? Poor people. Because the rich man is nothing but a layabout. Some people may be nice, but, as a rule, wealth spoils the individual. I think that we have come to the point nowadays where people ought to reflect and have confidence rather than be afraid.

The rich man, when he gets to be rich, his very first act is to erect an iron gate with a dog on the inside to protect himself, with rifles and guards. So much for the rich man and so much for capitalism. Whereas the poor man . . . Well! What has he got to lose?

Some people are smarter than others or more skilled, but everybody must work. We need cooks to do the cooking, and that takes cooking skills, and the gardening needs to be done and the fields need tilling and all this needs doing. Somebody has to know how to do carpentry. Who is going to do that?

Everything is work. Without years of journalism behind him, a journalist will never make a journalist. A bricklayer will make a bricklayer once he has thousands upon thousands of square feet of laid bricks behind him. A driver becomes a driver, not the second he is issued with his driving license, but after he has thousands upon thousands of miles of driving under his belt. A baker needs time to learn his trade, as does the pharmacist or anybody else. They don't fall out of the skies. The only thing that drops out of the skies is the politicians who repeat the same messages day after day after day. Like a broken record. But, generally speaking, people are hardworking.

On file

Throughout this time, I carried on working on demolition and construction in the slums of Nanterre. One day we set off to distribute libertarian propaganda and were arrested and then released at three or four o'clock in the morning. The police asked Clichy for a background check on me and were told that I was a good worker, and they dropped me home in a police car. From which point I have been on their radar.

From then on, any time some head of government paid a visit to Paris, I had to report to the police station in Clichy in the morning and again at night following my return from work. We finished off the Nanterre job and began a new one in Creil. We had been there for a long time, upward of a hundred of us on site, and one day we struck, demanding travel passes, lunch money, and traveling money. Between them, these represented a

heavy outlay for us and a fortune for the company. I was very well thought
of, and one of the site foremen, Monsieur Ventorini, a leftwinger, had a lot
of fondness and respect for me. The lads chose me to negotiate for them: the
offices were near the Madeleine and the top bosses and Monsieur Ventorini
were waiting for me there. After a bite to eat and something to drink we got
down to brass tacks. I had no experience as a negotiator and after having my
say and bandying around some figures that I neither knew nor understood,
Monsieur Ventorini piped up and told me, "Look to your own interests.
Tell us how much you want, and we can settle this between us and that'll
be that. Don't be a silly boy." To which I replied, "Monsieur Ventorini, you
are barking up the wrong tree." They paid everybody what they were owed
(and they owed us millions) and the job was completed.

Some friends of mine, Antonio Peralta and his brother-in-law, told me
gratefully, "We're starting out on our own, setting up our own tiling firm
and we want you to come in with us. We'll have all the work we can handle in Orly."

So I did. We started work on a number of sites as tilers, taxing work but
paid by the meter at a rate agreed between the bosses and the union. Tiling
was the only trade that could legally pay piece-rates. No one else had that
sort of a contract.

A trip to Spain

One day, after he had been released, Quico showed up at pretty much the
same time as Laureano Cerrada, a comrade who had organized an airborne
assassination bid in San Sebastián. Cerrada needed money to complete
the counterfeiting of phony pesetas and we had arranged with his son,
Floreal, that I would let them have some cash. When Quico turned up, I
took the bag containing the cash out from under the mattress and handed
it over. Together we organized my first tour of a number of places in Spain,
because, being a tiler, I had a lot of free time on my hands, and nobody kept
tabs on us doing contract work.

A new life began for me from that point: I was able to travel and to
meet lots of people: sometimes I would visit them on Quico's behalf and
others would drop by our place to see us, or we might meet up at some

pre-arranged location. Such interviews, especially with Quico, were not to everybody's taste, and these days I have a better understanding of this. We told them, "You've been a fighter, you've fought two wars for freedom and emancipation and now you accept everything without a word." They were people who, after a lifetime of fighting, had settled down with families and found themselves a reasonably comfortable niche, but the dead and the thousands of prison inmates, the number of CNT national committees discovered, and the political treachery by the governments of every country (or nearly all) weighed heavily on their minds.

Don't forget, either, the power and the respect commanded by the communists who took twenty-five percent of the vote in France, when everybody knew how they had actually conducted themselves in their dealings with us—more harshly than the Nazis did. Right from its inception, Nazism depicted itself as our enemy, whereas communism was the greatest fraud of all time and a lot harder for us to combat.

In those days, the French Communist Party not only commanded a quarter of the national vote but had many intellectuals lined up behind it. Nowadays its trickery and lies have cut its influence to under two percent.

For that first trip back to Spain, Quico had supplied me with several addresses in Zaragoza and Barcelona. I was to bring news to and fro and assist people with hard cash. I caught the train to Bayonne and then the tiny little train service, still operational, from Bayonne to Saint-Jean-de-Pied-de-Port (Donibane Garazi). From there I traveled by taxi to Arnegi. Some details I cannot recall, but I do know that by the following day I was in Zaragoza and the day after that in Barcelona. I brought with me news and cash and that was all, for I had no proposals to put to anyone.

In Barcelona I stayed at the home of my Uncle Blas and Aunt Felisa. After completing the mission Quico had entrusted to me, I chose to go for a stroll to familiarize myself with the city. I had very little spending money and I made my way to Montjuich cemetery. I knew that Francisco Ferrer i Guardia, Francisco Ascaso, and Buenaventura Durruti were buried there. I located the graves and took photographs of them. When I got back to my relatives' house and triumphantly told them about it, my uncle became very sullen. He had recently been freed from prison and had suffered greatly. On hearing of my adventure, he imagined himself back behind bars because those graves were under close surveillance around the clock, and he would be asked to report to the police at the drop of a hat. I left his home immediately lest I compromise him, and the poor fellow was relieved. Back in those days the Civil Guard sometimes lurked in the entrances of buildings where they could arrest whoever they wanted. This was part of the terror instituted by Francoism.

I returned to Paris and when I produced the photographs, Quico was delighted but told me that what I had done was rash and that I could have been arrested and that that would have been the ruination of me, the end of me. When you risk certain things and they come off, the success acts as a stimulant and inspires confidence; on the other hand, if you suffer a defeat in your initial ventures, it's very hard to take and could result in loss of morale and in your abandoning everything, including your beliefs.

I have often wondered what line of argument Quico must have employed that we hit it off and worked as a team, what with me being so inexperienced. Maybe it was the way I conducted myself? The gear was his, but I had known how to put it to use and had not gone off the rails, nor had my personality changed. My interest has always been in *being* rather than *having* and to this day I still say that I am a man who believes in nothing but believes in everything.

El Maño

One day Quico introduced someone to me. This was in the Place de la République, at the metro exit. We shook hands and then each went our separate ways, but we met up again at the "Luna" at No 5, Rue de la Douane. I could tell from the way Quico's friend spoke that he was from my own region: he asked me where I came from myself and I told him Pamplona to throw him off the scent, because in those days there was little in the way of precautionary measures. When I put the same question to him, he too told me what I wanted to hear, but we both knew that we had to come from places not too far removed from each other. One day the two of us were having dinner and he picked up on my being from Cascante and I gathered that he came from Murchante and was known as El Maño Loco (The Crazy Aragonese).

When El Maño was thirteen years old, he had been working as a laborer on repairs to the roof of the local church; it was February and very cold. He lit a fire for warmth because the mortar being used to insulate the roof was made up of red earth plus straw, which was very hard to mix, and it had to be trodden down by foot; the lad was frozen and would warm himself wherever and however he could. The parish priest, by the name of Legaría, soon showed up and without a word stamped out the fire, shrieking at the lad that he was nothing but a tramp and a shoddy workman. The boy's reaction was to give him a slap, call him a sonofabitch and take off. He caught the train in Tudela and headed for Zaragoza. He had family there and contacted the local anarchist organization. El Maño took part in a number of successful bank robberies, the proceeds of which were used by anarchist workers to subsidize strikes wherever they could and to help prisoners and to publish their own newspapers. One of these bank robberies went pear-shaped, however, and El Maño was arrested, tried, and condemned to death. For two years he faked insanity in the prison and ate his own excrement. In the end they took him to the insane asylum in Pamplona. He escaped from there and headed off to defend San Sebastián alongside [Manuel] Chiapuso and his friend [Félix] Likiniano. I had a real laugh whenever we were in the company of Basque nationalists and El Maño would tell them that they were over-reliant on prayer and that it was the *galleguicos* of the CNT who had saved San Sebastián from falling into fascist hands.

In Murchante, El Maño was known as Caracoles. Lots of people asked after him and some spoke well of him while others spoke ill. He introduced me to a number of Jewish friends of his whom he had helped, as well as to Likiniano and Chiapuso. They were great friends, and I am very pleased to have made the acquaintances of them all. Every year they used to spend their vacation together in Biarritiz and Bayonne. Likiniano was the man who devised the ETA emblem—the axe and serpent—with Demetrio, the man in charge of the international campsite in Biarritz. They and other libertarian refugees like Chiapuso and Asiain helped everyone any way they could, without distinction. And I can tell you that libertarians were a very significant support for ETA in its early days, feeding its militants—especially so Demetrio at the international campsite—and furnishing them with the weapons they needed, which the anarchists had but the Basques did not.

El Maño was an expert guide and he helped smuggle lots of Jews across the border. I knew some of them and later they helped him in one of his missions. He had been tossed into jail in Portugal and shared a cell with Alvaro Cunhal, the secretary of the Portuguese Communist Party. They had an opportunity to break out together, but the communist leader said that he would prefer it if the Party were to bust him out, so El Maño broke out alone and without incident.

During the Occupation in France, three members of the Pétainist Milice stopped El Maño and asked to see his identity papers, but what he produced instead was his pistol. It was him or them and yet again El Maño came out on top. After that he changed his documents, using the name Martínez now instead of Chueca. Later he specialized in helping smuggle civilians over the border via the Pyrenees. For those with money, the set fee was three thousand pesetas, fifteen hundred for the guides and the remainder for the organization. El Maño brought quite a few people across whom I met later, especially Jews.

While we were operating together, we carried out "recovery operations" as best we could. This is something I would rather not dwell upon for it pains me to think that I might have died on one of them or have taken somebody else's life. I also think that we had no alternative, that those were very difficult times and that in the wake of our efforts they became much easier with the risk of killing or being killed receding.

El Maño's cousin Sebastián, also from Murchante, was vicar at Tudela cathedral and frequently met up with him on the border; they would argue and could never see eye to eye. That is the way we were back then: we believed in the future and in a better world and we were fighting for that. We even believed that there would be no more need for locks or door keys, Civil Guards or judges.

Quico's end

I made a further trip as far as Barcelona via Perpignan and on this occasion some people bad-mouthed Quico to me. They said that he was not looking after the families of prisoners and had washed his hands of them, which was absolutely not the case.

Quico neither drank nor smoked; nor was he a big eater, because an operation on his spleen had left him quite ill. Everything we could raise was for the libertarian cause: on a number of occasions, we found ourselves short of money because Quico, who did not share out the proceeds, spent it on gear. Contrary to the claims of his critics, he was mindful of the prisoners' families. He shared out a lot of money to people who had nothing but who were battling to change the social system. He was not a daily visitor to the premises on the Rue de Sainte-Marthe, but would drop in from time to time, and he would also turn up at locations known to be under surveillance: bars, bus stops, and taxi ranks. He was a strong, dependable fellow with bushy eyebrows and hairy ears, with the flat feet of a cat, much like my father who was excused military service for that very reason. He was a libertarian and a trade unionist of integrity who never ever crossed the line to feather his own nest. That I can say with complete confidence and equanimity. He did not live the high life or dine out in fancy restaurants. Each month he would send his wife his pay-packet or an equivalent sum. I said he should send her extra and he replied, "If I were in a factory, that's what I would be bringing home every month." Everything else went to the cause.

Once I was along on a very lucrative hold-up with Quico, the proceeds of which were stupefying. Afterwards we went our separate ways. Quico headed for the Rue de la Douane and the fifth floor, whereas I headed for the site. The following day I learned from the radio and press the figures that were being bandied about by the bank manager and I grew uneasy, because the fact is that we had carried off only half of what they were claiming, and it occurred me that Quico might think ill of me. But no sooner had the bag been opened and the cash counted than he told me, "Don't fret, Nano. These bastard managers are always at that: they bump up the figures so that the insurance pays out more. Their wages are bumped up, thanks to us."

On one occasion Quico also talked to me about the communists. He was reluctant to say much on this subject, but on a number of occasions they had tried to kill him, and he managed to escape. He was afraid of nothing and knew all about weapons preparation and camouflage. In matters ballistic there was another highly expert individual in Dijon by the name of Pancho, real name Marcelino Massana. He was a very fine guerrilla, and I knew him, although Quico and he were older than me.

Quico Sabaté left me to my own devices. One day he decided it was time to go and I disagreed. At the time the requisite bases were not up and running inside Spain and I remember having told him that the waters should be tested first by those of us who were not well known. This could scarcely be said of him whom even the dogs in the street knew, and he was identified the second he crossed the border. The Civil Guard and the Army mobilized to surround him and there was little he could do. They killed him. I learned of his death from the newspapers and then from the radio; it came as a tremendous shock. I loved him and we had shared our lives for several years, discussing our fears and worries. He had told me the whole story of his life from boyhood onward. I knew his family, even though I would not recognize them now if I saw them. He gave me a great boost when he told me that he had needed a teacher—his brother José—to show him how to rob banks, whereas I had not needed showing. He told me that, in a number of bank jobs that had gone awry, he had made good his escape by a matter of seconds or thanks to a stroke of luck.

The four comrades who perished at the same time that Quico was captured, they on a farm and Quico in the town, are forever in my mind. Of the four the one I knew best was Madrigal; we were good friends and used to go out to dinner and dance at parties together. This is something I can never forget, because, although I was young and lacked experience, I had been against that trip.

Presses

Quico had introduced me to Piquer, the manager of a printshop in the Rue Jean-Jacques Rousseau. Piquer had had a terrible time in prison, for they had tortured him and pulled out his fingernails. We arranged with him that I would do some bricklaying in the mornings and in return I would learn how to manage an offset printer. It was the first printshop I had had dealings with; the idea that Quico and I had was to buy or set up a small printing press inside Spain or along the border, for the publication of newspapers and whatever else might take our fancy, since we were quite flush with money at that point.

One of my greatest delights in those days was "liberating" office equipment, typewriters, copiers, offset presses, and guillotines . . . whatever I could get my hands on, for it could all be moved on to Spain. The libertarian organizations were very impoverished at the time; youngsters from our organization would fill us in on the place where they were working or studying and, insofar as we were able, we would "liberate" the gear under cover of darkness. Most sought after were the copiers and typewriters and the premises concerned were nearly always admin offices.

One day we were told about a very significant location, some closely guarded State offices that had just taken delivery of a state-of-the-art printing press. It had to be moved by night and stashed and hidden well, because nothing like it existed in Spain at that point. The friend who worked there slipped me a key: it was a matter of getting inside and not breaking anything. The press measured 80 x 80 and weighed 110 kilos. I talked a comrade into lending me a hand. He was a guy who regularly spoke up at gatherings, however I had never felt very comfortable in such settings and debates were not my thing, although I know they may be necessary. At assemblies everybody is a revolutionary, but when it comes to running personal risks in the liberation of gear or securing of intelligence, there are not as many with a stomach for it. Talk is cheap.

The friend in question gave me his word that he would help me remove the machine and load it on board the truck. I arrived at the rendezvous point and waited but he never showed up. I went looking for him and for an explanation of what had happened, and he came up with some excuse. We agreed to give it another go and again he gave me his word, but I did not wait as I no longer trusted him. The night was very dark with lots of rolling thunder. I asked Anne to come along to drive the truck and keep a lookout while I got the machine out. I waited for the watchman to pass by on his rounds before promptly opening the main door and slipping inside. I made straight for the press, dismantled it as best I could, opened the window on to the garden and hauled it out that way before going back outside to tie it up with rope and was delighted to haul it over to the truck. Petty expropriations of this sort gave me a real buzz: money is an abstract sort of a thing, but managing to send something that can be of practical use, a piece of machinery, was something that I did not think of as stealing. It was more of a revolutionary act and entirely justifiable.

One day, about three years back, I happened to be in Tudela for dinner with some friends from Cascante and Pamplona and from Tudela itself.

There were about twenty of us in all, including Carlos Guardia and Fermín Munárriz, a journalist with *Gara*. The restaurant is a place called El Rancho Grand. We had our meal and drank and sang our fill, and when we asked for the bill, the boss said that it was all taken care of. We were dumbfounded because it was a sizable sum. I asked the owner to point out the kind-hearted friend who had treated us to dinner and he indicated a gentleman seated at a table with his wife and two daughters. I went over to have a word with him, and he asked me if I did not recognize him. I told him no and he explained himself, "You sent us a printing press and we did a lot of work on it. Thanks for everything." At which point I recognized him; we had seen one another lots and lots of times.

Such things have happened to me elsewhere as well. Back then, we in our groups were always at the ready, some to gather intelligence, some to act. Elisée Reclus put it very well, explaining how theft, when not carried out with an eye to laying hands on wealth for one's own personal use but rather to putting it to a social use, is not so much theft as an act of justice.

I set up as many as ten presses, with the backing of all the friends and comrades who worked on them. The interest anarchists have had in printing is common knowledge. It's one area of production for which libertarians have always had a bit of a penchant. Learning, communicating, writing, speaking, it is all useful knowledge for the printing trades. Not to diminish the expertise of teachers whose trade, as I have stated elsewhere, the fascists and clergy had a particular interest in stamping out.

At Sainte-Marthe I met several comrades who worked in the printing trade in a variety of capacities and every day they would bring us newspapers and books. After I developed my interest in printing presses, a small libertarian organization sent me—via Gérard Melinan—a request that I supply them with a metal door shutter for the workshop they had just launched. There had been several attempts to set the workshop alight, with entry having been gained through the rear, which was not well protected. At the time I was working in Boulogne on a deluxe job using top grade materials, so wasting no time, after night fell, I waited until there was no one around and with my van parked in a convenient spot, I removed the shutter from the heating unit, which was massive and heavy and fireproofed. The police arrived just as I was loading it up. They were taken aback, as I was myself, but they didn't pay lot of attention to me. Indeed, even they lent me a helping hand because, from the way I talked, I could not have been anything other than a genuine workman and a foreign one at that. Luck was on my side. The following day, a Saturday, we removed the fire-scorched shutter and fitted the new reinforced one to everyone's delight.

The firm's name was Edit 71 and it was in the Passage de Tlemcen. Shortly after that I partitioned off their laboratory, again using "liberated" materials. The premises were tiny and housed two large presses plus a huge guillotine. Organization-wise, it was a disaster; the guys were young with hardly any work experience behind them, and they were still green and short of money. Even so, every day they churned out heaps and heaps of newspapers and posters for all and sundry but most especially for the Spanish libertarians.

As I say, the print room was tiny, and orders were coming in from every direction. Those who did not have the means never paid and the rest covered the bills. When the business picked up, they set up shop not far away in vacant premises in the Rue Anaim. It was an empty shell, needing running water and toilets installed, rewiring, partitions erected, refurbished, refloored, and a new roof and so on. Our friends were excited about these premises because they were roomy but had no idea how to refurbish them. Virtually all the materials and eighty-five per cent of the labor were volunteered, and if it wasn't for that we would not have been able to afford even the metro fare. By this point our friends had learned a lot. What a delight it was. We thought we were gods, conjuring things out of nothing and "liberating" stuff without harming a hair on anyone's head. It was an age of miracles, so to speak.

But since the world is a small place, rumors soon spread, and I was approached on behalf of the *Imprimeurs Libres* from the Rue de Pelleport. There was a staff of fifteen there in the same circumstances as the Edit 71 guys had been. I dropped in on them and, between us, everything in the printshop and offices was sorted out.

Their rooms were also in dire condition, and I refurbished them. Things were fine at the time as each of us got on with his work; I was laying the bricks and they were operating the presses, and nobody had a clue who my friends were.

Another time, I was consulted about setting up a large press. All of a sudden, the bank that was going to give them the loan pulled out of the deal, so we approached the bank with which I was working, the Crédit Lyonnais, thinking that it might be easier to secure the loan from, but it too turned them down. Finally, the Île-de-France regional council advanced the loan, but all the work had to be completed first and only then would the council pay up. By then we had run out of cash and, since it was going to be a long time before we would see any payment, I made up my mind to pay a call on the man who would subsequently become minister of Justice, Monsieur Pascal Clément, who was a client of mine and a deputy. He interceded and the regional council advanced the loan immediately. Those presses are still in operation today, and they have lots of people on the payroll and they take care of much of the printing that's done for the left. The beauty of this story is that myself and the presses of the anarchist printers were rescued from difficulty by a rightwing Catholic politician, a future minister of Justice.

And there was another odd incident. When work began on the presses one Friday, I stopped by the house of the architect, Thierry Claude, to pick up the plans. The door was opened by his wife, a very beautiful woman and, while I had no idea why, she was very curt with me. I left with the plans but was utterly baffled as this was the first time I had ever met her. The following Monday I stopped by again to let the architect know that we had made a start on the project. I was nervous about running into such an unpleasant woman again. I knocked at the door, and she answered and, the moment she set eyes on me she started to shout at me and soon broke down in tears. It turned out that she was a forensic detective and had long had a photograph of me in her filing cabinet. When I had called on the Friday, she hadn't recognized me at all, but when she got to work on the Monday and opened up the filing cabinet, she realized that the bricklayer she had seen on the Friday was regarded—according to the note kept with my mugshot—as the greatest forger of all time.

I should say that I carried on working with her husband and that she and I eventually became good friends. Not only did I refurbish their home, but we saw each other on a frequent basis, and I cherish and have great regard for them both.

I also did some work for a press located in the Passage de Diou, a press that bore the name of Gilles Totin, a lad that was drowned near the Renault plant in May 1968. The manager of the press, a good friend of mine, later took on larger premises in which a cafeteria, toilets, and few other things had to be installed. I had friends among the workforce at these two last presses. The manager knew it and in the long run that created some difficulties between us. There are some things in life it is better for the boss not to know.

I also set up another big press by the name of Primavera. It was, like almost all the ones I have been talking about, libertarian, or at any rate, had libertarian leanings. Once, I was there picking up a plumber to deliver him to another site. When he climbed into the van, I noticed that he was carrying a copy of *Le Monde*, the first and only occasion I ever saw a workman reading that newspaper. There was a story on the front page about Cuba and I asked him, "What's happening in Cuba, José?" To which he replied, "Nothing of any concern to you, you turncoat." I flew off the handle and told him, "It's you workers who have changed. I'm just waiting for the day when you give me a kick up the arse, show me the door, and take over the firm yourselves, but you have neither the balls nor the brains to do that."

This particular workman is now living in Sitges and has regaled lots of people with this anecdote. The answer I gave him sprang from the libertarian education I had received from the CNT, which preached self-management.

All in all, I helped set up about ten presses, some of them quite substantial. Outfits such as Primavera, Edit, Ortograph, and Imprimeurs Libres ... I did not do it alone, but my enthusiasm and my ideals were crucial to their establishment. In many instances the materials used were taken from sites where I was working and very little of what was needed was bought. We also had a lot of help from other libertarian construction workers. As for those working on those presses, I was in their very good graces and if I asked for a job for libertarians or others they immediately agreed.

Coming to terms with the CNT

I don't think I ever really aligned with CNT thinking. I wasn't active in it, but for a long time we needed a card from the CGT's tilers' union (which was pro-communist), since it was the only tilers' union, and everyone had to belong to a union. Another factor was the tremendous influence that Quico had on me. I used to visit homes with him and of course it's one thing to be a revolutionary in your talk and another thing to be a revolutionary, like Quico, who takes up arms. There was a diffidence because the CNT national committee and Federica Montseny—no matter how much respect I might have for her—could not be squared with the practicalities of crossing the Pyrenees and going out and putting one's life on the line. Montseny was a highly intelligent woman, but she was even then a spent force. And most of the CNT committees were spent forces. There were very few people ready to put their lives on the line.

On a certain occasion, later, I went to enter Spain with a commission from the secretary of the CNT, a guy by the name of Pintado. The I.D. they gave me for the trip was a very shabby "liberated" document. I lost my temper and turned on him, "No wonder you send people to their deaths in Spain." Because it is one thing to give somebody a document for his use and quite another carrying it yourself when you know that your freedom is at stake and that your very life might depend on that piece of paper. And this was a very influential factor when the time came for me to connect with the CNT.

We used to venture into Spain with money and propaganda, essentially to help the dependents of libertarian prisoners and to pay for lawyers. In every organization, there is always somebody who gets blamed for things and becomes the fall guy. For us, it was Quico who faced a lot of animosity. There were some, prisoners included, who claimed that Quico had left them high and dry, which is a lie. In any organization it is the people in jail who suffer most, and although they get help, they never get all they need. So, I would bring in whatever I could and visit the homes where Quico had told me I should drop off a little cash, and I would deliver it. That was my task back then.

May '68

Just as there are today, in May 1968 there were a thousand reasons to protest and for bringing everything to a standstill in France. There have always been good reasons for a big general protest, so why did it erupt at that moment rather than earlier, and rather than today? This brings to mind certain phrases we used to use. We said, "You die when your number comes up, when your time comes," but we had no real way of gauging with certainty what the future would bring. And while death is a certainty, we can never be sure that people will come out and protest and fight to improve things. Turning points such as May '68 pop up when least expected.

At that point, the mainstay of the left in France was the Communist Party (PCF) with about twenty-five percent of the vote, and the CGT, the majority union federation, which was likewise communist. There was another party, the (socialist) SFIO, which had lost much of its prestige after several of its leaders had served in a government that carried out disastrous policies at home and internationally. The policy pursued by the PCF and the CGT stood out on account of its Stalinist inflexibility, its clumsiness and short-sightedness, which ensured that, in terms of their conduct and practice, they were neither leftist nor socialist even though they could call upon a strong, disciplined organization, unlimited propaganda resources, and all manner of political levers at the institutional level. Their greatest talent was for making life impossible for everyone in their own camp who opposed them. No one has ever mishandled power as badly as these so-called communists, which is why it is understandable that they have so little support from the people these days. The CGT commanded more support than anyone but only in the service of Russian interests and, at one point, took its orders directly from the Russians through the French party. The Socialist Party (SFIO), given its rightist line, could be discounted. That left only a tiny, younger, and more dynamic socialist party called the PSU that had a core of maverick students and its own trade union, the CGT-FO (Force Ouvrière), which had broken away from the CGT over the latter's performance and slavishness towards the Russians. But above all else, the PSU had a political leader of great stature in Pierre Mendès-France, a decent man who never succumbed to corruption and of whom we can state that he won and deserved everybody's respect.

The wounds of the recent war in Algeria had not yet healed and the entire process was still very fresh in everyone's minds. On the left, there was a climate of division and disorientation, with the added difficulty that many of us found it hard to express our views because the Stalinists would immediately kick in with their insults and there was the risk of losing one's job and indeed of physical violence. Back then voicing criticism meant opening yourself up to being written off as a traitor to the workers, or as a Falangist or pro-American. It was against this difficult backdrop that, at the recently built and newly opened University of Nanterre, teams of young students had begun to draft criticisms of how France had behaved and was still behaving in the wider world as well as at home. We had had centuries of theory, human rights galore, and a lot of progress had been made, but the Second World War still loomed large, as did the wars in Indochina and Algeria, not to mention France's behavior in the African colonized countries with the slave labor and the obligation to serve in the front ranks in times of war. The loudest opponents and critics of these policies had had their turn in power but had made no difference, so now they had lost any credibility. Some students toed the Maoist line, others were Trotskyists, and still others were up to their eyes in socialist and communist organizations. Between them all, they launched the so-called "March 22nd" Movement, the prevailing tendency of which was libertarian, and which had taken on board the experiences of the exiles from the Spanish CNT, in which one of the best-known student leaders, Daniel Cohn-Bendit, to mention but one, was well versed.

At the time, the Stalinists were strong enough to vilify and torpedo anything they did not control: anybody failing to toe their line was labelled a reactionary and an enemy of the workers. They had claimed a patent on representation of the working class as a body, although nobody could stop me and my friends from repeating over and over again, "I am a worker, but you don't represent me, and I do not want anything to do with you."

The University of Nanterre made a stand against the powers-that-be and the state, which is why it seemed logical enough to us to throw our weight behind it, even on matters in which it appeared not to be in the right. We figured, they may not be right today but they will be tomorrow, and in the meanwhile we'll have learned something about how to struggle at the least and how to take defeat. The issue had not been raised or the battle joined by the car plants, nor the construction or transport sectors, nor by any trade or agricultural or industrial union: which is why I stated earlier that whereas we all die when our number comes up, the fact is that we can never foretell when it will happen.

The fact is that it was all triggered by a student squabble over separation of the sexes, a squabble that the university rector tried to resolve according to his lights, his own outlook and code of morality. Protests followed, the police intervened, there was a crackdown and about ten students were charged, several of them friends of mine because they had been educated through the Spanish anarchist movement, and I had had frequent contact with three of them later as activists: Jean-Pierre Auteuil who runs a small publishing house these days; Daniel, now a professional politician; and Jean-François, a proofreader.

This all happened on March 22 and there was no way of telling how significant it was about to become. I believe it took on significance because of the behavior of the young and very bright Daniel Cohn-Bendit. Statements from the students aroused great sympathy from the wider public, whereas the then-secretary of the PCF, Georges Marchais, wrote the students off as spoiled brats and their leader as a German Jewish student. The fact is that the protests spilled over everywhere, and the strike spread from the universities to industry, all of it without any authorization or leave granted and in defiance of the express wishes of the Communist Party. The whole of France came to a standstill: the universities, transport services, the factories. Paris was left paralyzed, and all the big cities later shared the same experience.

Some days later, the communists stepped in, coming up with an alternative in an effort to raise their profile and an attempt to take the reins of a process in which they had, up until that point, played no part. Like the rest of the unions, the CGT jumped on the bandwagon too, after a fashion, relentlessly throwing slander and mud, spouting lies, and pulling the wool over people's eyes. Little good this did it, because nobody heeded the guidance it had to offer. Everyone was out on the streets, everybody was arguing and stating their opinion and whatever they knew and everybody, young or old, showed respect for one another.

People let out what was bothering them, without looking to organizations or parties of any persuasion, and the rallies started. The UNEF, the French National Union of Students (in which every sort of socialist, the PSU, communists, and Trotskyists had a presence, as had the anarchists, although the latter were not represented by a conventional organization) headed the first demonstrations, which featured red-and-black and black flags (where these came from I have no idea, any more than I could have dreamt that there were so many folk with a libertarian outlook). These days everybody acts independently but that was not the case then, and there is no denying that something new was going on, something that people were experiencing and enjoying. It was an eruption of freedom and a new urge to live.

And while the "usual suspects" carried on dismissing the students as bourgeois and as spoiled brats and throwing mud at their leaders, many of the university lecturers, writers, and intellectuals joined the movement. The Sorbonne was taken over and black and black-and-red flags were unfurled in the Odéon theater, and the actors came out in solidarity. There was an unprecedented climate of freedom and brotherhood.

By that point I was very emotional. You have stuck by your ideal through thick and thin but whenever you talk about it in public or at work, there were zealots who disrespected you and forced you, physically, to hold your tongue, which is never a pleasant experience. But now, the Sorbonne was overflowing with people, conversations and talks about Spain and self-management and libertarian ideas were proliferating and there was a new climate everywhere abroad. Sartre, long the intellectual adversary of Albert Camus and active in the ranks of our Stalinist foes, would converse with us and listen respectfully to what we had to say. He professed himself a supporter of libertarian ideas and acknowledged that my brothers, of whom a dim view was taken in Spain and who were penalized by the governments of Spain and France, had right on their side. And he even claimed to be an anarchist himself.

So much for the atmosphere in the Sorbonne. Outside, on the Boulevard Saint-Michel, the great poet Louis Aragon, another Stalinist, and director of the Communist Party paper *L'Humanité*, accosted Daniel during a student procession and told him that his sympathies lay with the students. At that point, Daniel grabbed him by the tie and retorted, "If you're with us students, how come you let that newspaper of yours insult us on a daily basis?"

It was a glimpse, a whirlwind of collective responsibility with everybody on a quest and working ideas through. At the Sorbonne, the home of the intelligentsia and right across the Latin Quarter there was a short flash of freedom and mutual respect. Regardless of all the drawbacks and obstacles that emerged, we were living out utopia and many a person found his path then and stuck to it, no matter how hard they found it to bear after harsh reality intruded once again and how often they lapsed into defeatism and also into despair. May '68 was a breath of craziness, an unsullied moment of solidarity, a struggle by the intelligentsia looking for peace and that urge to find out what lay behind all the division, all the personal selfishness and jealousy between nations, and all those people unfailingly fall apart after they achieve power. These were matters argued over for hours and days; I listened to conversations and talks given by a number of Nobel prize winners and lots of worthies, and I made the acquaintances of our Situationist friends alongside Daniel Guérin, a libertarian intellectual who would commit the latter years of his life to a quest for the truth behind the abduction of Moroccan trade unionist Ben Barka from the Boulevard Saint-Germain at the hands of the French and Moroccan secret services. I felt very far removed from them all, but I can tell you that I was excellent at using my pick to dig up the cobbles and tarmac from the streets. That is how things were during those days of hope; the swinging of a pick was considered a useful thing. Destruction may be necessary as an overture to construction later, just the way I had, in my working life, torn down the slums of Nanterre to erect better housing in their place.

But the ignorant and the under-skilled can make disastrous mistakes in such a heady atmosphere. I remember Jean Paul, a friend from Clichy, telling us one day that Raymond Aron, a "fascist," was examining his students and that we should go along and disrupt his class. About twenty-five of us clambered onto a truck, burst in, raising a rumpus, and effectively sabotaging the class. This was one of my most shameful acts, that I should have harmed a worthy man who was anything but a "fascist," but ignorance, stupidity, and poverty sometimes make fascists and Stalinists of us all.

The students and the March 22nd organization called a demonstration on May 13, and all of the so-called leftwing parties and trade union organizations joined in. The CGT, in particular, was not about to miss its chance. Until then, it had always been the doer and the undoer and it thought it had a patent on the present and the future. The demonstration moved off at two o'clock that afternoon from the Gare de l'Est, and the plan was to parade along the great boulevards as far as the arch of Saint Martin, then down to the Place de Saint-Michel and along the Seine as far as the Eiffel Tower. There was a massive, upbeat, peaceable crown at the Gare de l'Est, singing songs about the Paris Commune and some Spanish libertarian anthems, plus thousands upon thousands of flags, red ones and black ones. But the demonstration was not moving off. What happened? What happened was that, in accordance with their usual practice, the bigwigs from the Communist Party and the CGT tried to place themselves at the head of the procession. A lot was at stake right there for the future: the students, including Daniel Cohn-Bendit had lost all respect for them and dismissed them as Stalinists and told them that unless they were prepared to withdraw to a less prominent place in the body of the marchers, they could just piss off home.

It was then, at this demonstration, that for the very first-time, people who had for forty years thought of themselves as the lords and masters of the political left, were forced to back down, and a German Jew who was at that point a libertarian and a number of other groups unconnected with the CGT were catapulted into prominence. It was a premonition: a first step back by those who have since then continued to lose more and more ground, until these days they represent no more than any other grouplet.

The demonstration followed the agreed itinerary in a summery, party-type atmosphere until it came to the Champ de Mars. There the organizers stated that action committees should be formed everywhere to carry on with the general strike wave and to take it further. I had only recently got to know Anne and up until that point I had thought of myself pretty much as an outcast on account of my poverty and lack of education, accustomed as I was to living in the shadows. But now my eyes were opened, and I discovered that everybody was entitled to his say and to speak his mind and be himself. Besides, I was there with Anne whom I loved (and still do), which was something that meant a lot to who I was and the way I live my life. And there was another thing affecting the course my life was about to take: I was used to taking a hand in operations and matters requiring commitment, but what we were doing then was neither criminal nor dangerous; we were operating openly, in the light of day, in front of people and in concert with them.

As we strolled away from the esplanade in front of the Eiffel Tower (there was no public transport in operation), we came to the Place de Clichy and, at the bookshop on the corner, which is the Gallimard bookstore these days, we bought about fifty blank sheets and some thick-leaded pencils and set to work. There were four of us: a friend Robert Baldy, a conscientious objector who was living in London but who had taken a gamble and come over; his partner Marilyn; and Anne and me. Between the four of us we worked out what to scrawl on the blank sheets to call an urgent meeting in Clichy. A few days earlier, Jacques Duclos, a leading light in the Communist Party, had arrived in Clichy to give a talk at a school, and we knew, having attended it, that he had only attracted a crowd of thirty. What we had it in mind had nothing to do with that. The text we agreed upon was as follows: "Residents of Clichy and elsewhere, on the seventeenth at nine o'clock in the evening, an open rally will be held in the square outside Clichy council offices related to the current strike situation." This notice or poster was tacked to the trees, and we said to ourselves: if we can gather as many people on the seventeenth as that Communist Party bigwig, we will be doing well.

The big day arrived, and the rally was scheduled for nine o'clock, but Anne and I were on the steps in front of the council offices from eight. We began to see people milling around, wandering off and returning to the square. When the time came, the square was jam-packed; we had been expecting thirty people and here we had upwards of a thousand. What next? We, the organizers, were two people who did not know how to speak, because Anne had never spoken in public nor had she been seen at anything of the sort, and our friend Baldy had yet to arrive. I was in some bind. What a mess! All the politicians were there . . . the PSU to which Baldy belonged, five or six libertarians, the SFIO-controlled council, and the local CGT branch and Communist Party were there en masse. I was able to mumble something about our having called the rally to protest the repression at the Sorbonne: Baldy then arrived, and I breathed a sigh of relief, but it was at this point that the CGT folk and Party people started to chip in, bad-mouthing the students and especially that German Jew. There was a great furor: people could hear nothing, there was pushing and shoving, and insults were flung at me. Yes, the rally had been a great success but only half a success. The meeting was sabotaged, and we were unable to state our case and right up until one o'clock in the morning, insults were being traded. The lesson was not wasted on us: I realized that it was important to know how to talk and to have a megaphone available to reach out to all attending the rally.

The following day, I went out to the University of Nanterre, from which the 22 March Movement had emerged. Everywhere I looked I found cleverly subversive posters because the imagination was greatly to the fore in these events. There were posters opposing war, against some countries occupying other countries, supportive of education for all, critical of power or the powers-that-be, of the society of the spectacle and the consumer society. I had thought that it would be hard for me to gain access to the campus and meet people there. For one thing, I thought I would be greeted by older people whereas I was awaited by youngsters without labels or presumptions, who dealt with me in a very natural and friendly manner. They heaped praises on me, for some reason unknown to me, maybe because I was older than them or because they had sized up what sort of person I was or how I conducted myself. "I've come here from Clichy. We've organized a very important action committee there covering all age groups, workers, intellectuals, and students. We have enough in terms of numbers but none of us knows anything about public speaking and we need a speaker as a matter of urgency."

And so, between fifteen and twenty of us got together and talked amongst ourselves, but we didn't dare do it in front of a crowd because of our experience the previous day. We were eager to do something like that again, so we advertised that it was happening at eleven o'clock on Sunday morning. The young people who had greeted me, two girls and a boy, left me alone for a moment and then returned with a piece of paper bearing the name and address of someone who lived in Clichy. I wasn't familiar with him, but I was told he had just been released and was one of the activists from the Nanterre campus. Very pleased with myself now that we had our public speaker, I headed for Asnières to look up Maurice Lesaint, a libertarian friend who had worked a lot alongside Louis Lecoin on securing legal recognition for conscientious objection, including mounting a hunger strike that brought Lecoin to death's door, until he got what he wanted from General De Gaulle and Georges Pompidou. Lesaint was delighted to accept my invitation to come along to the council square to speak up for the students and the strike wave, and we arranged a time. From Asnières, I made my way to the headquarters of the CFDT, a union that was close to the PSU and that supported self-management: many of its members had a high regard for libertarians because they had always pushed for self-management. The most recent great experiment of the sort was the sit-in at Lip in 1973: the workers came out on strike, expropriated the bosses, and produced and sold goods and shared the profits. At the union

I found a young speaker for the Sunday rally, a comrade who still lives in the Rue de Paris, Jean Guéguin; he approached the strike committee at the Citroën plant to ask for a megaphone and to ask if anybody else wanted to attend the rally in Clichy. This was a bit of a novelty, for before Citroën got around to opening up its two huge plants in Clichy and Levallois, with much of the staff made up of immigrant workers, the CGT had had a monopoly on everything at the plant and it wanted nothing to do with students, nor would it allow anyone to set foot inside the workshops. But the action committee, made up of lots of trade unionists fed up with certain practices worse than anything the owners had done, opened up the gates to rival trade unions, as did the newer, younger workers.

By now we had everything we needed: experienced speakers, a megaphone, and posters tacked to the trees. We had a real sense of our own importance because we represented our local committee, the Citroën action committee, and others still. On a new poster, we listed what the speakers would be talking about and said that there would be an opportunity for anybody to put in their two cents. Everything was stopped and nothing was working, but people were chatting in the streets and cafés and there were always people arguing in the town square. That's how it was in Clichy.

Everyone turned up on Sunday except the speaker recommended by the Nanterre students. Suddenly, a very young lad arrived; he was very disheveled and fresh-faced. This was the student from Nanterre whose praises I had been singing even though I had never set eyes on him or heard a word from his mouth! He was the son of an English father and a French mother, and the moment he spoke we realized that he had a stutter, which was a let-down in terms of public speaking. But from that day forth, he participated in all our activities, and we struck up a friendship. He was one of the people arrested and charged—alongside Daniel and Jean-Pierre—with being behind the complete shutdown of the Nanterre campus to begin with and thereafter the whole country, something that, at first glance, seemed like nonsense. At the root and in the history of May '68 we can find all manner of contradictions, but the world kept turning all the same. Nanterre was at that point the main flywheel, but there are still little inexplicable cogs in existence that might, when the time comes, set bigger wheels in motion and trigger an immense movement absurdly out of all proportion with its origins.

I climbed on to the steps outside Clichy council offices with the square packed with people and, poor speaker though I may be, I introduced the Clichy committee and stated that anyone with anything to say was free to speak and that the megaphone was available to all and sundry. The meeting was going very well, and the speakers were well received; there were people there who disagreed with the strike and there was some arguing, but no one made threats and nobody provoked anyone else. Lesaint and our friend from the CFDT made intelligent contributions to the debate. And then, all of a sudden, the CGT secretary who was there at the head of the Communist Party branch, asked to use the megaphone and, once he had it in his hands, and just as everybody thought that he was poised have his say, he announced, "This megaphone is the property of the Citroën workers of Clichy whom I represent and I'm taking it." Nobody could fathom this: I who was at the top of the steps and very close to where he was jumped up immediately, grabbed the megaphone and cried out, "This megaphone belongs to the Citroën plant's action committee, and it is not for you to seize it. It is ours and you are not having it." Confusion ensued and there was a great stir in the square: the secretary was tugging one side of the megaphone and I the other, and I soon found myself surrounded by a tide of CGT and Party personnel. Wasting no more time, I landed a huge punch on the secretary, leaving him with a swollen, closed eye gushing blood like a stuck pig. The rally was wound up and for a while I walked on eggshells around the police due to his threats.

Little by little the fires of May '68 were petering out, but the flames of need were burning still, which is a necessary and a very important thing. Here, in western Europe, we may not go short of bread (although of course there are still a few who do not have enough to live on), but what we lack is imagination. We need to waken the imagination. To hell with rest. Life is all about activity and it is a privilege to be drained to the last drop as we strive to make life richer for ourselves and for our children and grandchildren.

May '68 brought with it hope, just when it was least expected. Today we know, more than we did then, that nothing is certain and that another explosion of rebelliousness within society might come at any moment. Beneath the still waters run dangerous currents and someday madcap, utopian notions of freedom will resurface; we need them to if society is to make progress.

Anne

I would like to say, if I can, what I think of Anne, the mother of my daughter Juliette. Anne is also my wife, for we are married and have thus far not sought a divorce, and our relationship is, in my belief, very positive. We are separate but always together through the sadness and the tears, the upsets and the rages, linked by an enormous love confirmed by shared practice. That is how it has been so far, and I see no changes on the horizon. Let me go further: I carry two loves with me . . . love for my daughter and for Anne.

No one can explain it, but love has brought me life—my life—but it has brought me suffering too. And it is not over yet; it carries on. Some say that there is no such thing as love, but love has spurred me on. On several occasions I have ignored or overlooked the demands of that love, but I knew what was required of me and what I felt was being asked of me. It is not for me to say but I have also been loved, and I think I still am, by Anne and my nearest and dearest. But I know I can be a handful and that putting up with me is a very complicated business.

I met Anne shortly before the events of May '68. She struck me as very young and very elegant, and I am only saying this so as not to indulge in the silly talk one hears from all and sundry. For me, it was love at first sight. Anne was then living in the Latin Quarter at No 5, Rue des Fossés Saint Marcel and for the first time in my life I heard somebody talking with profound passion about poetry and literature: about Arthur Rimbaud, Louis-Ferdinand Céline, and Albert Camus. Some years before, in her student days, if she was bored at home with her parents, Anne used to lock herself in her room and escape in literature until the boredom had passed. This is something I found out much later, when her parents told me. The only one of those writers with whom I was familiar was Albert Camus and, in terms of Spanish poetry, Federico García Lorca. Georges Brassens, Léo Ferré, and the line-up of singer-songwriters now deceased and irreplaceable—Mouloudji, Brel, and Cathérine Sauvage—loomed very large in my estimation. They were all libertarians and they all helped us out. I might even say that it was their poetry that brought me to Anne.

We were a very different pair, in terms of everything except our lives and what they demanded of us. When the May events came along, our acquaintance deepened. Anne has a very passionate nature and I remember driving her out near the Panthéon—the entire area under occupation by the CRS (*Compagnies Républicaines de Sécurité*). It was at one or two o'clock in the morning and when I braked, Anne shouted at me, "Step on it, step on it!" She was not at all fazed by the possibility that they might arrest us and thought I had braked out of fear. I had no reason to feel afraid, so I got annoyed and forced her to get out of the car. A few days after that, we agreed to a secret rendezvous at a cinema. The police cleared it out and beat the audience as we filed outside; Anne could not even walk. Covered in bruises and scabs, she headed home to Villenauxe-la-Grande in Champagne and her parents gave her a very tender welcome, seeing her in that state. She asked her father to turn his business over to self-management the way the anarchists had done in Spain. He asked her what self-management was and when she had explained it to him, he said, "Daughter, daughter, I think maybe you haven't taken enough of a beating yet."

At about the same time, Anne and a local artist set about publicizing what had happened in the Latin Quarter through newspapers, posters, and propaganda brought in from Paris. The locals took note of this, and rumors began to circulate that she was the leader of some terrorist group. Her parents were petits bourgeois, rightwing Catholics but that didn't stop them from responding to this nonsense with great dignity. They always stood by us.

Anne and I lived together in an apartment in the Rue des Pyrénées in the 20th arrondissement. We worked together and engaged in our Clichy action committee activities together, along with others. But when Juliette was born, we were living at 134, Boulevard Jean Jaurès in Clichy in the building where my sister Satur was concierge. Anne was working in Paris in a laboratory in the Rue Clignancourt at the time.

Franco was still alive then and, in our hearts, we were antifascists and anti-Francoists. Since Anne's appearance was impeccable and she spoke with no trace of a foreign accent, she looked after the rental side of things, in which being well turned-out is crucial. She would sign the leases on apartments we used for back-up and for whatever machinery we needed. She was in charge of filling out whatever documents we intended to copy, as well as a powerful machine for stitching documents together. Juliette also played her part in some of these activities. Whenever I need to retrieve all sorts of equipment and machinery from hiding places for delivery to Spain, Anne would help me and indeed she was the one who got the shipments clandestinely to their destination in our vehicles, crossing the border very carefully. Furthermore, when Bernard Kouchner set up Médecins Sans Frontières (Doctors Without Borders), Anne became active in that organization.

Anne did all these things as well as holding down her laboratory job. Her boss, Doctor Luc de Seguin, was a very humane freemason and leftist, who treated her very well and spoke up for her as the need arose. Anne must have put in about twenty-five years working for him; the pair of them were forever working. We were earning enough to live comfortably and were able to set something aside for a rainy day.

Anne was arrested and called upon to make a statement many times, most recently in 1996. Her biggest and most worrisome trial was in relation to the kidnapping of the banker Baltasar Suárez in 1974. She and a few others were arrested and charged, and she served a number of months in Fleury-Mérogis prison.

It was then that Kouchner stepped forward as a character witness for Anne and made the following statement:

"*Monsieur le président*, can you see among the accused this lady who will or will not be sentenced by the court you are chairing? This lady, who may well get five or ten years in prison, would, but for this trial, be in Kurdistan this very day, helping, easing suffering, and rescuing children and old people even as other humanitarians are doing at this very moment. This lady, who anxiously and nervously awaits the determination of this court, brings honor upon France and upon us all. She has already been deprived of her freedom for several months: I ask you and I ask the court to show every indulgence so that she may walk free as soon as possible and continue bringing honor upon us and doing the good that children and the elderly crave and are waiting for."

His humane and articulate praise caused a tremendous stir in the courtroom; there was tremendous emotion and several people from the High Court and from the jury were unable to hold back their tears.

Kouchner then left Médecins Sans Frontières to set up another NGO, Médecins du Monde and Anne went with him. She has devoted at least two months out of every year, plus trips abroad, to this professional work, for no pay beyond room and board, out of solidarity with the most vulnerable peoples of Asia, Africa, and America, prompted by humanitarianism and selflessness. She has made several visits to Thailand to support the Burmese refugees drawn from the Karen ethnic group and there she caught malaria and was very ill. She has also worked in several countries in Africa and was in Rwanda four intense months when the genocide was in full swing.

Retired these days, Anne commits six hours a day to Médecins du Monde. She heads up that NGO's Latin America team and mission in Haiti and is happy to do so and to be making her daily contribution out of conviction and solidarity. The only thing I can add is that it is a pity there are not more like her.

Income tax declaration

We'd go down to Villenauxe-la-Grande to visit Anne's parents, and her mother and I were the earliest risers. We used to have breakfast together each morning while the others slept on, so we had a chance to chat, and she would regale me with stories of the 1914 war and Second World War. In Anne's town, a POW camp had been built and a stack of German prisoners passed through its gates. Young Germans who were regularly visited and taken out to work in the fields and at other trades. Many families developed a soft spot for them. Stories like this taught me about certain facets of war and about the injustice of national governments.

Anne's mother was a highly intelligent person who had been a schoolteacher before taking over the bookkeeping for the heating company that her husband had set up with his brothers. She enjoyed nothing better than having us all around the enormous table: her sons-in-law, her own sons, her grandchildren, and a host of relatives.

That was where I had my first taste of oysters and first drank champagne. Anne was in quite advanced stages of pregnancy. At the crack of dawn, I would be off with Anne's father delivering estimates and collecting on or delivering bills to customers. They were nearly all champagne and liqueur producers. Needless to say, many times, we arrived back for dinner well satisfied with these customers' cellars and homes. I always say that back home all we ever think about is eating, drinking, and a singsong; well in Anne's town and home region that is how it was, with just one variation: eating, drinking, singing . . . and prayer.

One fine day, Anne's mother, in that way of talking the French have, an educated but hard-headed and direct woman, asked me a question somewhat worriedly, "Son, have you done your income tax returns yet?" I acted as if this meant nothing and made no answer. The following day, a Sunday, while we were at breakfast she tackled me again, "Lucio, have you made out your income tax return yet?" I waffled as best I could without answering her. I was not sure what she would make of my reply; our relations with the family were very good and I had no wish to lock horns with any of them over my beliefs or outlook. The week after that, again in the morning, while Anne's mother and I were breakfasting, she said to me at the earliest opportunity, "Listen Lucio, I haven't had a wink of sleep all week: I am very worried because it looks to me as if you have not done your income tax return and that worries me. It is a very serious matter, and you can get in big trouble. You're going to be living together so get it done as soon as you can, or I can do it for you if you'd prefer." My response was that I had never made one out nor had I any intention of starting, seeing as I am opposed to taxes on the grounds that they subsidize war and the arms industry, which I think is unfair, and ordinary people are to blame for that. I bombarded her with arguments logical and illogical and I was quite nasty about it, talking thoughtlessly and clumsily. I insisted that governments ruled through their record of crime and violence against poorer peoples. It was a rant that fitted in with my ideals and anarchist education but it was brutal, shambolic, and inarticulate, and although I was right on a number of points, I realized that it was upsetting and disturbing to Anne's mother, as well as to me.

Shortly after that I made out the declaration. Up until then I had been living in a tiny apartment in Clichy and Anne in the Rue des Pyrénées, but we had just moved in together into 134, Boulevard Jean Jaurès. We made out the statement from the Rue des Pyrénées address and I figured that if they were looking for me, they would try Clichy, whereas at my new address I would be in order with the courts and that that would spare me problems in my life and spare the family. Confusion had me perform what I regarded as a betrayal of my ideals, and I submitted my first ever income tax return.

That must have been in 1973, and I thought my statement would slip past unnoticed, but problems started to crop up before two weeks had passed. On coming home from work one day, I spotted an eye-catching notice posted on a neighboring building announcing that on such and such a date a wardrobe, a radio, four chairs, and some dishes would be sold off at public auction. They belonged to one Urtubia, Lucio, residing at 134, Boulevard Jean Jaurès, 4th apartment on the left. I looked around and saw more posters and I did my best to tear them down. I felt as if I was gasping for air. Such things annoy me and piss me off and it was as if we were back in the days of the Holy Inquisition, with the public auctioning of three of Monsieur Urtubia's chattels. It was a horrible feeling, especially when I was trying to begin a new life with my daughter Juliette and with Anne.

My sister Satur was concierge of the building and looked after Juliette for us. A number of men had arrived to put up the notices, and they had in tow a police inspector, a court officer, an official from the Finance ministry as well as a locksmith, in a great show of strength. My sister, intimidated, thought it really was a case of a public execution and that I was to be burned at the stake. All of this passed over Juliette's head and she slept right through it, being very young at the time. They posted the notices about recovery of taxes from the entrance hall right up as far as the fifth floor. Once the henchmen had gone, Satur tore down all the notices in the stairwell thinking that they were the only ones posted, but when she discovered that they had also put them up in the street outside (something she had never even dreamed they would do), she was sickened even more. She found it shameful that they were putting her brother's belongings up for auction.

When I got upstairs to the apartment, I found that they had been inside and had left behind a summons ordering me to appear at the tax recovery office to sort things out. I had never made out a tax declaration as I thought it was unjust and immoral to pay taxes just to fund wars and criminality. For seventeen years I had been receiving forms inviting me to do a tax return and I had always sent them back marked "Not known at this address," "Away traveling," or "Deceased." They had also forced entry into my place in the Rue Castères but in those days I was a free agent, living alone and without a pot to piss in. That was swell; I felt like a wealthy man and life was all joy, getting by on very little but with my needs met. The story of the poor cobbler who had no shirt and who spent all his days singing to himself while his wealthy neighbor was overwhelmed by the worries created by his wealth came to mind. That was how I had been before Juliette came along and before I fell in love with Anne.

Some of the firms I had worked for tried to dock my wages in order to pay my tax, but I was not up for that and told them, "Pay me my due and I'm off. I am not about to shell out good money for people to be killed and to fund wars." And then I'd switch jobs. There were lots of others like me and they were not all anarchists. Many of them were Christians.

The following Monday I showed up at the Finance office as instructed by the note they'd left. There were several people waiting for me there, among them the chief inspector from Clichy: I told them as best I could that I wanted to sort out my tax status and was ready to pay 500 francs a month or whatever arrangement we might come to. But two of the big-wigs told me that I had been making fools out of them and that I owed them seventeen years' back taxes. According to the law, tax debt is wiped out after five years if it was the Inspectorate that had been negligent in collecting it. But since, in my case, they had been pressing me for many years and I had not coughed it up, they could force me to pay every penny. Just my luck. It was out of my hands now and I was left dumbfounded, feeling really, really sick and not knowing how to answer. Crushed by the steam-roller of the law.

That was how things stood when somebody gave me the address of a woman to whom I could turn for help and a solution to the problem looming over me. I made my way to the regional tax office, knocked on the door, stepped inside and the lady in question was on the telephone: without hanging up, she asked me what was up and in my straight-taking way I told her, "I'm here because they're intending to sell off my radio, chairs, and a wardrobe. I have a young child and I am married, and this is all because I owe some taxes. But I'm looking for a way to sort things out."

The lady carried on talking into the telephone while she heard me out and then asked me how much I owed and told her: "Seventeen years." When she heard that, she told the person at the other end: "I have to go, I have to hang up. I have an intriguing case here." She asked me why I had let so many years go by without paying any tax and I replied, "Question of ethics, Madame." She asked, "What do you mean, 'ethics'?" So I told her, "Well, do you think everybody has the same ethics as the baby Jesus? I have my own set of ethics and I am not prepared to shell out to kill people."

The fact is that the woman was greatly taken by my case and told me, "What I am about to do I have no right to be doing, but I'm going to help you." And she took me in hand. She helped me write up the necessary letters, dictating the contents to me because they were not supposed to help nonpayers and she told me that this would have to remain between the two of us. That was my salvation, and, in the end, I had to pay out very little, next to nothing.

Juliette

At three o'clock in the morning one day in 1970, Anne realized that her water had broken, and her mother brought her by car to Clichy, to the Les Allées clinic in the Passage Léon Gambetta, where she gave birth to Juliette. Before all that I had told everybody time and time again—especially Anne's family—that if we had a boy, I would name him Germinal. Later, as a joke, I stated that Anne's mother had prayed for it not to be a boy so that he might not be saddled with that revolutionary name.

Moving into 134, Boulevard Jean Jaurès where my sister Satur was the concierge was a stroke of luck for all concerned, as my sister used to help us with the girl and in many other ways. She lived on the first floor and we on the fourth.

When Juliette was old enough to attend infant school, Anne used to take her in at nine o'clock in the morning before traveling on to work in her Citroën 2CV. I started work very early at six o'clock in the morning and would collect the child from school at 4:30 p.m. When it turned warm, Juliette liked to pop into the St Vincent de Paul church. I think she did this more than anything else because she had heard me speak ill of the Church. Another practice of ours was that when school got out each day I used to buy her a *réligieuse* (a chocolate cake) from the bakery as a snack. That was our way of life: we worked, we shared, and we received. We also bought ourselves a Volkswagen *combi* in which we would go wherever the fancy took us: between one long trip and another, we toured all the Nordic countries. These days I can appreciate and am profoundly grateful for the happiness of those years.

One day in May 1974, as I was leaving the restaurant to return to work on the site behind the Hilton hotel, I was arrested by a number of police officers. Anne was picked up the same day. We later discovered that the police were linking us to the abduction of the manager of the Banco de Bilbao branch in Paris. I was unable to go and pick Juliette from school as I usually did (she was then four years old) and neither, obviously, was Anne, so it was the police who collected her and brought her to Satur's home. The police urged my sister not to open the door to anyone for there was about to be a plague of people and reporters bothering her. I ought to say at this point that the police behaved better than the reporters who, as ever, wrote whatever fantastic tales they saw fit.

For several months Juliette was fatherless and motherless although she could count on Anne's family and mine who did a great job of shielding her. She spent some time in Cascante with my own family. The kid was told from the outset that we had gone to London to work and would soon be back again, but she was never told that her parents were in jail. Anne was freed before me but was banned from leaving the country and so was still unable to see her daughter who was still in Cascante. When we were finally able to pop down and see Juliette (by clandestine means in my case), my sisters came to the outskirts of town with the little girl to meet us and Juliette refused to even look at us. She was barely four years old and had taken offense at our absence. She took the view that we had deserted her, and she bore a grudge over this. That was our interpretation of it.

Juliette was raised in our ethos of clandestinity; she used to help her mother in preparing a thousand different things in secret locations. On several occasions, she came to see me in prison, and she also witnessed the house searches carried out by the police and she answered questions from some people whose identities we were never able to establish. What we know and what the girl knew is that she was never to use our home phone. Sometimes it was a considerable walk to the nearest phone and from a very early age she knew to check if there was anything odd going on behind her. Whenever she was traveling on the metro, she used to switch seats for no real reason just to check if anybody was tailing her.

At the time of the big trial for the kidnapping of the banker Suárez, the headmistress of Juliette's school and all the schoolmistresses, as well as her harp teacher, showered Juliette with attention and sympathy. Brigitte Hemmerlin, a lawyer, collected her childish testimony in a book *Paroles d'innocents*, devoted to the predicament of the children of detainees. Some years later Juliette took part in a TV show on the same subject and spoke very well and in a very convincing fashion and displayed great maturity and self-possession.

I could tell you so very many things about her. These days she is married to a lad from Cascante who runs the Atelier 71 company, she works as a teacher of Spanish at a high school and has two children of her own. We love them all madly, but we are still at odds with one another, most likely on account of my difficult nature.

On the job

When I started out working in construction in France, the first thing demanded of any bricklayer was significant physical stamina. Working hours were long: eight in wintertime but a lot more during the summer months.

Upon arrival on a new site, our first order of business was to erect a sort of very lightly constructed, simple wooden hut so that we would have somewhere to change our clothes, with a padlock to protect our clothes and belongings. We also put up hooks—a wooden board and nails—for hanging up our clothes. In winter it was a real ordeal to get changed in the mornings as well as in the afternoons when we would wash up, because there were no sinks, and we used the icy water from some standpipe. The foundations of the buildings we made by hand using pick and shovel; a few firms had begun to use more modern gear but nearly everything was done by hand. In many firms, the initial spadework was done by squads of navvies who were in plentiful supply and who were all unionized in the CGT; they were anarcho-syndicalists, generally very pugnacious and, in theory, very well paid as compared with the other trades.

After the foundations, the latrines were dug, a huge pit two and a half meters deep and a meter and a half across, covered over with sturdy boards leaving a hole into which everything was directed for as long as the work lasted. If the job dragged on and the hole filled up, a second one was dug adjacent to it. The basic foundations were of stone and mortar; the latter was mixed by hand, except in the case of more modern firms, which had access to cement mixers. One way or the other, the mortar was a blend of cement, sand, and rough aggregate and we used to break into a sweat filling the bucket because we had to slide it along with our foot every time.

The load-bearing walls supporting the construction were made of large rocks with a skim of mortar; not only did we have to hand mix the stuff before application, but we also had to hoist everything up by hand-operated pulley. The pulley was used to lift everything, materials and water alike. Once the construction reached a given height, the flooring was installed at each level using strong wooden planks secured at each end by thin but very strong brickwork, and cement was poured into all the gaps. Next came the construction of the internal walls, roofing, and plasterwork. Outside work was laborious and dangerous, for the gangplanks were very rudimentary and secured with ropes that were not very safe. These conditions applied from start to finish; people in this line of work were tested by the physical demands, the cold, the heat, and foul weather. A lot of drink was drunk, and red wine and the building trade went hand in hand.

Years later the building trade was modernized with more differentiation between trades and an easing of working conditions. Now we were roofers, cement-layers, and tilers, and so on. All these trades were taxing, but the cement guys and tilers had the heaviest work of all; the former because they were forever working in damp conditions and when it came to laying down the cement they had to dart around, sweating. Compared to the other tradesmen, the cement layers earned a very good living, but their work was exhausting.

The tiler was in charge of finishing off the floors and walls. Floor work was always very tough; by contrast, when it came to finishing a wall with tiles or the like, there were tradesmen who never even bothered to change their clothes because they never, or hardly ever spilled anything, and their apprentices did all the prep work for them. That trade took off when it had to tackle large surfaces; my first tiling job was in Orly, and it was there that I learned the job from the more experienced comrades on site. We also did big jobs for Prisunic and other superstores. In those days a tiler would do three times as much as he would today, and all by hand. If we were working outside of Paris, we would report for work on the Monday and not return home until Friday afternoon; we worked whatever hours we chose because we were paid piece rates, so much per square meter, in accordance with rates that had been agreed between the employers' organization and the CGT union, the only union catering for tilers. When working away from home, we used to try to finish the job as quickly as we could so that we might get back home as early as we could; we were the ones who set the working hours, but we rarely did less than a twelve-hour day. That way we were able to finish the job in under a week and take home a very respectable wage.

Very often these working arrangements brought us into dispute with foremen and charge hands because we might be earning twice as much as them and that generated hostility and jealousy. When working on the tiling of tower blocks, we had problems getting the materials brought up. If the structural builders were still on site and their equipment was still in place, everything was fine as we could come to some financial arrangement with the crane operator, and on the Saturday or the Sunday he would hoist whatever we needed up to the right floor; it was all down to coordinating jobs and greasing palms.

Floor tiling was really heavy work: all of the work lifting the floor and levelling things out prior to laying the tiles was done on one's knees and in damp conditions. When there was no crane to keep the materials coming, we had a tough time of it because everything—cement, sand, tools, flagstones, and tiles—had to be lugged up the maybe twelve or fourteen floors manually. Whenever there were ten floors to climb, we worked in three-man teams; the first ganger would load a bag of cement or sand on his shoulder and climb until he could hand it on to the next stager and then head downstairs for another bag; and so on. After three or four such climbs you needed a sit-down and a bit of a breather.

The work back then was a lot tougher and more intense than it is these days. There was still the odd Frenchman to be found on site, although most of us were Italians, North Africans, and Spaniards. Not only did we work longer hours than they do these days, but there were practices and training that have now been lost. Workers formed cooperatives; people wanted to be free, and on site all the talk was of self-management. Analysis and explanation of how that preoccupation fizzled out would be sorely needed. These days the tradesman has more money and time to himself, but I do not think we are any freer now than we were back then. What does freedom mean?

My own boss

The best way of learning how to endure the contradictions of working life and to adapt to work is to start very young. Everything has since become much less burdensome and easier, or I think so anyway, although by my guess this doesn't suit everybody. I mean the hard graft, unpleasant drudgery, the sort of work one does out of necessity, without any taste for it and just to eke out a living; the individual engaged in something he enjoys is a quite different beast and his work is not so much work as pleasure. But very few find pleasure in the work they do to earn their living. This is something quite hard to achieve, and harder still to acknowledge. For someone to get to that point they have to start working at a very early age.

Anything I might say on the subject is because of what I went through, practiced, and shared with friends and acquaintances of mine as I grappled with what life threw or what was thrown at me. I can't recall a single work colleague that I regard as an enemy and I have good memories of them all. With some, I am connected by an enduring friendship and, with others, by mutual regard.

During my twenty-five years as a bricklayer, I dreamed of moving beyond working for someone else, of not being ordered about by undesirable bosses. From time to time, I managed to strike out on my own, without going legit, sometimes on my own and sometimes with others. As for the cooperative I tried to launch after I got out of jail, as I recount elsewhere, it never took off, which was a disappointment and a learning experience for me. Each of my friends was a revolutionary, which is one thing, but being bricklayers, carpenters, and laborers is quite another.

My outlook underwent a complete transformation back then and a friend and I made up our minds to set up a small firm of our own, the idea being to make our living without working for wages and to manage ourselves. For months, I spent all day at work on site and, at night, after work was over, I would visit clients and draw up estimates. Everything was going well, and my friend did what he could; he was the manager, but we took very different views on things. Friends and partners were one thing and even though we had known each other for many years, the situation became very strained, and the company collapsed due to our inability to see eye to eye. It is possible to be an excellent workman but a very poor boss, even with the best of intentions on both sides.

One day, a gentleman born in Madrid who had set up a family firm decided to put it on the market. The firm's name was Caro, the family name. It boasted a Mercedes truck, its premises, all its materials, and its workforce. Among the latter there was a highly efficient and discreet secretary in Madame Belloy and a Galician from Villagarcía de Arousa, one Benito Ferreiro, a great friend of mine and a fine worker but one inclined to be timid. On one occasion I invited him to become a partner in the firm and he admitted to me that he did not have the gumption to take on the responsibility.

The Caros lived near the little Spanish restaurant where we usually had dinner and that's where we heard that the firm was on the market. We did the business and bought the little firm outright at a very decent price.

The greatest assets of any firm are the quality of its staff and the excellence of its administration. The early days were hard because in those days I knew nothing about red tape, laws, budgeting, and so on, and I knew that ability to work was one thing and ability to run a firm quite another. Madame Belloy became my teacher; she had always worked "on the q.t.," either for Caro or for her husband's painting and decorating firm. As regards to this new venture of ours, all our employees were "official" except for Manuel Dasilva, a Portuguese apprentice who was very young. He's still with the firm today, some thirty years later. Everybody started off on very decent wages. Initially it was some time before I took a wage and the first money we made went to pay off the truck.

On one occasion, working on Paco Rabanne's private residence in the Boulevard Aragon, Manuel's mallet sent a fragment of wall flying and it landed on the neighborhood electricity transformer. It was as if a bomb had gone off. The lad was stunned, and the neighborhood was plunged into darkness. There was a real song and dance made about it. The following day twenty trucks arrived to repair the damage and we promptly made Manuel "official" although he was no longer on the scene.

During the negotiations to purchase the firm, Monsieur Caro introduced Monsieur Thomas, a man who is etched on my memory. He was a very wealthy but very hard-working man. We were introduced to each other and hit it off. After that, I spent many a Saturday and Sunday in his company. As in my own case, he had never had the chance to move back home to his native Auvergne; he had a house there, but he only managed to spend the odd day there, every now and then.

Monsieur Thomas, his wife, and children ran—and still run—a big estate rental agency and are available around the clock should any problem arise in the accommodation they manage. We have been working with them for over thirty years, with never a problem. Their outlook and my own are very different, but they are in the office at 7:30 every morning. Thanks to them a lot of work has come our way.

The friend with whom I had set up the firm took charge of the managing of it, since I couldn't do it because I was awaiting a court decision. We were such different people that eventually we decided to go our separate ways. He preferred for me to carry on with the firm, so I found myself out on my own. I faced a lot of problems during those early stages, but I was convinced that with due patience they could all be sorted out. I used to work Sundays as well, because I had no one to rely on to do the books for our projects and budgeting. I could feel that I was making headway, not that the money was rolling in, but I was making headway on my own account, and no one was being abused. Since I enjoyed what I was doing, it was not work as far as I was concerned. Overnight, I stumbled upon the delights of working on something enjoyably humane and good. When working on something that brings you satisfaction, it doesn't matter how exhausted you become, because the effort is no burden. Indeed, it is a pleasure.

I also stumbled upon the delights of going out with friends for a snack or to dine in fancy restaurants, and I have been a regular at the same spots many years. There is nothing presumptuous about my belief that our workers earned a very good living and they still do today, under José Luis, my son-in-law.

Other workers were added to the complement and within years we had about thirty people. The firm itself expanded and became two separate ventures: Atelier 71, which handled the bricklaying and foundation work, and Deco 71, which handled the carpentry, painting, decorating, and plumbing work.

The discretion of Madame Belloy, our company secretary, was especially important: whenever she was summoned by the police to provide certain information, she never said anything. She was very brave since, had she "coughed," workers such as Benito and Manuel would have quit the firm.

I had some problems with people sent or recommended to me as workers because of their lack of skill, as they had never worked in construction before and had to be shown everything from the basics up, including how to sweep up. Many had dropped out of school; others had never had the need to work and were over twenty years old and spent forces. They thought that working on a building site was easy, but they soon learned different, as it takes many years of practice and hard work to learn any trade. Some people applied for work but lasted barely an hour or a day. I remember one Italian friend, Gino, who was due to start work at 8:00 a.m. but showed up at 10:00. I set him to transporting some materials with a wheelbarrow and after eight to ten trips he said to me, "Lucio, I haven't done a anything in the last ten years and you, my friend, are not going to make me work." He dumped the wheelbarrow and walked out. The poor fellow had no luck; he left for Nicaragua and over there became ill and died. That particular friend knew thousands of things but building work—seemingly insignificant things like sweeping up or taking down a wall, things one has to learn to do well and that require considerable hard work—was not one of them.

There is widespread ignorance of construction work and lack of respect for the trade. Logically, that sort of exacting work ought to be well paid, and oddly enough, pay rates back home in Navarra are better than they are in France right now.

For a long time, through friends and lawyers and contacts, a lot of young men in prison would ask me for what we term a "promise of work," a document normally requested by the courts before they will authorize or grant their discharge from jail. On a few occasions, I had to do the same thing myself and I know that prisoners who had no one to offer them this sort of support took longer to win their release.

One of our intentions in launching the firm was to help refugees by issuing them documents and offering them a chance to pick up a trade and earn their living. It is a special privilege to have helped reintegrate these people into society just by putting my signature to a few papers containing a promise of employment. It has not always been as straightforward as it might seem, but I believe I have been partially successful. I have already mentioned some of the difficulties I encountered in certain cases. Being a small firm, it was hard for us to place workers. In a big firm, a worker who knows nothing can be hidden among other workers and nobody notices whether he knows what he is doing. And, on the larger sites, the client is not present.

In most instances there were no problems; I was able to take on lots of ex-cons and refugees. Luckily, I can say that, despite all the work and all the problems, I now have lots and lots of friends whom I met through work. My greatest problems were with workers who didn't work for long enough to pick up their trade and learn how to respect it. There are people hell bent on getting rich but who, if they were to be paid based on the work they do, would starve to death. On one occasion I had a run-in with a fool who used to bicker with and abuse everybody else, quite apart from the fact that he did not have a clue as a tradesman. I am forever saying that there is no manna from heaven and that there is a price to be paid for everything; in order to be free, one must first be a slave. And there is another great truth in the fact that a man with a trade can tell the world to go take a hike, so to speak.

As I see it, running a firm is not just about making money. The boss is the driving force and should take care over the ethos of the firm, ensure that there are welcoming, well-appointed, and clean premises, tend to his staff, his customers, the bank, and so on. He should realize that the earnings are not his but belong to the staff and that all he gets is the leftovers after everything else has been shared out.

Not that I think my life as a boss is in any way shameful; I have always considered myself a worker answerable to the firm rather than as an entrepreneur. And I have loved the workers alongside whom I have worked a lot more than they have loved me. I always dreamed of a different modus operandi in some firm where there was more brotherhood, sharing, and inventiveness. A firm that would invest the profits, rather than their being gobbled up by one individual. But it's tough; if it wasn't, everybody would be a boss. I reached for freedom when the time came, though it was a very special kind of freedom. Up until I retired at the age of seventy-two, I worked every day of the year, putting in at least twelve hours every weekday and at least six on Sundays. This was a personal triumph: everybody pursues his own brand of freedom and I have had to put in more work just to have my freedom. I am firmly persuaded that we all need to fight harder to be free. Freedom and revolution consist of ongoing effort.

To conclude, let me say that nobody should think himself any better than anybody else just because he started a business that is a going concern but equally no one should think that running one is easy either. The only thing I can say without fear of contradiction is that for a firm to be a going concern, a great deal of effort is required. As the saying goes, "Let the master look to his assets or sell them off."

At no time, either as a workman or as a boss, have I ever worked on the construction of prisons or military establishments, but I should say that I was never offered any such jobs. Some of my customers were out and out fat cat fascists, while others have been marvelous. Among them I number several close friends, photographers, bookdealers, or writers. The lousiest person I ever had as a customer was one wretched reporter from the newspaper *El País*. I presented him with an estimate for the job and, taking advantage of my access to discounted home electrical goods, I installed the full range of them, just as I did the bathroom cabinets, which set me back a fortune. But because those were not included in the original estimate, he refused to cough up for them. The matter was allowed to rest at that, else it turn into a serious matter, but I have not forgotten about him.

Job satisfaction

It gives me a real buzz to stroll through Paris and see sites that I have worked on, or to know that just over there there may be an aesthetically pleasing former job of mine whose occupants are happy with work carried out well and acknowledged as such. Feeling useful and making one's contribution toward life's pleasures are a source of pride.

In the Rue de Saumur, we did Blondine Compte's Libre de Lire bookshop, which was later expanded after the adjoining pharmacy was bought out or handed over. Most of the local children visited the expansion to read, and Blondine would hold readings for them once a week. Activities were held in the basement for adults. It was a success and still is, and I derived great satisfaction from this. Another huge inspiration of a bookshop, the brainchild of my friend Thierry Claude, was La Joie de Lire, no expense spared but accessible to all. The owner, Martine, resembles Blondine in terms of courage and know-how; both women live and breathe books and literature and it is a delight to see them at work, putting all their energies into these pursuits. They can both easily be found on the premises very late into the night.

Across the street from the Collège de France at the Sorbonne, we did the Éditions de Minuit bookshop and the nearby offices in the Rue Palissy. During the war, Minuit brought out a number of books that made life really awkward for them, but they can be happy and take pride in the fact that they had a hand in the advancement of intelligence and freedom. Monsieur London, the founder of Éditions de Minuit, had been very active in the Resistance during the Occupation years and had great affection and sympathy for the Spanish anarchists. I had the good fortune to be able to chat with him about this on many occasions.

Another rewarding experience for me was our refurbishment of the headquarters of the Ligue des Droits de l'Homme, the place where a number of agreements of great social and political significance were signed, like the ones in 1936. Back then the Ligue's secretary was Victor Basch, who was to be shot by the Germans a few years later. Basch had helped Louis Lecoin with the Durruti and Ascaso case when these two had been implicated in the death of Cardinal Soldevila. The refurbished premises were opened by Mitterrand and the façade displays two marble plaques, one dedicated to the president and the other to the two architects Didier Richard and Cantal and to my firm, Atelier 71. The press and media gave considerable coverage to the job, which was a boost to our spirits.

Finally, there was the magnificent Gallimard bookshop in the Rue de la Convention, one of the largest bookshops in the whole of Europe, covering two stories and a total area of some two thousand square meters, if memory serves. One day we were finishing off some flats near the bookshop in the Rue Chambéry and I went for a bit of a drive. Glancing in at the display window, I spotted a photograph of myself large enough to take up most of the display; I stopped the car and got out, touched. Some notes had been put up beside the photograph that said: *This great man and great bricklayer built our bookshop.* Not so long ago, some friends making a documentary dropped by to see the bookshop manager, Monsieur Turion, who told them, "It pleases us to think that at a time when every policeman in France was looking for Lucio, he was building us our bookshop, and that we now have his book on sale here."

I was also very delighted and proud when we did the Paco Rabanne arts center. In the Place de la Réunion I did another arts center, La Mouette Rieuse, which is devoted to poetry and song, especially the music of my friends Léo Ferré, Brassens, Jacques Brel, and all the libertarians who used to help with anarchist festivals. In Ivry there are premises named after Léo Ferré, and their creator, Julien, stated at the opening, "This center is being opened thanks to Atelier 71."

To conclude, let me say that the Espace Louise Michel exists because Atelier 71 exists and, if it wasn't for the firm, we would never have been able to open it.

My homes

It was at No 32, Rue Castères that I first met my friend and comrade Quico Sabaté. I lived there for a number of years, but when my sister Satur arrived with my two nieces, Romerito, and our sister Ángeles and brother-in-law Juan Cruz, it was too many of us for the small flat. For a time I moved into the hall but then, if anybody arrived, they could not get in and if anybody was wanting out, they could not do that either. My brother-in-law Juan Cruz found a job in a factory and the two girls went off to school. My sister then found premises where she could work without any difficulty, as I did myself; my sisters found work as maids, and I worked as a gardener or took whatever I could find. This has always been one of my gripes: it is no fun working in lousy conditions just to earn a living but it is even worse being without work of some kind. All revolutionary struggles and advances have been the handiwork of workers, and the anarchist movements grew out of work and out of the workplace. Unless there is a world of work bubbling under society, no progress is feasible and we are headed straight for disaster, no matter which political party is in government.

I eventually moved into the home of some friends, still in Clichy, at No 3, Rue Marc Saignier. It was a sizable apartment and it belonged to the Clichy council; I helped reappoint it and in a very short time we had a fabulous apartment. Since the friends in question were fond of me and we got along so well, I was able to start taking part in the activities of the Clichy libertarian group. They used to churn out propaganda on a roneotype machine, and the walls around Clichy were covered with libertarian propaganda. My friend Lesaint, from Asnières, knew the streets like the back of his hand, so we always knew where the police or indeed the Communist Party (who were always the first to report us) might pop up. In these conditions, the entire libertarian group would gather in our apartment to lay the groundwork for our activities—Jean Guéguin, Silvio Matenci, Claude Roche and his family, quite a number of people. We also used to get together with some Trotskyist friends from Vie Ouvrière (known these days as Lutte Ouvrière) like Michel Gaudichot, Robert, and others. These were very active militants and we got along well together, as we did with some other Trotskyists from the Lambert faction. They all came to our place several times and their leaders would give us talks, all shrouded in mystery and hush-hush, except when we were having dinner together and I had to half give one of them a piggy-back downstairs to the street. Some Irish friends also dropped by the place on several occasions in search of books.

After I got to know Anne, my sister found work as a concierge at 134, Boulevard Jean Jaurès, which came with a two room flat plus kitchen. She left the Rue Castères immediately, and the bedsit was left empty but was soon filled again with machinery and archives belonging to the Juventudes Libertarias (Spanish Libertarian Youth), smuggled in from Brussels. My sister Satur told me that the landlord of her block had an apartment to rent, so I refurbished it and added a nice kitchen and bathroom and that was where Anne and I first moved in together and where we raised Juliette.

Soon after that, Anne asked for an appointment with the deputy mayor of Clichy, Monsieur Métayer. At the rear of Clichy Council offices there was a huge tract of land and a convent that I had been inside lots of times because the wall had collapsed, and from time to time I and other friends had arranged to take a look around inside. The council had some apartments built there and Anne was there to apply for one on behalf of my sister Satur. It was a tough interview with a lot of raised voices, but Anne did get the apartment. It was at around this point that we were arrested and taken to prison over the abduction of the banker Suárez; Anne was freed after three months, but I was not. Anne got back to work immediately and was invited to buy out the Clichy apartment. Arrangements were made and the purchase went through. I was released from prison a few months later and went to live there with Anne.

Friends from the Juventudes had relocated the machinery and books, and the Rue Castères bedsit was free again. For a time, we installed my friend Llamedo and his pregnant partner there until they could find a larger apartment. I was then working by day and active by night and I came up with another small apartment in Clichy at 3 Cité Nouvelle. By that point I had launched Atelier 71 after coming out of jail and dropping my plans for a cooperative. Those were the days when we had "boltholes," or hideouts, and I used several of these for a number of activities, but I also lived and slept at home on very many occasions.

I used to leave very early in the morning for work. In my line of work, it is said that the wages are made during the morning time. One day, around eight o'clock, several police officers arrived looking for me, and Anne told them that I had left for work a good two hours earlier. They didn't believe her; they were after me for some very serious matter, which had nothing to do with a mere tiler, so they arrested Anne and took her away. Juliette was left to her own devices in the apartment and when I rang at one o'clock that afternoon, as was my custom, for an update, Juliette told me that the police had been by looking for me and, having failed to find me, had taken Anne away and that Juliette had heard nothing from her mother. Meanwhile, she had gone down to the public phone kiosk and had tipped off Olga Rabaneda and our lawyer friend, Thierry Fagart. I immediately decided to head for the area in search of news and it was there that I learned that Anne had been held for some hours under a warrant issued by a certain judge, on charges of forgery and sale of administrative documents. I left work and as mentioned previously, went underground. After interviewing Anne, my lawyer friend went to the office of the highly disgruntled judge and made a complaint that the police, acting on the orders of the judge, had arrested his client and friend, an outstanding individual, who had been subjected to ill treatment. The judge's reply was snappy and very harsh. He stated, "Your client, Madame Urtubia, is no doubt a very good person, but her husband is no angel. I have issued a warrant for him to be tracked down and arrested and as soon as he has been detained, I mean to lock him up because he has committed a very grave offense."

Within days we discovered what had happened. Back when I was being held in La Santé prison, I made the acquaintance of a Moroccan who was a casualty of the same nonsense as most of the inmates, because, as I always say, prison was invented for the poor and for petty offenders. Somebody in the cell told me that the Moroccan was under arrest for counterfeiting money. The next day, I approached him, and we started to go for walks in the yard together. I quickly established that he knew nothing about anything and that his real offense had been stealing a suit of clothes. We also chatted about the Polisario Front and arranged that, once he got out, we would meet up again and that I could sort Polisario out with passports, driving licenses, and identity documents for only a thousand francs when the going rate was ten thousand, on the condition that I had a minimum order of a thousand documents. I was delighted; it would bring in some money for us and would be helping Polisario. Once I got out of prison, we did meet up and I passed him a sizable batch of documents as a sample, though they were not for sale. The fellow had never seen so many documents in one batch and instead of honoring our arrangement, he set about selling off everything that I had entrusted to him. The police found it easy to pick up his trail and find him. They arrested him, but he knew absolutely nothing about me but did let slip that one of my lawyers was Roland Dumas and that I drove a red van. Even after three months under arrest that was all he could give them. I promptly moved away from Clichy and from my usual hideouts and wound up in the home of some of my friends, Marie and Patrice, in the Rue Custine in the 18th arrondissement. I spent very little time venturing outside because there were now three very serious warrants out for my arrest. I dropped one of the judges a letter telling him that, just as soon as I could and once I had summoned up the requisite courage, I would surrender myself to the courts.

As a precaution I switched from the Rue Custine to the 12th arrondissement, to the Rue Brèche-au-Loup (I think that was its name) to the home of some friends, Mario Durán, an Argentinean surgeon, as well as a great painter, and his partner Hélène, a very likable, affectionate intellectual. I spent some time with them and when I started to worry that I might be found there I went back to my previous friends who were living now, not in the Rue Custine but in the Boulevard Ornano and I spent some time there too without mishap. But it was a hard time for me and not being able to see Anne and Juliette was a real pain.

For a while I ended up close to the Place des Abbesses in the Rue Germaine Pilon; one time I was burning some proof traveler's checks there, ones that had failed to pass quality inspection, when the chimney caught fire. Before I realized what was happening, the firefighters arrived with the police and hammered on the door. I bundled up all the half-burnt and yet-to-be-burned papers and stuffed them under the bed and neither the firefighters nor the police caught on. My luck had held but, just in case, I left the premises and rejoined Mario and Hélène in Brèche-au-Loup for a while. I made Mario a present of a rather elderly Peugeot 403 and he headed down to Nice in it for a few days' painting. Feeling very weary, he pulled off the motorway to catch forty winks and attracted the suspicions of the police. Since his papers did not match the car that he was driving and since surgeons do not usually drive old, clapped-out cars, the gendarmes arrested him, and he had quite a job explaining himself.

I moved back to the Boulevard Ornano for a while. One day I arranged to meet someone who had been hounding me with business propositions but whom I did not trust. He insisted on dropping me off at home in his car, but I got him to drop me off well away from where I was staying so that he would be clueless to the actual address. A few days later, very early in the morning, I got up to head out to Montparnasse to keep a rendezvous with some Argentinean friends. As ever, I stopped for a coffee at a tiny bar from where I could scan the area for anything out of the ordinary. Out on the street, I spotted a fellow in his thirties, which is the usual age of police officers assigned to surveillance work, so after finishing my coffee, I ducked into the metro, watching in case he followed me. I was standing on the Montparnasse-bound platform when I spotted him facing me, ready to catch the metro going in the opposite direction. I acted nonchalant. But when I emerged from the metro at Montparnasse who should I see among the crowds but the very same individual. He had fooled me into believing that he was bound for somewhere else and once I had boarded the carriage, he may well have crossed the tracks, boarded the same train, tailing me. This was really something and I was greatly taken aback because many people, even those of us who consider ourselves courageous, would never have dared do that.

Having established that I was being tailed, I had no option but to leave the place where I'd been staying. I moved to another place nearby in the Rue Ramey, into the building of my friend Max Llamedo. He lived on the second floor, and I moved on to the fifth. I hardly ever ventured outside and then only on essential errands. Many days passed and I saw no one. There is the hitch: you may be sure of yourself, but you can never tell if the people you mingle with are being followed. In the places I stayed during this time I had nothing that might compromise me or my protectors; all, or nearly all the gear had been moved many kilometers outside of Paris. However, there was still one cache in the city itself, in the home of my friend Jérome, a crate filled with administrative documents and another crate containing a large sum in cash. I weighed up all the pros and cons, and finally one night, at four in the morning, I loaded all this gear into a suitcase and removed it to the home of a very close friend of mine, a female journalist. I headed home and that very morning two gas company employees showed up to read the meter; they did a really good job, and I was never sure if they were actual company employees or police.

At around seven o'clock that evening, my journalist friend and I showed up at the home of Roland Dumas. My friend was carrying the suitcase in order to avert suspicion and when we got there, I said to her, "You sit over there. Sit there for ten minutes, then walk away leaving the suitcase behind. Don't fret. Somebody will be along to pick up the case." That was the day of the second round of the presidential elections won by François Mitterrand, so the streets and my lawyer friend's offices were swarming with police, but it all went off swimmingly: somebody collected the suitcase so discreetly that I myself missed them, and my friend went off to work while I made my way home again.

My friend Jérome's mother, who also lived in the house where I had left those two crates of gear, had previously opened them up and seen the contents. She never breathed a word to anyone, but when she had another look later and found that the crates were empty. She asked her sons about it, who told her that she had been dreaming. But there was no convincing her, although she was always the soul of discretion.

I stayed at my fifth-floor hideout for quite a while, without ever feeling safe. When a comrade of mine called Gonzalo was arrested, I paid a visit to his lawyer to ask about his case, and when I read the charge sheet, I realized that my friend had been arrested in my place. "As a result of confidential intelligence," the document recorded, the police had been keeping surveillance on the home of the accused "waiting for one Lucio Urtubia. The latter entered the house and was photographed, but he was dressed in such a fashion that we failed to recognize him. When the reel of snapshots was disclosed that night, our agents recognized him and at six o'clock the next morning they entered the home in the belief that Lucio Urtubia was within, which he was not." When the place was searched and compromising matter belonging to Gonzalo discovered, he was arrested.

Eventually the inevitable happened. The police can make a hundred mistakes, and nothing comes of it, they just start all over again; but in our case a single mistake spells disaster and ruination. One morning at around nine o'clock, I emerged from my hideout, no longer a safe house since that visit by the phony gas company workers, not that I could be sure. As I was blithely making my way along the Rue Labat near the Rue Ramey and Clignancourt, I suddenly heard someone call out to me from the opposite sidewalk, "Lucio! Lucio! Don't move!" I glanced across and saw two men a few meters apart with their gleaming revolvers trained on me. It came as a real shock, and I was stunned. Other police officers immediately raced toward me and told me to put up my hands, frisking me. One of those in charge said, "We knew you wouldn't be armed and have no liking for guns." There was a van drawn across the Rue Labat a bit further along, cutting off the traffic flow. They invited me to get into a car and took me to the Place d'Italie police station, not even bothering to search the apartment where I had been staying. This was because they knew that I would not have had anything there and they knew that because they had already paid me a visit while I was out. The only thing they found on me was the phony papers I was carrying. I needed to tip Anne off as to what had happened, so that, after a while, I asked very respectfully at the police station to let me phone her so that she might pick up Juliette from school, since I was not going to be able to do so. The police officer who had overseen my arrest, a fair-haired guy of Italian origin, flew off the handle and screamed, "When are you going to stop making monkeys out of us once and for all? Show us a bit of respect, bluffer. You say you're the one that collects Juliette and we've been waiting every day for six months for you to do just that at the end of the school day, planning to follow you if you showed up to see or get her, and not once did you put in an appearance!"

The officer carried on screaming at me for hours on end, regaling me in a very exaggerated way with all the offenses of which I was being accused and with what lay ahead of me. Then, out of the blue, he suddenly said to

me, "Here, call her and tell her whatever you please." I spoke with Anne
without mishap and was able to fill her in on my location. Then they hauled
me in front of the judge who had issued the warrant for me to be tracked
down and arrested. The judge questioned me for quite some time in the
presence of my lawyer friend Thierry Fagart. At one point I was asked why
I was involved in so many very grave illegal activities that might send me
to prison for many years. To which I replied, "Everything I do, your honor,
is inspired by moral considerations. I imagine that under the Occupation
you subscribed to the same moral standards as I do." The judge was taken
aback at this and had never dreamed that I would give him such an answer.
He pondered for a moment and then said, "Monsieur Urtubia, your life has
been quite some success. My own, let me tell you, has been quite a failure."

At the time I didn't understand that. Later I found out that at about this
time a detainee whose case was being handled by the judge had taken his
own life in La Santé prison and that this had struck home with him; no one
can take pleasure in something like that. Not that I have any illusions, let
alone believe in anything, but, whether it was on account of my answer, my
lawyer's plea, or the judge's conscience pricking him over his having failed
to order the release of the detainee who killed himself, or a combination
of the three, the fact is that I came out of this affair quite well. That's how
the courts work, and one can never tell. The judge makes his decision and
that is that. No one can contradict him or explain away the inexplicable.

When this was all behind me, after nearly a year of worries and ups and
downs, hiding out in the homes of some friends, I was eager to learn more
about the "confidential intelligence" that had put my adversaries on my
trail. At the police station I saw photos of the shops where I used to stop to
check if I was being followed before I ducked into the houses. If they had
taken all those photos of me, it was because they hadn't been able to work
out exactly where I was staying and maybe because I had never allowed
that fellow about whom I had had my doubts to drop me off outside my
place but had always got out elsewhere—just to be on the safe side. Another
important point was that that individual was the only person I knew who
frequented Gonzalo's home, but I couldn't prove a thing.

One day there was a very important theft of arms from a regimental
depot. No one knew who the perpetrators might have been. I paid a visit
to my suspected "plant" and quite casually and candidly told him that the

theft had been the handiwork of some friends with whom we were often seen, and he told me that they had had no hand in the affair. The next day, the gutter press headlined the news that the arrest of the perpetrators was imminent, according to a very reliable source, and told of the phony details I had confided to the suspect, which confirmed my suspicion. Later, a police officer who had mounted surveillance on me for a long time and whose wife, as it happened, was Spanish, offered me conclusive proof when he showed me a photo of his informant. I had my revenge when I told him, "I knew it. Next time you see this guy, tell him that he owes me his life, because, if I hadn't intervened, other comrades would have made him pay for his treachery."

PART FOUR

FOR THE CAUSE

The GARI

The emergence and organization of the GARI (Grupos de Acción Revolucionaria Internacionalista/Internationalist Revolutionary Action Groups) to counter the repression in Spain, a repression acceptable to and countenanced by the entire planet, was a David-and-Goliath struggle. GARI members lacked funding and experience; they were all workers and there was not a single professional politician or "drop-out" among them; all they had to rely on was their hearts and their ideals of justice and selflessness.

Salvador Puig Antich, an activist with the Iberian Liberation Movement (Movimiento Ibérico de Liberación/MIL) had been executed by *garrote vil*, and several prisoners—among them, Pons Llobet and others—were about to be sentenced to death. As is the case even today, some prisoners were sick behind bars. Several of us groups got together and resolved that we would not tolerate any further death sentences, at which point somebody came up with the suggestion that we should kidnap some bigwig. Obviously, the people with the contacts are not fringe elements but working people. If you work, you have contacts and you meet people, especially in trades such as my own, where you go out on a decorating job, go out laboring, or go out laying carpets or tiles. So, whether by me or by those around me or by whomsoever, the decision was made to seize Señor Suárez. There was no question of doing him any harm; the point was to get it across to the Franco government that there must be no further executions of prisoners and no more death penalty.

So the first operation by the GARI was the kidnapping of the director of the Banco de Bilbao in Paris, Baltasar Suárez. A team of youngsters planned out and researched the operation and, one morning, as the banker was on his way to drop his children off at school, they snatched him at gunpoint. The children were taken to a small room and their father bundled into a huge wicker hamper that was then loaded into the trunk of a car. The kidnappers handed him over to another group so that they had no way of knowing where he had been driven and had no way of keeping tabs on his whereabouts. That second team then entrusted him to the care of those who were to stand guard over him. It was all done without any brutality, or at any rate, so I was told. The custodians treated Suárez well and humanely, in stark contrast with the criminal conduct of the Spanish government, which was only to be expected, for Señor Suárez's abductors were anarchists rather than fascist thugs. The actual kidnap victim himself later recounted that he had never tasted such mouth-watering paella dishes as the ones cooked for him by his guards, which is something states might learn from: humane treatment for those whom they deprive of their freedom.

What were the GARI hoping or asking for through this operation? First, the abolition of the death penalty in Spain, which in those days existed in a form—the *garrote vil*—that dated back to Inquisition days. This was the method by which Salvador Puig Antich had been executed. GARI was also calling for the release of ailing prisoners since, inside prison, they could not be given the attention they needed if they were to make a good recovery. These were humanitarian, incontrovertibly decent demands in keeping with the anarchist morals of their makers; those friends can hold their heads high. Also, having the director the Banco de Bilbao in their keeping, they demanded money, something that I saw as unremarkable. These guys needed money and they were not looking to go on holiday with it.

The youngsters who mounted the operation did well in pursuit of humane ideals and without a thought for material gain; their demands were discussed, and the banker freed without being harmed. Later, as is often the way, somebody did overstep bounds and reprisals followed. I was arrested at work by the police and was held for several days in my work gear, denied a change of clothing. Not that I feel any embarrassment; quite the opposite, it is a source of pride to me.

The GARI carried out a host of operations throughout France and they also issued many publications over a long period. They disbanded at their own choosing, and we may say that it was a highly intelligent organization.

After nearly eight years, a number of us were tried over two weeks at the courthouse in Paris but we were acquitted. The entire press lined up behind us and rallied staunchly to our defense and I must say that, insofar as the charges they leveled against me went, the police were barking up the wrong tree. The location they mentioned, Arnaud Chastel's home, was not the location where the banker was held and there were further mistakes made, but that is not to say that the police are stupid. In this matter they got the location wrong, but I have to say to this day I do not know, nor do I care, where the kidnapped banker was held. What I can state loudly and clearly is that the treatment he received during his abduction set the bar for the police and for Spain's Civil Guard.

One of the groups snatched him, bundled him into the hamper and handed him over to the keeping of another group, and I was put in charge of issuing communiqués to the press. One morning—I had just gotten up—I spotted that the police were tailing me. I headed for my workplace—this was at six o'clock in the morning—and I changed and slipped out through the rear of the site and phoned some people to tell them that I was "very unwell." And then returned to the site. The police followed, keeping me under surveillance; they are crafty and know their business. That afternoon I made my way home, collecting my daughter Juliette. I popped into a nearby café, which is still there, and the police loitered nearby. I sat down and ordered a beer. I was there with Juliette, and they could all see me, and after a short time I pretended that I needed to use the bathroom. There was a rear exit and I slipped into another café and made a second call, this time saying that I was having "real problems with my health." The police were oblivious to this. I could have warned them, but as I say, what is intelligence? People who were supportive of us, academics, very educated folk never picked up on the signals and never realized that there were regiments of police trailing behind them and keeping them under surveillance. And the police are not kids. I have put them to the test on thousands upon thousands of things and when they arrive, they ought to play it very smart. If I managed to get away with a lot of things, it was because even Anne and our girl and our closest friends knew nothing about my hush-hush activities. If people know, you can't get away with it. Anne was indicted for sending demands to the Spanish Embassy (I cannot remember on whose behalf), one of which called for an end to the death penalty. Another was asking for a bit of cash that might be put to good use. And when that cash was successfully collected, they followed her, and she unwittingly brought the police to us. The charge against Anne was because there had been an insertion in *Le Figaro* newspaper stating, "*House to let in Benidorm.*" She was to insert the same message in a different paper—I think it was *La Vanguardia* in Barcelona—and so went to the post office to mail it. The police later traced the ad, put two and two together and then charged her.

I would not want to give the impression that after so many long years of repression, it is a thing of the past, never to return. It is all a very complicated and difficult business, but these days you can go to a French courtroom without fear of being arrested and beaten for your trouble. You may well submit a complaint and it goes no further, but at least they do not torture you when you reach the courtroom door, as was the case in days gone by. And let me add that very rarely are we protesters 100 percent in the right, but there is an endless stream of cases of beatings, deception, and political crimes brought to light by chance or accident.

We ought to recognize that justice is non-existent, nor *can* it exist. There is a semblance of justice but, if that semblance was not there, things would be even worse if we took justice into our own hands all the time. In the case of the banker kidnapping, carried out by youngsters with grown-up morals and for a good purpose, there was a trial held some eight years later and all the press regarded this as a scandal, the last fascist prosecution brought in France by Francoism. But the kidnapped banker put us all to shame when he refused to show up on the day the case was heard, proving his humane and principled character as well as his intelligence. The eleven or twelve of us who were in the dock had nothing to do with his kidnapping. We only knew the banker's face from the newspapers and television news. Even if that gentleman had turned up, it would have made no difference, for we knew nothing about his abductors and captors or about how they had done about things. I take my hat off to them; as an operation, it was stunning and the outcome brilliant for all concerned.

I have no problem with this or in the expropriations recovering certain sums of money from a bank, through intellect and eschewing all violence, because we all know what the banks stand for. What goes around comes around. On the one hand, we have unscrupulous banking abuses and, on the other, operations mounted by us in order to retrieve the very money they strip us of.

Where abductions are concerned, there can be no excuse for violence, but we must not lose sight of the fact that there are some who use violence their whole life against others and without scruple. And if violence is kept to a minimum and applied with humane intelligence, I see no problem with employing it in pursuit of a greater good. After all, violence and pain attend our arrival in this world.

Before we venture into certain places we need to know if the ground is firm and will take our weight. Likewise, we need to know that there are certain actions that, even if they turn out well and bring good results, get us nowhere. And there are others that, while we may not have much to show for them, add up to successes. We should all have it in us to act judiciously at certain points in our lives if, by so doing, we can avert tremendous dramas and unfathomable, repugnant deeds.

A perfect job

There was a time when I had every single one of the police agencies on my heels. During that time, I took it upon myself to make ready three vehicles with full documentation for a big operation and started to look around, exercising the utmost circumspection. The aim was the simultaneous abduction of three consuls by the ETA *polimilis*.

I had a friend whom I had met in La Santé; he worked at the flea market and knew all about getting ahold of cars. I told him that I needed three and pronto. "I'll pay well as long as you have all three of them ready on the same night." He agreed and headed for the garage where he could get them from. In the end, he couldn't deliver. Without writing off this first avenue, I looked around for others, and at midnight I had a meeting in the same location with another acquaintance from La Santé, a good mechanic whose wife was from Corella. He had a bona fide garage plus an "unofficial" place where cars could be resprayed and transformed; he had a squad working for him and he kept them supplied with high-powered luxury cars. He used to buy registrations and license plates of crashed vehicles and had some Portuguese friends who used to steal very nice cars and switch the paperwork and so on. One day the police, who had their suspicions about him, took over the street the garage was on and pretended to be taking precise measurements, but in reality, they were taking photos of all cars entering his premises displaying one number plate and then re-emerging with a different one. When they got tired of taking photos, they sought him out and asked him where such-and-such a car was and were told, "Can't help you."

That sort of vehicle was of no use to us; we needed cars that could pass unnoticed, discreet "cheapos." When it became apparent that that source had petered out as well, I reverted to my first friend, but he had still not been able to solve my problem, so I turned to a Portuguese garage owner in Clichy and told him the same as the rest: that I needed three cars very urgently and would pay a handsome price but they had to be very nondescript cars. The following day I took delivery of the first one and he brought the second a couple of hours after that, the third arrived that same night. We readied the cars as best we could in Clichy, and my friends, as arranged, arrived to pick them up. All the preparations had been carried out in a very short time under the conditions that I was living in at the time, with all the police hot on my heels. One of the cars broke down and was out of commission as far as the operation was concerned; my friends were forced to forcibly commandeer a replacement vehicle because the whole plan was predicated upon the involvement of three cars.

So three bigwigs—three consulates from three European nations serving in Spain—were abducted at the very same time. The following day, the press reported a flawless operation carried out by "pros" with access to bottomless resources. As if the organizers were big banks, as if the people involved had had police training! The whole thing was done on a shoestring budget and with every possible precaution being taken, for the people involved were averse to violence and terror. The same could be said of all the idealistic revolutionaries I have met. When things have gone badly, those same people took it hard, and I have seen people get sick because they got things wrong. Not that things always do turn out for the best; sometimes they do, sometimes they don't.

The operation I have been talking about went off well. It was carried out by idealistic workers who had no ties to anybody abroad. Two very prominent personalities called me to express concern for the kidnap victims. The two were Roland Dumas, my lawyer, and the president of the French

Republic, François Mitterrand, who were off skiing together. They called me at three in the morning: "Lucio, you've kidnapped Kreisky's nephew." Bruno Kreisky was then president of the Austrian Republic. "The Republic of Austria has been very proper in its treatment of you and the Basques. Do not harm him. Ask whatever you like, but do not harm him." I jokingly replied, "We're going to ask for a truckload of guns." Roland Dumas confirmed the whole story to my friends from San Sebastián who were making the documentary *Lucio*.

In the end, the three kidnap victims were freed without a hair on their heads having been harmed. To celebrate our success a few of us went out for a paella washed down with a good bottle of Rioja. We were elated. Nobody hurt, nobody arrested, just a renewed appetite for further action and for doing whatever was feasible because all things are possible where there is determination, courage, and an ideal.

Today I can state with equanimity that I knew all the action groups that existed then. I think we still need them; they are no less needed than everything else that makes up politics these days. It was my good fortune to know them and associate with them; Italians, Uruguayans, Spanish and French anarchists, Basques, Argentineans, and several teams of Irish. They all had their reasons for their struggle, and they all had their ideals. They were fighting military dictatorships, be it Francoist or in the Americas, and all the groups concerned were regarded as terrorists by every government. I think rather than terrorists these groups were idealists, that their primary motive was standing up against tyranny and making a stand for freedom and justice. Like everybody else, they had family, and they had their sentimental side. They were young and many of them paid a very high price—in terms of jail time—for their selflessness, solidarity, and passion for freedom. Everything must be paid for and comes at a price, and the ideal of emancipation and a measure of destruction (necessary in the construction of an ideal that many can neither appreciate nor cherish) come at a very high price.

The Argentina World Cup (1978)

In Argentina the military had seized power and were the masters of everything. The coup was led by General Videla, and a ghastly nationwide repression followed. Thousands upon thousands of people of varying persuasions were jailed without trial, while others were shot, tortured, or bundled onto planes, drugged, and dumped into the ocean. Many went into hiding or fled into exile. One group of European and South American libertarians and antifascists decided to put their knowledge and resources at the service of the Argentinean people. There were Tupamaros and breakaway Montoneros, Italians of various persuasions, Germans, Basque *autónomos*, and other Spaniards of sundry persuasions, some living as refugees in Belgium and others in Germany. They decided to kidnap the French and world soccer idol, Michel Platini, in order to force the cancellation of the World Cup and thereby salvage the world's honor rather allowing it to disgrace itself by going to play in Argentina. Leftwing newspapers and general left opinion at the time was that a boycott of the soccer championship was needed as a demonstration against the repression and a show of solidarity with the victims, a blow against a global festival about to be played out in a country besmirched by criminality and torture. And this is why we favored the kidnapping of that soccer idol.

A few groups had cash, the proceeds of a number of operations; others had nothing but their wages, but these were placed at the disposal of the collective. Everybody contributed whatever they could; a bank account was opened, some comrades were put in charge of leasing an apartment, others of getting ahold of the requisite vehicles, all through phony documents to protect their identities away later. The vehicles were a station wagon and a van. The plan was to kidnap him without any violence, and the operation's success relied on that.

Each group had its own well-researched mission and once the operation was under way there would be no contact of any sort between the different groups. Weapons would not be loaded but were to be used solely to intimidate; nonviolence was a *sine qua non* if they were to succeed, otherwise young people around the world would turn against the perpetrators.

Everything was ready and waiting: the apartment, the paperwork, the vehicles, and the friends who were going to take part. The biggest hitch was that we didn't know where Platini lived, so five people in two vehicles set out for his training ground, and the five registered separately at two different hotels. The following day one of the teams monitored the practice field and spotted the target when he arrived for training. And they watched as he left again. The day after that, the other team that was in position to tail him as he left the training ground. Platini set off in his big, fast car; the other car followed at some distance so as not to attract attention but was forced to give up after ten minutes having lost sight of him. The footballer was a very fast driver, and his car was far superior to the ones his pursuers were using. The following day, it started all over again, but again they failed to tail him all the way to his home. It was now the weekend and trying again on the Sunday was out of the question, so both groups went out for a stroll that day. They started all over again on Monday, but the problem was the same: they couldn't keep up with him. But they wouldn't deviate from the plan and resort to violence, as nonviolence was crucial to the operation being a success, propaganda-wise. Recourse to violence was tantamount to failure and, so, very reluctantly, the plan was scrapped.

On his return to Paris, a friend reported that there was another VIP—French team coach, Michel Hidalgo—who was due to spend the weekend at his country home and, most likely, a few extra days before he flew to Argentina. The operation was resuscitated and since all the infrastructure was already in position, it was quickly decided that they would go after this new target.

Meanwhile, there were horrible reports in the press, the message being that politics was just going to have to take a back seat and that the sports tournament simply had to proceed. Proceed—even though it meant legitimizing an immoral and murderous military dictatorship in the eyes of the entire world.

The two teams sprang into action again, well supplied with cars, hotel rooms, and walkie-talkies from friends from Italy. Day one arrived and the two cars took up their positions, one pointing in each direction as there was no way of knowing what direction Hidalgo would head toward. Out came the VIP with some other people and one of the cars tailed him. The same happened the following day and the day after that, and we deduced that such-and-such was his regular leaving time but that he would not be alone. We prepared to strike, knowing that the chances of success in these conditions—time pressures and without violence—were minimal. We did have one advantage over the others, which was that we were not going to be asking for any money as ransom, which would reduce any sentence we might receive should we be arrested. Even with all the drawbacks, we couldn't walk away from the operation because that would have been a betrayal of our beloved Argentinean friends. Solidarity was everything as far we were concerned.

Without further delay, we decided to strike. As planned, one car and its occupants hid in a wooded area, and some spotters used the walkie-talkie to let us know about the target's departure and that again he was accompanied with other people in a big family car. After a few minutes, their car approached, and we moved ours to cut it off. They ground to a halt. As I said, the only thing we had to make an impression on them was one unloaded gun, and surprise and fear sometimes provoke people to unexpected, maverick reactions, and that is what happened. One of the passengers in the car—our target—threw himself at us and a struggle ensued. He got ahold of the gun, which he believed was loaded, and he aimed and prepared to squeeze the trigger. We managed to escape so, at the end of the day, there was no violence, but there was also no kidnapping. Had the gun been loaded, the consequences could have been very serious with loss of life on one side or the other, which is what we decided to avoid from the start. We got back into our car and, since we had a good driver, managed to get away safe and sound. We promptly dumped the vehicle and took the train home.

The next day's press spoke of an act of terrorism, but the groups involved held a press conference and explained that, had their intentions been what they were being accused of, they would have resorted to violence and would hardly have shown up with an unloaded weapon. We later found out that the coach was haunted by the fact that he had tried to shoot us.

There is little more to be said about that operation. Those with the means to act—governments, political parties, and trade unions—could and should have done something to prevent the World Cup soccer tournament from being held in a bloodstained country. But every country—without exception—took part in the games, and every one of them should hang their head in shame. They should have been setting the example and acting to prevent thousands upon thousands of disasters. They did nothing, nothing on this occasion and no one lifted a finger on behalf of Argentina except for us, a few poor idealists. Back in 1936, too, virtually all the leading nations took part in the Olympics in Berlin, including France, which was under a Popular Front government at the time. Only one parliamentary deputy—Pierre Mendès-France—spoke out against participating in the Games in Hitler's Germany. No one else, not the socialists or communists, raised any objection. A number of athletes took the very honorable personal decision to decline to participate and instead took part in the parallel antifascist games held in Barcelona.

Those of us who tried to trigger a boycott of the World Cup tournament were not wealthy; we lacked the financial resources for our operation. That's how life was for us, and funding was always a problem with no definitive solution. In this particular operation, each group or individual contributed whatever they could. There was quite a bit of intercontinental solidarity back then and we use to swap news and mingle with each other, sharing our expertise and our lives. I still believe that operations like this are needed; the downside though is the price to be paid for something done with good intentions.

Lending a hand

From time to time I was asked to do the odd favor by one of my many friends. No matter who the beneficiary might have been, I had a certain "infrastructure" in terms of documents I could access. I had thousands upon thousands of the things, and one does not dole them out one at a time. Instead, they are issued by the fistful, according to the need. If the recipient had cash, he would give me some; if not, well, we could sort it out next time around. That's how we operated and there was never a problem. Then one day, sometime around the time of Tejero's attempted coup in Spain in February 1981, the *polimilis* kidnapped Javier Rupérez, leader of the UCD party, the party of Adolfo Suárez. At three o'clock in the morning my lawyer Roland Dumas sent a visitor, even though Dumas had no idea if I was involved. I was told that if there was anything I could do to establish contact with the kidnappers, they were ready to negotiate. So I put the person in charge of the kidnapping, whom I cannot name here, in touch with Dumas right then, at three in the morning.

At the time, Dumas, a clever operator, was negotiating to have Picasso's *Guernica* transferred from New York to Madrid. He said to Suárez, the Spanish premier, "I know some people in Paris, and I can sort this out." He didn't know for sure if I was involved, but he wasn't wrong to approach me. I was able to put them in touch, and by noon the negotiations were under way. That night I joined the fellow in charge of the kidnapping at the Casa Alcalde restaurant (owned by someone from Lekeitio) for a dish of paella and a good bottle of wine. He told me tearfully, "I really hope we can sort this thing out, or else I'm going to have to kill him." This was their first kidnapping, and, in the end, it was all worked out.

I knew of another attempted kidnapping in Paris, this one of a socialist republican named Calviño. He had headed up an arms-purchasing commission for the Spanish Republic, but when the war was lost, he had been left with a lot of money on his hands, and a certain group of anarchists, war wounded themselves, approached him to ask for a piece of it. As they were asking him for it in the middle of the street near the Champs Elysées, the police arrived and arrested them all. So, we, being anarchists ourselves, and just to inject a little fairness into the proceedings, decided to kidnap Calviño, a Galician by birth. It was at this point that Fernando, the activist I mentioned in *Lucio, l'anarchiste irréductible*, stepped in. He made himself the bait and stumbled across Calviño on the street, supposedly entirely by chance, to engage him in conversation. In the end it proved pointless, and we didn't manage to pull it off. Fernando came with me to London on some expropriations we carried out there. He was a Felipe, a member of the FLP and a highly intelligent fellow who later held very high office in Madrid, by which time he had joined the PSOE.

Another affair I was asked to help with was when the Tour de France cycling race was approaching its finale in Paris with Miguel Indurain the race leader. I was invited to the celebrations, which were attended by lots of friends from Navarra, as well as the mayor of Pamplona, as might have been expected. A few friends of mine from Pamplona—including Javier Osés, the builder who came up to open my place in Paris—and Manolo Lezana and a number of other anarchists and semi-anarchists, asked me about the chances of tailing the mayor during his stay in the French capital. The word was that he was using the race as a cover to attend a meeting of President Chirac's party and to carry out a few sketchy money transfers and deposits. At the time there was quite a stink hanging over such things in Pamplona and all I did was lend my friends a helping hand in their little inquiries.

Recuperations in Catalonia

One day, back during the time of "recovery operations," we received a tip-off about the cash payroll of a leading public institution. It turned out there was a check—payment of the institution's entire monthly payroll—accompanied by a completed withdrawal form.

I was told that we had a check from a Catalan doctor made out to that institution and that it could be cashed at any of the banks and savings funds within Catalonia. In Paris I quickly prepared forged copies of the checks and other papers and anything else we needed. I stuffed them all inside the tires of my car and smuggled them as far as Barcelona. There, I was met by about twenty militants in the home of an anarchist comrade, one of the leading lights of the time, back in the early 1980s, who, albeit with the best of intentions messed everything up. We brought the tires indoors and spread everything out on the table. The "recovery" of the money was due to start the next day. We had already given the militants a run-down on the proper procedure and picked out a range of banks, savings companies, and post offices, and provided them with every detail they needed for the operation to be a success.

It was the same system that would be followed for traveler's checks. There would be people cashing them at fifteen to twenty different locations at precisely the same time and once they had enough cash, they would step back. I had instructed them, "On the dot of nine o'clock tomorrow morning, we must set to work." They replied, "We should hold off for at least forty-eight hours." They were not seeing clearly, still had a lot of doubts, and didn't believe that my way was the safe way. I told them that a delay was out of the question and that by the following day—without fail—they must start cashing checks and doing it quickly. They talked among themselves and decided not to proceed. As I went to bed for the night, I told one of them, "Raúl, get me as many ID cards as you can and I'll start myself in the morning: if there's anyone else willing to start, let him get on with it." The first person to start popping into the banks was me, since I was more experienced in how to handle the paperwork.

As a side note, I remember on a different occasion, I found myself in a post office cashing some checks made out to "the bearer." The staff smelled a rat and grew suspicious, so I snatched the check out of their hands, thereby saving everybody's bacon and bringing the operation to a halt. I was the one supposed to give the nod to the rest of the comrades to spring into action.

But to get back to the business in hand: the Catalan comrades told me no and that was that. I went to bed and at one o'clock in the morning I was awoken by the leader of the group, Luis Andrés Edo, who had had second thoughts and now believed that the operation should go ahead. We made a start the next morning and it all went off well. By the time all the banks and savings funds closed shop at two o'clock that afternoon, we had netted about 35 million pesetas: all that for just one morning's work.

Along on that operation was a lad who had been a cook in Segovia prison, a free man at the time, and a friend of Luis's and mine. Although we are no longer friends. The fellow was an ordinary prisoner and he netted 3 or 4 million pesetas that morning. To cut a long story short, he said to the others, "Here, you can have this share, I don't need it." This struck me as a nobler act than I saw from the libertarian activists themselves; his act of solidarity won me over. However, my friend, the libertarian leader in Barcelona, was neither a tinker nor a worker nor an anarchist nor anything else. And this is something I hold against him, and lots like him. I have had to endure some very serious problems because of people who pass themselves off as very prominent, heavyweight anarchist militants, but let me down when push comes to shove and who, in some instances, have even betrayed me.

Traveler's checks

I can't say where this idea first came from, but I have said before and will say again that I was never on my own; there was a lot of people in on it with me, pros from the printing trades. I was the dunce in the pack. True, my actions were carried out with an honesty that earned me the respect of people from all sorts of places and ideological outlooks, but that was all.

We had an infrastructure unrivaled by any other revolutionary organization and our forgery operations were going extremely well. At one point, it occurred to us that we should counterfeit US dollars, that being a currency a lot easier to forge than other jobs we had done, such as ID cards or passports from various countries. The films and plates were ready and

being stored in two different workshops under the watchful eyes of important friends. But we knew that we were facing a twenty-year jail term for
counterfeiting the dollar, if anything went wrong, so we dropped the dollar
idea and turned our thoughts to traveler's checks instead. Since they were
not the official currency of the United States Federal Reserve but issued
by a private bank, getting caught would bring a lesser sentence. This was
something that had been done before and we still had access to checks from
a variety of banks, some of which were no harder for us to counterfeit than
soccer tickets. But we didn't land on the easiest ones; instead our attention
settled on the First National City Bank of the United States, which was
probably the mightiest bank in the world at the time. It had and must still
have something like fifty-thousand bank branches covering virtually every
country of the world. Taking on such a giant with what little we had was like
trying to repeat David's experience with Goliath, but that was us.

I traveled to Brussels and bought thirty thousand francs' worth of City
Bank traveler's checks, using phony documents, of course, but ones that
were undetectable. The infrastructure and templates we already had; all
that was missing was to manufacture them. As ever, our equipment was
useless if we didn't know how to use it, if we didn't learn to put it to use,
patiently and taking our time. It was quite difficult separating all the colors
and arriving at a top-quality photoengraving, and my task then was confined to making sure that no evidence was left behind in the labs. The work
was done during the night or on days off and, over time, we managed to
produce some very high-quality proofs. I purchased the paper and whatever
else was needed, acting under the guidance of the pros, and I oversaw the
various preparatory tasks as I was the only one conversant with the different
stages of the whole process, whereas the specialists focused on one stage
only. This was all very exacting work, but when you are driven by an ideal,
you take pleasure in it. I wound up staying overnight in the laboratories
and that meant bedding down on the floor out of sheer exhaustion; but I
couldn't sleep. Instead, I took the utmost care when it came to squirreling
away all the proofs and film from the laboratory or printshop.

Once everything was in place, we set about printing, using phony documents, as ever. It was quite some time until we had things perfect and then
we had to dispose of the defective proofs, and anything left over from the
printing process. I took charge of that: I would gather it all up, clean up, and

remove to a safe location anything left over from the process, burning it so that not a trace remained. At first glance this might seem an easy enough task but in reality it was very hard because even gestures and movements leave some trace. Fire was the only solution. I carried out the burning however I could, on building sites, at discreet times, or in deserted locations. In the end we were left with some 150 kilos of traveler's checks and our two friends from Barcelona, Eliseo Bayo and Luis Andrés Edo, were in the know.

We cashed in the documents by the book or as a single check, and the cashier would check these against his or her lists. Since there was nothing untoward about them and the serial numbers of the checks were not listed as having been stolen or gone missing, not flagged in any way, every one of the banks paid up without a problem. The system was foolproof; without violence of any kind, we had come across a source of funding for all revolutionary groups and movements across the globe. We were operating right across Europe and South America, in two-man teams, one to cash the checks, the other to keep watch. People would produce a phony ID document or passport with the traveler's checks and at every bank we raked in two, three, or four hundred dollars and sometimes, indeed, a lot more than that. Everything had been worked out in advance and each team visited about fifteen pay points. Depending on the city in question, they could keep this up for two or three days in succession, but the usual practice was to stick to a single day and then drop out of sight. For instance, one team headed for Marseilles with fifty traveler's checks and got to work there while another would simultaneously head for Lyon with another fifty and do likewise there. This was a comprehensive money-raising operation. If anything untoward occurred, the lookout's task was to immediately call a certain phone number so as to bring the entire operation to a standstill. The money was shared out as follows: one-third for the team on the ground, one-third went on infrastructural expenses (cars, machinery, accommodation, and manufacturing costs), and the remaining third on solidarity.

We had been using these methods for several years and everything was going splendidly when, one day, City Bank branches around the world were issued a notice to the effect that they should no longer pay out on the checks. Whereupon the managers declined to make full payment on anything handed in at the cashier's window: they would only pay out fifty or a hundred dollars. This caused tourists a real headache as they were carrying money on them but could not change it whenever they wanted to. Quite a stink was raised by the bank's customers, especially in America, and then nobody wanted to buy City Bank traveler's checks.

When the bank suspended payment on traveler's checks, we had just run off some forty kilos of paper and the problem now was what to do with it. At the time, I had serious doubts about some people whom I had always looked upon as brothers. They were more into politicking than the politicians and they were all talk, but when it came down to practicalities, to actual activity, they did nothing; they were neither workers nor bandits, nor anarchists, nor revolutionaries.

One day the friend with whom I had been a cook in Segovia prison told me that he'd come across somebody in Spain who was ready to buy up our entire backlogged output of traveler's checks for 30 percent of the face value. I thought it over and it seemed like a good deal to me; this way we wouldn't be placing anyone in danger and would recover a substantial sum of money, but I did find it odd that a contact of the sort should pop up out of nowhere. My pal arranged a "meet" at the Hilton Hotel in Paris. The pair of us showed up, and the would-be buyer strode up to my friend requesting some samples of the merchandise, namely, a few books. This was the buyer from Spain whom we had been expecting and I knew immediately that he was a cop. As best as I could in my panic, I fetched the car and dumped the entire package of phony checks in the Pantin cemetery, in a hiding-place where I had occasionally stored loads of "goodies." I canceled on my friend and said, "I told you I wanted nothing to do with those guys from Barcelona, but you are one of them yourself and you're useless. A dead loss." I escorted him to the airport and off he went. Three days later he called me again to tell me that this was a serious deal and could be relied upon and that I had let my nerves get the better of me that time. One way or another, he talked me round and called on me once again to a further rendezvous in the Grand Hotel in the Place de l'Opéra. There, an American introduced himself to me and we chatted and chatted over the next couple of weeks. He was conversant with libertarian ideas and the Paris Commune, the Spanish revolution and Durruti. More so than I was. I put him through his paces, and everything was as it should be. After two weeks of talking, I still couldn't smell a rat, so we decided to trade a suitcase of traveler's checks for a suitcase of US dollars, as follows: we would sit at the Les Deux

Magots café in the Boulevard Saint-Germain, where Sartre and Paris's most celebrated intellectuals were wont to gather, and he would be in the Café Bonaparte right opposite. Once we saw each other, we would pick up our respective suitcases and trade when our paths crossed.

I was up very early the next day to visit to the cache and stuffed my suit-case with traveler's checks. Unbeknownst to my sister Satur, I had rented two garages under phony names in the building where she lived. Nobody knew a thing. When I entered my sister's home, which was on the first floor, the police followed me and could see that I had gone upstairs, but there was a false staircase in the back, and from there I went downstairs to the garage. I had been very discrete about renting them and I used them as a storage depot. It must have been about seven o'clock in the morning by the time I got home, and I knew that I was being watched. Anne had just gotten out of the shower, and I remember telling her, "Get dressed, the police are down-stairs. I've got a suitcase-full of dollars. Take your car and slip in behind my van, and once we reach the Rue Villeneuve, which is narrow, stop your car and behave as if you've had a breakdown." We did just that. Anne stopped her car and pretended she couldn't get it working and the police could see that I, further ahead, was getting away. They spluttered with rage but there was no way they were getting past.

I was running a little scared at the first rendezvous; we did the swap and I raced to drop off the suitcase in a girlfriend's office. The swap had gone smoothly, so I heaved a sigh of relief and put the earlier events out of my mind. You never know at the time if you've gotten away; it is only later on that you finally discover the truth. When they tailed me that morning, the police knew what I was up to, but they still had no proof and couldn't catch me red-handed since Anne played her part so well.

We met up again with our friend from Barcelona and the American and, after a few days had passed, we decided to repeat the operation in the same location, it having gone so smoothly for us. My friend and I sat down to breakfast in Les Deux Magots, the suitcase between us, and all of a sud-den, a swarm of arm-banded and armed police swooped on us, grabbing the suitcase and hauling us off to the Interior Ministry. The Catalan guy conducted himself very well; they had been using him without his knowl-edge. There I was accosted by several ranking officers keen to make my acquaintance; their tone was cordial, and they made much of the marvelous traveler's checks stunt that had baffled them for years: "Well executed, discreet, no use of violence, the handiwork of idealists and workers." They congratulated me, telling me that it was an extraordinary worldwide operation—they were prompted by their own dislike of Americans—but they did their jobs. I pretended to know nothing. They told me that I was the most famous man in the world at that time. One of the superior officers leaned over to tell me, "The leak came from Barcelona. We have a fax." It was only then that I realized that I had been betrayed. Who could have exposed me? It had to be somebody who knew me. There were serious interests at stake here so why had they turned me in? I have no idea. All I know is that the bank, the First National City Bank, declined to pay out on customers' checks, that there were some excellent counterfeit checks around, that they were swamped by them, and that the bank's prestige was plummeting deeper with every passing day.

Later I spoke at greater length with "Captain Barril," the former commander of the GIGN (Groupe d'Intervention de la Gendarmerie Nationale—National Gendarmerie Strike Team) and a member of Elysée Palace's "anti-terrorist cell."

This was his version of events: "On July 1, 1980, the central anti-counterfeiting bureau was tipped off by American Express and the Spanish police about a significant transaction due to take place in Paris involving a criminal of Spanish nationality. The French police had no difficulty identifying the man capable of launching such an operation. The close surveillance mounted confirmed the scale of the deal: three million dollars in phony First National City Bank traveler's checks were about to change hands. Stage one was the handover of a sample to prove the quality of the revolutionary anarchists' counterfeiting work, a sample that Lucio would be handing over to the buyer, one Sarra Papiol.

"The police followed up this lead and Lucio knew it. Between tails and evasive action both sides tested the other's ingenuity with a range of stratagems. On the morning of July 9, 1980, Lucio and Sarra Papiol were arrested on the terrace of Les Deux Magots while sitting down to a hearty breakfast that they never got to taste."

The good captain's account is wide of the mark. Sarra Papiol was not the buyer, nor could he have been, having arrived in Paris without a penny in his pocket; the alleged buyer of the dollars, for whom we were to have waited in the Café Bonaparte, was never arrested, for a very good reason: the "operation" was not the result of a tip-off received at some central office but a trap mounted from Madrid by someone with enough detailed knowledge to make it feasible.

That was a dismal time in prison for me, and Thierry Fagart prepared a masterly defense. He dropped by to see me one morning and told me that the judge wanted to see me in order to wrap up the charge sheet before January 10, at which point I would have served a full six months on remand. While the judge had to wrap things up by then, I would have to linger on in prison until I had served out the sentence handed down by the court; but if the drafting of the indictment was delayed, I would be granted conditional release.

I suggested to him that I should injure myself so that they would have to take me to hospital, and I could therefore avoid making a statement before the judge. Thierry said, "No, I have a better idea. Get set because there'll be a special escort here to get you at one o'clock." And there was. At two o'clock, the judge ushered us into his chambers, and in strode Roland Dumas with other lawyers and he briefed me in a few seconds, "At the end of the arraignment, the judge is going to ask if there is anything you would like to add. You say yes, and then for the charges to be dropped."

I had no idea what was about to happen. The arraignment took several hours, and at the end, just as Roland Dumas had told me, the judge turned to me and asked if there was anything I wanted to add. I replied, "Yes, madame. Drop the charges."

The judge became flushed. Roland Dumas and the other lawyers surrounded her desk and flagged up the procedural irregularities that Thierry Fagart had uncovered. It would take the judge quite a bit of time to straighten things out, but I was back on the street within the hour, released on probation.

Betrayed

There is nothing that compares with the torment created by the treachery of someone you thought you could trust. Life loses all meaning, the world goes to hell, and all the colors meld into a dark gloom and disappointment.

To withstand this, one must be strong and stand tall, because in such circumstances there is nothing you can do.

That's how it is. Taking one's own life or somebody else's, somebody dear to you, with whom you have shared your life, your ideals, the good times and the not-so-good times through the years, someone who you thought you shared the dangerous ambition for which you time and again risked your all, is no remedy.

When and how did this criminal and ghastly aberration set in? And why? You cannot fathom it; it is unfathomable because those who were au fait with what you were planning and who were able to snitch on you are the very people with whom you would face anything and even give up your life.

And in those circumstances, one begins to reflect and think as our repressive opponents do: you become suspicious of everything and everybody.

It wasn't your daughter or your wife that let you down. There are three people better informed about the things for which you have been reported. One of the three was arrested with you, at the very same time, endured the same interrogation, and runs the risk of the same sentence as you. Thanks to luck or guile, you are free, and they've locked him up. You carry on with the struggle and you help him every way you are able, as is only right: you help the family, warn his friends, and find him a lawyer. Then one day, from the lawyer, you get wind of the chances of an escape, but a sizable sum of money is required. You seek out the money and do what's needed. It must be handed over inside Spain, they tell you. You crisscross the border clandestinely, either in person or through a friend; you risk your life and liberty. Word reaches you that the money has arrived where it needs to, that everything is going well, and that the last and crucial rendezvous will take place in Zuburu. He will be arriving by boat. Six of us friends show up with three cars. For some reason, no one shows up for the rendezvous. You head home, scared and somewhat compromised. Three cash instalments were paid and must now be in hands of the Police. At least nobody has been arrested. Maybe they have no interest in arresting us. We probably weren't important enough.

One weekend, the same friend, who had been freed from jail some time previously, arrived from Barcelona to get a few bits of gear from a secret apartment we had been using as a storeroom. The key-holder was, unbeknownst to us, on a stopover in Fontainebleau. Unable to gain access by key, we refrained from breaking down the door lest we arouse suspicion, so called it quits for the day. We arranged that, the following week, we would meet at five o'clock in the afternoon to retrieve the gear; if the key-holder failed to show for any reason, the rendezvous would be put back until eight o'clock and, should he fail appear again, until midnight. There was no deal involved; when it came to gear or documents, those who had the money could pay and those who had none used to help us out as best they could. That was our modus operandi.

On the Saturday morning, I set off for work and about noon I picked up the gear and left it in a cellar at my house, hidden in a sack of potatoes which was now was quite heavy as there was quite a lot of gear. I went back to work and at a quarter to four o'clock I headed home, not wanting to miss that first rendezvous. I was startled to find a piece of paper stuck in the keyhole of my front door; I unfolded it and found it contained a rash of insults and death threats. There was still a quarter of an hour before the rendezvous. Stressed, I made a call to Barcelona and my friend's son answered. "Where's your father?" I asked him and he replied that his father was in Italy. "Ask him to call me immediately," I urged him. As soon as I had hung up, I called my friend. I explained the position to him, and he told me, "The guy you phoned is tapped." I asked, "What do you mean 'tapped?'" "The police are listening in." In a funk I went down to the basement, grabbed the sack, and moved it to safety. Then I made my way to the CNT local and sought out several friends, because I thought the police would be coming to arrest me that night. A number of people came to the house, but nothing happened. At eight o'clock I received a phone call with more abuse and death threats, and this was repeated at midnight and again at five the next morning. The abuse was always the same and the caller said I had been sentenced to death.

I had a rough time over the next few days. My friend later explained that he had gotten somebody else to drop by the house to collect the gear. That was the first mistake. No one should have been there other than the friend who I knew. He did not feel up to the task and sent other people in who got scared at the last minute and made an excuse for themselves, saying that I was the one who missed the meeting though there were *three* agreed-upon rendezvous times. Even though they had missed all three, we did not.

This was very serious business since there were so few aware of our activities. Upon learning that I had been turned in by somebody who had been a friend of mine, someone I just refused to see as an enemy, some comrades talked about evening the score with him and taking matters into their own hands. That was going too far: the failed escape bid into which six of us had been drawn, the sums of money handed over to the police, the sending of criminals to fetch weapons when he should have gone in person, unaccompanied, and the blowing of the whistle on the traveler's check counterfeiting. Why? Maybe it was because the Americans had paid him a pile of money.

On two occasions I expressly vetoed any revenge: the first time in this situation, which was a very serious matter, and the second time when a police inspector, who had spent a really long time dogging my every move, showed me a photo of the traitor. I told the inspector that he should tell his nark that he owed me his life, that I had stopped other comrades from taking revenge because I am no criminal and no thug and still believe in what my friends and revolutionary forebears have passed on to me.

You have no idea how hard life can be when you feel betrayed. But time moves on, and it makes you, if not quite forget, then at least more understanding. Maybe somewhat more cowardly or more intelligent. In every society people are a mix of strength and weakness, dereliction, enthusiasm, selflessness, meanness, and kindness. In situations like this the best course is to remember the positive, the constructive side to everybody, which is crucial if you're going to keep on struggling and living.

Later, no one wanted to know anything about this person who carried on posing as an anarchist campaigner, writing the odd book that I never bothered to read. A number of attempts at a rapprochement were made, some through the good offices of a person who knew us both, the Bolivian trade unionist Liber Forti, who said to me, "Lucio, please. I'm asking you. Let's go for a coffee with Luis Andrés." To which my answer was that I hate no one, but I can neither forgive nor forget and, even though I hold Liber in high esteem and regret having had to refuse him the favor, I spurned the overture. He thought he was something that he was not, that's all. But there are worse things than that: a sellout, for example. He sold me out and he put a price on my suffering. What that price was I cannot say, but the facts are there, and I think the complete story will come out someday.

Three-star hotels

Some people who don't know what they're talking about but who have an entrée into certain media circles, refer to today's prisons as "three-star hotels" to which prisoners are eager to return because they treated so well there. They say that people inside are fed well and don't have to face the problems of earning a living on the outside. By which they mean that the inmates are spoiled, and those who have been through the system transgress over and over again because they *want* to be in prison.

I'm no expert on prison and I've been lucky enough not to have spent a *lot* of time inside. Besides that hole in Cascante, a room in a grain store where they used to lock up us boys who caroused through the night or the tramps and beggars who had nowhere to sleep, the prison I remember best is La Santé. I was locked up in Cascante twice myself, but I don't remember ever having to sleep there. We used to refer to the jailer as "Huete the Gimp" on account of his limp. On one of my secret visits to the town, undocumented since everybody knew me, and carrying phony papers would have been even worse, a gang of youths heard that I was in a particular house with my family. Meaning no harm, but maybe for fun or as a gesture of kindness, they turned up that night to sing "The Marseillaise" outside the door. A Falangist known as "Pepe el Hojalatero" summoned the Civil Guard and the whole group wound up in jail. They were all, or nearly all, the sons of respectable families, right-wingers among them. One of them, Joselito, caught a chill in Cascante jail that night and died a short time later.

I also had the good fortune, or misfortune, to see the inside of Tudela jail, which had proper cells, each holding several inmates. The gaoler dealing with me was an official from Cascante, and in those days they wore the scarlet *boina*. I ended up there because my mother could not come up with the ten or fifteen pesetas I'd been fined; she brought my meals every day.

From that brief incarceration I moved on to detention in Vera de Bidasoa. They brought me there from Biarritz or Hendaya in the car they described as "the salad basket" as far as Endarlatza and there I can tell you they unloaded me. I had taken barely a few steps into my native Navarra when they asked me for my papers, hauled me off to the police station and, after several hours of questioning, but without any violence, the police or *comisario* decided that I should be locked up in the town's jail. I was wearing decomposing, repaired rope-soled sandals (*alpargatas*) and was filthy, not having washed for several days. In Vera's tiny jail, Senor Antonio . . . I think his surname was Porto . . . would bring me a pail of water and some apples. I remember that there was a French guy with me whose homeland was seeking his extradition and he explained to me as best he could that they were taking him back to France to be shot. This fellow wept uncontrollably as he brought me up to speed on his arrest and extradition. That's the only thing I can remember about Vera: that fellow and the gaoler who treated me very humanely, bringing me water and allowing me out of the cell to pick apples from the jail's orchard.

Once in France I received a citation from a gendarme in Clichy; I reported to the station at seven o'clock on my way to work and the gendarme who opened the door told me off because they didn't open until nine o'clock and I should call back later. Off I went to my job, returning around ten o'clock in my work clothes. I thought all they wanted was for me to fill out a form or some short formality, but the moment I was inside, they shut the doors, and I was surrounded by several gendarmes who handcuffed me. Nobody said a word to me; they took no statement from me; and I had no clue about what was going on, given that I had gone there voluntarily, leaving work in order to report to them. After a few hours they took me to Nanterre. Since it was the weekend the prosecutor or whoever had summoned me wasn't around and they locked me up for three or four days, I can't remember which. I have little to say about the place that would be of any interest, except that my arrest came out of the blue and I was still in my work clothes. After taking a few statements from me, they moved me to Bois d'Arcy jail, a huge modern jail, and I was able to get in touch with Anne and my lawyers. Thierry Fagart was away for the summer, but the moment he found out he stopped in to see me and told me that they'd be moving me very soon to La Santé to stand trial and that I would probably be released because he had taken the required action before coming to see me. During the few days I spent in Bois d'Arcy I saw little and learned little, except that the jail was modern and new, and the staff and wardens were new too. From there I was moved to La Santé, where I was able to see Anne, Juliette, and my lawyers and then I was brought to the courthouse. There, my mind at ease on account of the confidence my lawyer inspired, but uncertain and a bit scared, I listened to a thunderous indictment from the prosecution, complete with the gravest and worst charges imaginable. "All of which is true," he stated, "but we also have testimony and evidence assuring and confirming to us that Lucio Urtubia is a splendid worker that few can compete with in terms of his morals, and in this instance, I have no objection to Monsieur Lucio Urtubia's returning to his work." And this, for the time being, ended my adventures in Spanish and French jails, but I want to devote a separate chapter to talking about La Santé, the Parisian prison, where I was several times, and some of the acquaintances I made there.

News from La Santé

The first time I landed in La Santé was back in 1974 at about nine o'clock in the evening. On leaving the Quai des Orfèvres for La Santé, the black maria carrying you resembles nothing so much as a can of sardines; your anguish wells up in your throat and oozes out through your eyes, and nothing can convey the accumulated sadness and foul mood that sweeps over you; at times you feel that you could smash anything. But this feeling evaporates once you are within the walls of La Santé and received by the authorities; for that is your last glimpse of order or of the guardians of law and order. On that particular night, a bunch of us were unloaded there, most of us poorly dressed, with the sad faces of starvelings, and a few also with pinched faces and half-closed eyes as the result of having taken more than just one slap. We looked like a herd of bewildered animals driven along by push and shove. Behind those walls, the guards function like robots; it is all mugshots, arrest numbers, fingerprints, registration, off with your shoes, and they leave you nothing or next to nothing. They talk to you like broken records, strip you down and force you to walk three meters naked just to sign something. A jailer hands you the pile of gifts the prison gives you: a filthy blanket, two tiny sheets, one towel, a bowl, and a cutlery kit that includes a tiny penknife, a fork, and a spoon. The blanket is heavy from the amount of disinfectant powder saturating it. They march you to your cell to the sound of shouting and as you shuffle along you come upon other inmates with the saddest faces looking for whatever, for whomever. Every guard carries a huge bunch of keys, the keys to the cells, but they do not have the keys granting access from one cellblock to the next, that is, the guards are also prisoners. What a job!

The first thing I noticed in La Santé was the sour, dank smell; on the floor, pools of filthy, soapy water oozing from some sort of shower or aged toilet up above and clinging to us. On every side, ropes and iron mesh were secured to safety nets to prevent prisoners from throwing themselves off the third story, just to end it once and for all. "This place is like a circus," I said to myself.

And when you reach your cell, the jailer opens the door for you and promptly steps back two or three paces, a precaution that experience has made standard.

The cell back then, and I don't think it has changed at all since then, consisted of two bunks on either side and bedding for four inmates; in the center, four stools and a table that occupies virtually the entirety of the free space. It is used for meals and for doing simple, badly paid work. Off to the left there is a toilet bowl and a point of light in the ceiling. No washstand. The guard points to the bunk that is yours and you climb up. After a visit to the doctor to fill out another form, you're off to the barber and a shower.

If you are a smoker, your first contact with the other prisoners or detainees involves asking them for a cigarette; if they are kindly, they will give you one. If you need to write, they lend you paper and stamps. And they'll lend you toilet paper as well. The cell is gloomy with one window very high up, protected by several iron bars and a wire mesh. The filthy walls are off-putting, the paint peeling with crude doodles and messages scrawled as well as some yellowing images stuck to them. These are taken from sports papers like *L'Équipe* or pornographic magazines, these being the literature most frequently circulated among the prisoners. There is always clothing hung up to dry, the floor is grease stained, and the table is almost always covered with dishes and mugs from mealtimes. As a rule, it takes until about four or five o'clock in the morning before you can relax, because the wheels of the rubbish carts and the bins in which the food is transported have never been oiled and they make an infernal racket, a racket that is part and parcel of life and that also keeps you (though not everybody) alive. As the last remaining hours of night slip by, the noise intensifies and grows until it become thunderous, whereupon the guard opens the cell door to the accompaniment of that very special jangling of keys, says "mornin'" and carries out a count of the inmates in the cell. After listening several times a day to the screech of opening doors, we are eventually able to tell which cell is being opened.

Then comes breakfast, nearly a liter of milky coffee to start with, albeit with no coffee in it and the milk of an almost greenish hue, but it is something and we make do with very little. Within minutes, we are summoned amid screeching and earsplitting whistle blasts to our morning exercise in the gym, which lasts an hour. In winter, since it's very cold and still dark, not all the inmates venture out into the yard or what we describe as the yard—often a very cramped and horrible railed-off area some thirty to forty square meters in size to accommodate ten, fifteen, or twenty people. And, day in and day out, the routine is the same at this hour: several prisoners play cards, except in the winter or when the temperature plummets because they have to sit on the hard ground. Once the exercise period is over, at eight in the morning, we head back to the cells, and many head back to bed, while others read or while away the time as they wait for the mail, the highlight of the day, and absolutely vital if we are to keep feeling that we are alive. Many inmates never get a letter; in some cells one inmate might have a subscription to a newspaper and the others take turns reading it.

Noon means lunch, usually greeted with the hope that it might be an improvement on the previous day's fare. The meals, for meals they are, are jailhouse salads, vegetables, some sort of purée made quite some time ago and as hard as concrete. Ten minutes later, it's all over and you head to bed again; the dishes are done by whoever's turn it is, as agreed between the occupants of the cell. One hour after that, the door opens again, and coffee is delivered. Then comes siesta time. The radio is going all day long and generally there is not much conversation because the inmates are very poor in every respect, which is why they are prisoners, because prison is made for the poor.

Prison produces not men but boys with the mentality of boys. If prisons produced men, they would have been closed down long ago. The enforcement of justice is also, we might say, infantile, these days at any rate, pending the discovery of some other methods or solutions that are more economical and comprehensible to all and that might shape men. During my time in La Santé, we had a prisoner in our cell who had been there for five years; he was a martyr to intestinal problems and was afflicted by awful bouts of diarrhea. The sink was shared among the four of us and was used for washing and shaving as best we could every morning as well as for doing the laundry and dishes. The toilet was thirty centimeters from the dining table and practically touching it and every day as we sat down to eat or were in mid-meal, our afflicted cellmate would have to answer an urgent call of nature. His guts were forever gurgling, and we used to turn the radio up really loud in order to drown them out. We could do nothing to counter the stink, but at least we were spared the "soundtrack." In the early days this was what really got to me: I would be having a bite to eat, and this guy would be at the very same table answering a call of nature. At night taking a piss was also an ordeal. On your first day you are urged to wash your hands every time you have to take a piss, which is reasonable enough, but there are some that spend their days and seem to have no purpose in life other than watching to see if their cellmate washes his hands every time. And there was a nightly drama too over flushing: the racket woke everybody else up and they would swear at whoever it was who had flushed, but if he didn't flush, the toilet would stink. One night I witnessed one such drama: one prisoner tugged on the flush chain, waking up another prisoner who jumped up and punched him. The whole thing finished with their fighting it out.

One of my cellmates was Serge Teissedre, who had been charged with the murder of Prince de Broglie. Teissedre claimed to be innocent, as did I and every other prisoner and detainee. Teissedre was very down, very demoralized, and had made several applications for bail, but the judge was in no hurry to grant it. With his consent, I wrote to the judge concerned, Chevalier, to inform him that I could see that my cellmate was deeply depressed and that I feared that something bad might happen to him. When he didn't respond, we decided to make our move: we got ahold of a medical book and familiarized ourselves with the more fragile body parts in order to convincingly fake a suicide attempt. We pored over the book and made of it what we could. While the jailer was finishing lock-up for the night, I used a well-filed knife with a point like a needle, scraped it across Teissedre's neck and left a long slash. But the blood oozing out struck me as little more than a trickle, so I made a deeper slash at which the blood began to gush. I banged the stool against the cell door, my cellmate was rushed away, and they saved his life. The judge wasn't moved, and we geniuses found that we had miscalculated our mark and had made our cut where no incision should ever be made—in the most dangerous spot.

On another occasion I had grown fond of and sorry for a Tunisian lad, Kanzari, who was jailed on drug charges. They searched him one day and discovered a discarded packet of drugs on the floor; he claimed that it wasn't his and I laughed at him because, just as he had said, it looked like I was to blame. One morning I bumped into him and noticed he was dressed like a Cuban or West Indian musician: he was on his way to trial. He hugged me fondly and told me that he would be out by that night because he was innocent. I acted like I believed him, and the following day I bumped into him again, downcast and feeling suicidal; they had sentenced him to four years. In order to shake him out of it, I told him I was going to help him out and I did: Anne and I found him a lawyer, and in a retrial and his sentence was halved. To thank me he sent me a postcard from within the prison. It bore the image of the Virgin Mary, said that he, a Muslim, was praying to the Virgin and to all the saints to help and watch over Anne and Juliette . . . Something along those lines. The prison censors thought this was some sort of a coded message and hauled me up in front of the *pretoire*, an internal tribunal. There was no way for me to explain it all away. They were not listening to me, and since I had no legal counsel, they sentenced me to some months in the cells. It would be laughable, if it wasn't so sad.

In prison, I got to know an electrician fellow, from Senegal I believe, who landed in prison after he set about tackling a few jobs around his house one Sunday. His neighbor took exception to the noise and called the police who asked him to produce the receipt for the drill he was using. He told them that it belonged to his employer and that the foreman had lent it to him. They called the foreman who was afraid to tell the truth because he'd get in trouble with the boss. Things took such a turn that the Senegalese lad, the only real innocent I have ever known, served several months for nothing: another injustice in the courts.

A reporter once asked General De Gaulle what he thought of the prisons, and he replied that they were "France's garbage dump." "And once the garbage dump is filled . . ." the reporter pressed him, "What will you do then?" "We shall open up more garbage dumps," De Gaulle retorted.

Any prison is cleaner than La Santé. You have to have been there to understand how dirty it is . . . Everything is filthy, black, stinking, all the corridors murky. Anyone who steps inside loses all self-respect and trudges everyday through all the filth dumped there by a thoughtless, blinkered society. Punishment is merely a form of vengeance that cannot be squared with any sort of class consciousness or science. After all these centuries of there being prisons, if those responsible for the administration of justice were capable of gauging what they have achieved, they would be shocked to find that, rather than curing, they have added to and multiplied the evil in the world. Prison is one of our worst afflictions; society has the wherewithal to protect itself without resorting to this breeding ground or gangrene worse than cancer, and worse than any of the diseases by which we are afflicted.

Repression

Gentlemen, you can crack down as hard as you like. You can jail as many people as you like and deploy as many policemen and jailers as you like, but you are not going to solve anything. Repression, money, and power can never resolve issues that you're going to have to confront some day.

The violence that exists today and which you administer is nothing, yet. There is too much talk about it, and so-called leftist politics helps to gloss over it and play down rebelliousness. That won't last forever though because you cannot go on buying off poverty with alms, which is what so-called social assistance, loans and subsidies like unemployment benefit actually are. Your watchdogs will always be outnumbered by the throngs of dispossessed who today are cowed by terror, but your highest damns are not going to be able to hold back waters that, if they carry on rising without an outlet will eventually sweep away everything in their path. And when that happens, the people will single you out as the ones responsible for the disaster and will give you the punishment you deserve; they will step into your shoes and do what you have been doing in order to get out of the situation we're in.

The rich get increasingly richer and the poor ever poorer. A tiny band of parasites hijacks our common assets for their own advantage and loots the public coffers. The necessities of life and the environment are put in jeopardy, for the typical purpose of bringing further advantage and profit to the usual suspects, short-term profits doomed to be pointlessly frittered away.

We have arrived at a point of no return and repression is on the rise because there are no alms left to give and the usual means of lulling us to sleep don't work anymore. The wait may be a long one, but our patience has grown too. And, whether we know it or like it or not, mightier than patience is impatience, the formidable weapon of the poor, which is always at our disposal.

Palestine

Adversaries of mine have written several books and quite a few newspaper articles about me; they must have spent days and weeks on my trail to accomplish all that. The detective in charge of monitoring my every move was married to a Spaniard, and every Saturday and Sunday he would quietly attend a get-together of Spanish workers. Years later he told me that whenever they met in the detective's home, the people tasked with tailing me used to talk with each other about "Lucio's treasure." That legend came about when a financier from Barcelona Football Club, grateful for my help, gave me a signed but blank check on which I could have written whatever figure I wanted. I never tried to cash it because I never knew the man whom I had helped, nor had I realized that the scrap of paper, which I had assumed was a meaningless gesture, could be turned into hard cash. But the police drew the conclusion that I was a multi-millionaire.

Answering "Captain Barril"

In all humility, allow me to reply to a very significant figure from the gendarmerie who had quite a bit to say about me in the book *Les archives secrètes de Mitterrand*. Paul Barril, who oversaw the Groupe d'Intervention de la Gendarmerie Nationale (GIGN—National Gendarmerie Strike Force) contends in that book that my activities were protected by the administration headed by François Mitterrand. This is not true; I had no protectors in pursuing my activities alongside my idealist friends, and no agency of repression, land-, sea-, or air-borne, was ever "in" on them. I regard myself now, as then, answerable to no one.

What Barril says is unbelievable and inexplicable. I can see that every one of the highest authorities, who were charged with protecting the president of the French Republic and the wider authorities, behaved as my adversaries rather than as colleagues of mine. Every last one of them works on his own account without deference toward those it is their duty to protect.

Barril speaks of my friends Régis Schleicher and Jean-Marc Rouillan. Let me tell you that if the courts ever set them free, they'll find a lot of doors open to them. First and foremost my own. I can tell, Captain, in all candor, that even if Régis has done anything I disapprove of, it isn't for me to judge him, and he is not paying for that but for his staunch solidarity.

Jean-Marc Rouillan of Action Directe received assurances of a pardon if he were to turn himself over to the authorities. He found out before turning himself in that this was a set-up they'd concocted in order to arrest him, and he almost got away. The "big noise" who had laid the trap was left high and dry after having bragged that Rouillan would be caught "for sure." Rouillan was eventually given a nineteen-year prison term and Schleicher twenty-three years. The mistakes we make give us pause for reflection. I don't sit in judgement of anybody, and I would never venture an opinion, except in instances that affect me directly and I am knowledgeable about. As far as I have been able to find out, the courts got it wrong in the case of my friend Régis. I have been up against the courts and the police so many times, and I have always been treated with respect. I take pride in how I have conducted myself. But if the police had tortured me or if they'd tortured Anne or Juliette in front of me, then maybe I might have had it in me even to snitch on Nôtre Dame de Paris.

If I were in your shoes, Captain, I too would feel very hostile towards and crave vengeance against Jean-Marc Rouillan, who ran rings around you. But it is interesting how our fate can change in the blink of an eye. Rouillan managed to escape your clutches, but if you'd managed to arrest him, your life would have been changed utterly, and would have been very different from the life you lead in Africa, rubbing shoulders with African heads of state. Our life can be turned upside-down in an instant; it only takes a second. But for the Rue des Rosiers outrage, in which my friends played no part, had they not been arrested they could have boarded a plane to La Paz. Everything was in place, the visas and the tickets. Friends were waiting for them in La Paz. All the arrangements and preparations were part of a determined effort to capture Klaus Barbie and, if possible, haul him back to France, and let no one say that this was impossible. They were released after a short time, and I can testify to the courage and intelligence needed in order to mount our friends' operation, as well as to the solidarity for which they paid the price, and I can state that the idea was conceived by the libertarian movement in Paris as well as in Pau. The funding? Well, all the agencies of repression now know where it came from. Actually, we had plenty of funds, but there were lots of other things we needed as well, because the money problem is never-ending. Just like life, in general, we solve one problem and right away another raises its head. I am better placed than anyone to assure you that the "recuperation" operations never originated in our libertarian circles.

Barril hints that I helped out the Socialist Party. For a start, I cannot see why he would mention the Socialist Party above any other; besides, we now know that socialist parties have access to much easier ways of subsidizing and funding themselves. If I helped or have a duty to help anybody, it will be my own kind—libertarians, the people who have made me who I am, friends of mine and no one else. My sponsors and day to day work are what have enabled me to make a more than adequate living, but it has cost me an enormous number of nights and days locked inside labs and printshops. Once we have what we need and have an ideal, there is lots of time for toiling in the workplace and underground. There are people who spend as much time on recreation, sports, or in cafés as they do working, whereas we—and here I speak for myself—we devoted such time to the cause.

That's the way it was and the way we were, and no one, absolutely no one, was behind us in the Pau job. The fact is too that in those days the police repressors dared to talk of Lucio's "treasure." That is nonsense and it always was, for I had nothing. All I managed to do was to protect and delicately stand guard over a collective resource, using whatever strength and stamina natured bestowed upon me.

One fine day, a bigwig repressor summoned up the courage to say, "Lucio, we will never stop keeping surveillance on you. Never." This was the general attitude of agencies specializing in operations to counter antifascist groups, which they equated with violent groups. Among these agencies, which were very close to the president of the Republic, was the

"Elysée anti-terrorist cell," which ran the French Gendarmerie Nationale's strike force. All this is very well explained in Captain Barril's book, which devotes quite a few pages to my own revolutionary activities. By following the activities of all these police and judicial bodies, interestingly, we can better appreciate the individuals and groups (sometimes very few and very unlucky) that they were shadowing. These groups were endowed with tremendous courage and an ideal, sometimes massive intelligence and a childish ignorance. Clearly, it must have taken all these traits to involve oneself in a revolutionary operation, which is why revolutions are made, especially and for the most part, by young people. A revolution needs this twenty-year-old's blend of inexperience and rampaging strength. Propelled by this human motor, it fleshes out the yearning for a changed life. Utopia is something that scarcely exists but as it takes root in an unbending world, its power is multiplied one-thousandfold; even then it falls short, and it needs thousands upon thousands of young dreamers to multiply their strength. Maybe the strength of the libertarian groups lay in the different way we had of organizing ourselves: compared with our rivals, our resources were insignificant, but even in the face of all such difficulties, the problems we stirred up were great.

If you get the chance, you should read Alain Hamoun and Jean-Charles Marchand's *Action directe: du terrorisme francais a l'euroterrorisme*. As for Barril's book, he claims to know but does not, especially when he talks about an infrastructure being set up like a mini-state within the State, an administrative infrastructure underpinning counterfeiting operations. If we read the book in question, *Les archives secrètes de Mitterrand*, it is like misperception heaped upon misperception and great notions of one's own importance. But then I know only too well that had luck, or, as I would say, the unfathomable not been on my side, things might have taken a turn for the worse and my downfall might have been fatal.

Captain Barril depicts me as international socialism's Mr. Bountiful and a financier, the creator of one big international libertarian network. Let me respond to that according to my knowledge and to what I am. For one thing, Monsieur le capitaine of the Gendarmerie, you are wrong; you do not know me at all, other than through the "tales" and notes of various authorities; and you are one of my adversaries, my enemy. I do not have the slightest confidence in your practical or bureaucratic capabilities, nor in the mental faculties of all the courts' agencies of repression. A working man like me places no trust at all in any authority figure, even should he purport to be a socialist or a republican, for, the instant he achieves power, even the best person turns into a bad one. Power corrupts people and warps them, and history can bear witness to that: no man, having attained power, is an exception to this rule. Which is why I am opposed to power, all power.

This is the soundest proof of my never having sought to or been able to subsidize any political party. Quite simply, it runs counter to my beliefs and my thinking. By the way, Monsieur le capitaine, I believe you wrote all that nonsense about me because you know nothing about me or about my life and you have no notion of what a libertarian bricklayer is. The truth about my life is what I have recounted here and what appeared in the book, *Lucio l'anarchiste irréductible*. I am a believer in the truth, and I want it to be known, free of all animosity and of all score-settling.

I stand ready to lose my liberty in order to defend it, whereas the only thing some people stand ready to defend is their privileges. And in order to defend liberty, other people have opened their doors to me and so was born an entire network of idealistic artisans and workers on a scale of which the agencies of repression could never have dreamed. The creation of an infrastructure made up of professional workers who share the ideal of self-management and a spirit of honesty was essential. Such honesty is untainted by expropriation; we take what we need. Just as there is nothing so banal as building a bathroom with "borrowed" materials in the home of a friend who has no bathroom, so it is with secretly printing up documents that might help some people out in difficult times of persecution or producing banknotes every bit as good as the dictators' banknotes and using them to propagate freedom instead of fostering repression. This is also part of what I mean by self-management.

It takes workers trained in some industrial skill, workers with experience and expertise to reach that capacity for subversion and to lose respect for governments and private property like that. It takes year upon year of slavery before one can dare aspire to be free, and that all requires practice. You, Monsieur le capitaine of the Gendarmerie, cannot conceive of a plain building worker possessing all that latent professional intelligence and revolutionary spirit. All I am doing is carrying on and perpetuating a morality, an education, and a practice passed on to me by my Spanish anarchist friends. It was them that taught me to lose all respect for private property and to not line my own pockets with the proceeds of expropriations. We never took an accountant along on recovery operations; everything was made by weight, when it came to manufacturing, or by handfuls when it came to sharing, depending on one's needs. What a delight, giving open-handedly without keeping count! In situations like that there is the risk of somebody getting corrupted, but it never happened; just as our Gendarmerie officer says in his book, we all carried on with our hands grimy with cement and stinking of paint and in our day to day lives, nothing changed. What a delight, knowing that the color of my van and the racket it made were famous among the antiterrorist police agencies. Let me quote Captain Barril's own words:

> A modest Volkswagen van, one of those "hybrids" in fashion in the 1970s. Orange and bearing the license plate 9968 CV 92. Its driver a bricklayer-cum-decorator-cum-tiler, a native of Navarra. The racket from its engine sets the vehicle apart. Lurking in the darkness, the men from the RG (Renseignements Généraux— General Intelligence) at police headquarters didn't even need to follow the *combi* without letting it out of their sight; the racket from it was enough . . . . To this day, Luis Urtubia Jiménez is a living legend within the revolutionary anarchist movement, thanks to his reputation for invulnerability. This militant is one of the chief driving forces behind the "Organization" described by the chief of the Elysée cell in his lengthy memo to François Mitterrand regarding the financing of international terrorism.
>
> Between January 1980 and December 1982, hundreds of millions of dollars' worth of phony traveler's checks flooded the whole of Europe and places much farther afield, in an unparalleled onslaught behind which there was a tiny gang of highly talented counterfeiters, as well as men involved in the highest levels in international terrorism. Nothing and no one seemed able to end their activities, to the extent that, rather than be forced into shutting up shop, First National City Bank, one of the world's biggest banks, opted for a negotiated settlement. One of their leaders, Lucio, caught red-handed, was locked up in prison for less than

six months, during which time the counterfeiters' onslaught did not let up one bit. The judicial fall-out from his trial was confined to a token sentence.

Barril goes on to offer us his own estimate of the overall funds raised through the phony checks: some 240 million francs, or around 36 million of today's euro. Above all, he points to the two "fairy godfathers" who lovingly tended to Lucio, the die-hard, throughout his protracted battle with the courts: "One of François Mitterrand's closest collaborators Roland Dumas, and one of the highest placed judges in the land Louis Joinet, cofounder of the Judges' Union and architect of the 1981 Amnesty Law and, today, premier advocate-general of the Court of Cassation, having served as legal advisor to three socialist prime ministers: Pierre Mauroy, Laurent Fabius, and Michel Rocard."

Barril could have tossed in a few more details about these two figures. Before working alongside Mitterrand, Dumas had been a friend to Spanish antifascists and his own father had been shot by the Germans for his part in the Resistance. Leading judge Louis Joinet is a man of great intellectual and practical freedom who lives as modestly as any working man and has five sons and twelve grandchildren.

Barril insinuates that I paid these men handsomely for their favors, thanks to the fabulous treasure I had hidden, but the only thing I ever gave them was my courage and my libertarian ideals. Barril is astounded that a matter of such import was buried by the authorities with such ease; and the man making this statement is none other than the captain in charge of the Elysée's anti-terrorist cell, a trusted confidant of the president of the French Republic.

Barril doesn't believe that the reason why I was able to evade capture and notice for so long is because of my intelligence and ingenuity, and so imagines that I must have had protection from people in power. I am no more intelligent and ingenious than anybody else, and as I've said, my greatest possessions were my working whites and my bricklayer's trowel. I do find it quite astounding that these claims are coming from a police officer when the police raided my workplace a thousand times over and always found me on site, not to mention that they had me under surveillance from the time I left home until I returned. Anyway, I want it on the record that

I was always treated with respect, which is only logical and to be expected, for we were not living in 1970s Latin America.

So how I was able to fly under the radar for so long? The police specialize in petty criminals who frequent questionable locations and splash money around even though they may not have a job or any apparent source of income. The people who subscribe to the same ideals as me are workers; bricklayers, mechanics, miners, taxi drivers, people drawn from every sort of trade. They do not hang around in gambling dens, cabarets, or cafés, and they still report for work on the day of an operation or the very next day. That sort of life is harder to monitor although I always say that no one should think himself any cleverer or craftier than the police. I can assure you that of all the comrades and friends it has been my good fortune to know and associate with, and who have risked their lives and liberty on many occasions, I cannot think of a single one who has made his fortune at it.

And Monsieur le capitaine is beside himself with indignation when he talks about the "deal" that my lawyers, Louis Joinet and Thierry Fagart, cut with the City Bank's representative, Geoffrey Heggart and his chosen advisor, Yves Baudelot:

> Swamped by phony checks, the bank had decided not to honor its own checks anywhere in the world. This was a decision with very grave consequences: not only were holders barred from cashing the checks, but the bank's reputation was in danger of collapsing beyond recovery. The only big fish caught in the police net, one of the supposed masterminds behind the scam, was Lucio who, realistically, should have paid a heavy price for his involvement: no matter how well things had gone in his favor, he should have got at least five years in prison.
>
> First his lawyers and then the socialist government set a thousand procedural devices in motion to ensure that Lucio would evade the proper judicial reprisals for his activities. A real fairy story. They "amicably" thrashed out the terms of a spine-tingling deal. Under the benevolent sponsorship of the socialist government, Lucio bought complete impunity by handing over the plates and part of the gear he used to manufacture the phony traveler's checks, but there were no guarantees that the checks would drop

out of circulation quite yet . . . And Lucio threatened that if City Bank rejected the deal, he would carry on swamping the world with his phony checks!

The handover of the plates took place in late October 1982 in a hotel near the Champs Elysées. The switch was conducted with the utmost secrecy. Lucio was afraid of a last-minute ambush and of being caught red-handed, so to speak, but Geoffrey Heggart, the First National City Bank's security chief, was a perfect gentleman and blithely caved in to the "friendly" pressures brought to bear by the many well-meaning people determined to close the book on the affair. Lucio even received compensation for "ceasing his activities"!

The gendarmerie captain's righteous indignation is rather laughable. He "emphatically" recommends the Bernard Thomas book, *Lucio l'irréductible*, to his more skeptical readers and adds, naively shocked, "They will find there extraordinary information and details that I would never have imagined could be published one day."

What most scandalizes one whose trade is state secrets is the glare of publicity. But in this instance, there was no "state secret" involved, only an honorable commitment swapped by two parties and one that was honored to the letter by both sides.

Régis Schleicher

I am writing this in Paris in the year of 2006, a few days before my friend Régis is to be tried for attempting to escape from the prison where he has served twenty-three years.

I know we hear this from everybody in prison, but my friend is paying for something he didn't do. I thought of myself as innocent, and I am not about to repeat the reasoning that I have set down in writing elsewhere. In all honesty, I do believe that there are plenty of reasons for setting Régis free and if, during the trial scheduled for a few days from now, I could address the court as a character witness, this is the statement I would make:

Monsieur le président, I could so easily have found myself in the same position as my friend Régis. If you will allow, let me explain to you why I am here, a free man, when the courts held me culpable of some very grave deeds, or crimes. I hold that I was spared a conviction due to what García Lorca would have called my *duende*, blessed good luck. Nobody has ever quite managed nor known how to account for it. Several theories have been put forward but not even I, the primary beneficiary of it, know the true facts.

Monsieur le président, I made Régis's acquaintance in prison in a very tight spot: we were sharing a cell and sharing our punishment. I had my *duende* and I benefited from the understanding and intelligence shown by a few judges of rightwing and leftwing persuasions. I might easily have been sentenced to very many years in prison, but instead I was set free and that put an end to my worries and my fears. After that I was able to launch two firms employing around thirty workmen and ten craftsmen who have added to the county's wealth and put bread on the table for forty families. I can tell you, Monsieur le président, that I cannot disentangle my courage in setting up those two firms from the understanding that I was shown by the courts. And I will also tell you that, in addition to those two firms, I have gone on to open a small arts center in one of Paris's least favored districts. I live there and my door is open to everyone, and youngsters can drop in on me any time they like.

You have helped me become what I am and that is a source of some small pride for us all. I say small because, compared with what has yet to be achieved, what I have contributed has been very little.

Monsieur le président, when Régis arrived in jail some twenty-three years ago, he was a youngster, and, like many youngsters around the world, his motives were rather different from what they are today, although he is still the humanist he always was. I can see the paradoxes in him that brought him to share in our aspirations and, at the age of twenty, it is very hard to keep a rein on such paradoxes. Now my friend Régis is almost sixty years of age and is utterly changed. He has very little time left to sit on a park bench or in some café with a newspaper in his hand, downing a beer or a glass of wine as he watches people pass by. This is something I rate very highly, something that no one should deny us: sitting there, a free man, enjoying the caresses of a sun that shines down on every one of us.

To conclude, Monsieur le président, I can tell you that the ideals of Régis Schleicher, Action Directe member, these days boil down to regaining his freedom, spending his days in the warmth of his elderly, widowed mother, and plying his trade as a proofreader. What the courts did in my case—and they were not wrong—you can do for my friend Régis, and we will all come away winners, including the courts—thanks to their understanding—and society at large.

Journey into the past

I do what I can, and I tell it as I remember it, but. . . Let me reiterate what the poet said: If only I knew how to write! That line refers to a woman who cannot quite convey her feelings to a man she loves. I am aware myself of the very same need to preserve the memory of what I have been through and to pass it on, modestly and without pretention, to others coming after me.

Some friends from Guipúzcoa have been working on a documentary movie about my life. They have urged me to remember things and write them down because the personal safe deposit box that is the memory needs to be maintained and exercised, lest it lose what it holds.

But there are times when the memory looms in front of you and you see it clearly. On October 19, 2006, I went with my friends, the documentary makers, to visit Roland Dumas, the great lawyer, minister of Foreign Affairs in the Mitterrand cabinet, and the man who helped me out in trying times and whom I have had occasion to assist myself. I was impressed by his powers of recall, the number of anecdotes and facts he could dredge up. And he knows how to write too. The following day, October 20 it was, the whole film crew journeyed to visit a man, a friend of mine these forty years, who at one point helped me get rid of all the clandestine infrastructure that we had been using for forging of all sorts of documents, as per the agreement with the courts. He and I spent an entire day burning huge heaps

of all manner of equipment, just as I had pledged to do. At the time—this
was during the early 1980s—I was fifty years of age, an age when one is in
one's prime and more than equal to all the work I was involved in but an
age at which care must be taken because one is starting, albeit unwittingly,
to decline generally.

I have always been a really energetic person, but I have also been hasty
and never had the patience to put my affairs in order. I was reluctant to
return to the place where I had burned nearly all the infrastructure we
were using, but everyone badgered me so much that in the end I did. It
is located some three hundred kilometers from Paris, and we went there
with the whole film crew. We found the house easily enough although it had
changed a lot, now modernized and very attractive. My friend was waiting
for us and almost immediately, and he set a batch of stuff on the table to
be filmed. I had had no idea and it had never even occurred to me that it
still existed; I was stunned, but he said that this was only a tiny fraction
of everything that was still in storage there and that, once we had finished
filming it, he would bring out more and more of it.

Among the gear that was emerging, perfectly preserved and wrapped
to prevent deterioration, was the photogravure of the dollars that we had
been planning to counterfeit—a plan we dropped on the advice of some
friends—as well as plates for most administrative documents in Europe;
and stocks of such papers already printed, complete with the appropriate
dry or inked stamps and gold leaf seals. At one time these had proved very
useful to anarchist and antifascist circles. Our friend also produced an
entire run of brand new traveler's checks ready for cashing, along with all
the corresponding plates. There was a degree of nervousness as I watched all
of this subversive gear emerge that I had assumed was long gone. It was this
that was the basis of the authorities' talk of "Lucio's treasure," and time and
again when we read or heard this, we dismissed it as exaggeration calculated
to impress public opinion and justify their activities. What was now in front
of our very eyes, captured on film and then burned immediately, actually
did amount to a treasure, some very delicate craftsmanship created with
a lot of courage and intelligence, and prepared thanks to the trust shown
by many people, the approach being that each of us had a specific job to do
and all shared responsibility for the end product. Attempts at infiltration
always failed except within Spain, but no warehouse, no machinery, and

no cache were ever captured. And when I gave the authorities my word of honor, many others undertook to lend me a helping hand; highly intelligent people, very much of the left, honorable people who had never soiled their hands and whose personal dealings were impeccable. I am stating this for the record and will not be naming names. They know who they are, but it all comes flooding back to me and I am taking this opportunity to express my gratitude to them one more time through this none too diplomatic way I have of stating things. Politicians say one thing and do another, but we are not like that; a man's word should be his bond, and in the case of all the people implicated in this affair, it was. And so all the gear forgotten about and uncovered now twenty years on was brought out into the light of day, filmed, and immediately consumed by the flames. I had thought it gone already, but the important thing is that, over the years, no one had passed it off or made any use of it; I had come to an arrangement with my friends, and they lived up to the trust they placed in me and that I had placed in them. This is what we were made of.

Even as all the gear that symbolized a whole stage in my life was burning, my thoughts were of the hours, days, months, and years that it had taken to put it all together. Very few were privy to it or knew the full story. Some may say that it was a sacrifice, but I found it a pleasure and the pleasure of making something invests one human being the strength of many, and turns him into something different, a saint or a demon, depending on whether he acts for good or ill.

Nowadays the fascism that spurred us to mobilize no longer exists in Spain and the work we did would be meaningless now. But I am grateful to the courts for helping me to turn over a new leaf and move on when the punishment hanging over my head was a very heavy one. The judges who had a hand in arresting me caught on to the fact that I was a working man, an idealist who never derived any personal profit from my actions; society came away the winner too, because I went on to establish two building firms, creating employment, and generating wealth. I also set up the Espace Louise Michel, an arts and historical center with anarchist roots. There are those who say that the Espace points the way and that if there were many such *espaces*, lots of things would not have been forgotten.

My own experiences can and should be turned to advantage like this. I am firmly convinced that many who are behind bars today would do likewise, should they regain their freedom. They are idealists and creative workers: if they have been punished enough already, further detention is pointless. If they are to be returned to society their labors and efforts might bring forth a lot of useful fruits.

PART FIVE

FRIENDS AND FOES

Paco Rabanne

His real name is Paco Rabaneda, and I know his whole family. When I was jailed in La Santé, a group of my friends organized an art show in solidarity with libertarian prisoners in an exhibition hall on the Île de Saint-Louis behind Nôtre Dame de Paris. I was released in time to attend the opening. Among the artists who had organized the whole thing was somebody from the Rabaneda family, as well as Mario Durán, the surgeon and great painter who was cofounder, with Bernard Kouchner, of Médecins Sans Frontières and, among many others, my friend Reinaldo, the sculptor from La Ruche Française. It was there that I was introduced to Paco's sister, Olga Rabaneda. We chatted for quite some time and, as I was just out of prison and out of work, she suggested that I do a bit of work on her home and completely refurbish her apartment in the Rue du Four.

She was very pleased with the result, and we became fast friends. Later, I did another two apartments for her brother Pacífico and her sister-in-law Monique, and in no time at all I was on friendly terms with them as well. I also got to know his mother who lived in a château that Paco had bought. I had no idea then just how famous Paco, whom I saw occasionally at the workshop, was.

We chatted over time and got better acquainted. The Rabaneda family comes from Pasaia near San Sebastián. Paco's father was a republican officer arrested for loyalty to the Republic, and shot. I got to read the letter he wrote a few hours before his execution, a farewell note to his wife and children. As you might imagine, it was an impressive document. After his father's execution, his mother left for London with Paco and her other three children, Olga, Pacífico, and I think it was Libertad, or some such

175

fashionable name from that time. They left on the same ship as other Basque children and, on reaching London, found that the English were reluctant hosts. Their poor mother somehow made it to France with her four children and settled in Perpignan. There, too, they were neither welcomed nor well treated, as these were the days when republicans crossing the Pyrenees were being penned like animals in concentration camps.

In the end the authorities sent them to Brittany and the family managed to get back on its feet there, one step at a time, thanks to their mother's hard work as a seamstress. What she and Paco's sisters managed to save covered the costs of his education.

In the building where Pacifico lived, there was the Le Vieux Colombier theater, premises with a lot of history but now deserted and in ruins. Without saying a word to anyone, we set up a company to restore the theater, with partners Anne Urtubia, Olga and Paco Rabaneda, and my architect friend Jérôme Gerbert. We sorted out all the paperwork and set to work. We did all this out of a love of culture and asked for no help from the authorities, but a few French VIPs got wind of the venture and did what they could to smooth the way.

One day, after I had set up the Atelier 71 company, named in honor of the Paris Commune of 1871, Paco asked me about the chances of the company working on his workshops and offices. This was a big job, and it opened a lot of doors for me. Paco bought some huge premises with a glass roof that could open. I was told that the carpentry in the roof was by the engineer Gustave Eiffel and, during the Great War, airships or balloons had risen through that opening.

I have seen lots of expensive premises, but this was a real wonder. It needed restoration and refurbishment and was full of the accumulated rubbish of years of disuse. Paco made plans for a huge arts facility with twenty areas for music practice, double-partitioned soundproofing, two stairways leading to the apartments, a concert podium, bathrooms, kitchens, and a garden area. It was, in short, a big job on premises with tremendous potential.

While I was in prison, I set up a cooperative with this job in mind. The cooperative was made up of revolutionary comrades but then came proof of what I always say: being a revolutionary is one thing and being a bricklayer quite another. The fact is that the co-op fell apart and I was left on my own. In the end the work was undertaken mostly by Basque refugees: ETA militants, *polimilis*, *autónomos*, and anarchists. They were without papers, which the police knew, and I saw to it that I was able to hire and pay every one of them, using the following line of argument: Why let them steal just to feed themselves, when there is work to be had?

The police agencies kept us under constant surveillance while we were working on site. Though we were free to come and go, have lunch wherever we wanted, etc., they were monitoring us as a form of intimidation mounted in a very high-profile way, with a number of people, myself included, being followed around. At the time I was very well known given my police record and the work I did, so we decided it an honor and a source of pride to find ourselves under very respectful police surveillance.

We built the center in an act of solidarity with Paco, the great fashion designer, who has never had a capitalist spirit, and whose bank account back then didn't have millions in it. We advanced him the requisite loan and joined forces to build this arts center. Sometime later I visited a few places in Spain to get money for Paco. Stores had been opened in several countries and a Paco Rabanne brand been established, but he was in dire financial straits. We came to an arrangement with those stores, and they advanced whatever they could to help him weather his difficulties.

I am not really familiar with my friend's work, nor could I put a price on it. What I learned from Guy Laroche, a client of mine, who I built two shops for, one in the Avenue Montaigne and the other in the Faubourg Saint-Honoré, as well as doing a few odd jobs in his home in the Rue Pierre 1er de Serbie. "I'm not creative, nor am I an artist. There are only three people in France deserving of that description, and one of the three is your friend Paco Rabanne."

That is what Paco is like, not merely a great artist but a man very generous towards his friends and always sound. I am very fond of both him and his sister Olga who really came through for me during my time under arrest; she never forgot me and helped me as much as she could.

The center was opened by Culture minister Jack Lang, and it had the capacity to accommodate eighty drama and music groups at the same time. Paco gave preferential treatment to African and West Indian groups because he figured their needs were the greatest. His neighbors didn't really like it, some because of the music and some because of the smoking and still others because of their being Black. The fact is that the minister himself, who was so happy to open it, eventually shut it down, preferring to pander to his voters rather than to the poor, Black performers who found the place an ideal practice hall.

Arnaud Chastel

I met scientist and astronomer Arnaud Chastel in a bookshop in the Place de Clichy. He was browsing through the section on nineteenth-century subversive books that dealt with revolutionary events in France. I was interested in the same books, and we were very soon chatting and exchanging addresses and phone numbers. A few days later we got in touch and had dinner. Arnaud was not just a complete intellectual, but he was a "star" in the field of astronomy, and more especially in the study of the Sun. He had spent several years working in an observatory in the United States and was greatly renowned both there and in France. He was a man with a very radical mindset, very much the Situationist as well as a great admirer of the Spanish revolution and the anarchist collectivizations. He had read everything he could find on the subject, revolutionary books and pamphlets. And he also had a great interest in manual labor, and I think that's why my outlook and modus vivendi caught his interest. He could do anything and learn anything, and one day he asked me to come with him to a gambling den, a casino, assuring me that, mathematically, it was perfectly feasible to gamble and win. He and I swanked it, dressed up like gangsters in dark, pinstripe suits, breaking the bank.

Arnaud's father was the historian André Chastel, a lecturer at the Collège de France, a great and world-renowned expert on the Italian Renaissance. From a very modest family background, it cost him great effort to rise to the heights that he achieved and that's why André was very demanding in everything, including toward his own son. For his part, Arnaud was a prodigious intellect with wide-ranging knowledge; and besides that, he wasn't afraid of anything. As he saw it, publishing a book or a pirate newspaper was not just a reasonable thing to do but necessary. He delighted in crossing boundaries and, if there was a price to be paid for doing so, he was ready to pay it.

One day Arnaud asked me about the chances of manufacturing a flying machine, a sort of remote-controlled toy plane capable of ferrying a cargo of explosives wherever one might like and detonating it at a distance. I mentioned this story to a journalist from the magazine *Interviú*, a friend of mine at the time who later proved a complete disappointment to me. The idea really intrigued him and, on returning to Spain, he published a big sensationalist article in the magazine, a total concoction of his own making, announcing that the king of Spain had escaped safe and sound from an attempt on his life during his winter holidays in the Pyrenees around Canfranc, no less. The article went into comprehensive detail about the remote-controlled explosive device that had allegedly been used in the attempt on the king's life.

Arnaud had begun taking flying lessons in Montargis, a town some sixty kilometers south of Paris. One day we had a phone call from there, informing us that our friend had had an accident with the plane he was flying and had been killed. His parents wanted to retrieve his corpse and bring it to Paris for burial with great religious ceremony and pomp. Arnaud's wife put her foot down at that, so about ten of his friends set out to collect him in my Volkswagen *combi* van. Once we returned to Paris, we were joined by another fifty people. We all headed for the Porte de Choisy cemetery where a still larger crowd gathered. We were all sadly recounting stories of our time with Arnaud and then escorted his body as far as the enormous pit that had been dug by the gravediggers. At the end of a simple ceremony, all those attending were handed a rose and then the body was laid to rest.

We began to disperse and were a good hundred meters from our friend's grave, a pretty sizable band of us, including my very downcast friend, Thierry Fagart. All of a sudden, I heard a female voice screaming for me. "Lucio! Lucio! Arnaud's relatives are having a Mass said for him!" This came as a shock since Arnaud had not held any religious beliefs for many years, and his wife and friends had agreed that the funeral would be a secular one. Wasting no time, we all raced over to see what was going on. I led the way and soon spotted, gathered around the open grave and with their backs to us, Arnaud's father, mother, and two brothers alongside a priest dressed in his Mass vestments, right down to the chasuble. I shouted, "What are you up to? Your son was against this, and you are disrespecting him. Have you no shame?" Others began to raise their voices too and a big scene unfolded. Seeing us, the priest turned in a panic, snatched up his briefcase, and still wearing his Mass vestments, scampered like a hare through the graves and crucifixes, and that was the last we ever saw of him. Arnaud's brothers did nothing, but his father began to screech abuse at us, using the foulest language imaginable. Arnaud's mother, who was also calling me names, suddenly jumped me and the pair of us fell into the grave. She clawed at my neck leaving me with several scratch marks and I, unable to defend myself, was bleeding like a stuck pig. Our friends offered us a hand, Arnaud's mother and me, and hauled us out of there. So much for our friend's funeral; it was a surreal display.

When Suárez the banker was abducted, Arnaud had been jailed due to a police error. I had been working on the installation of a bathroom on the Boulevard Soult. Some days earlier, when the banker was kidnapped, there was a knock at the apartment door at half past ten in the morning. I answered and there were young people there who said they were decorators; strange because they didn't have even a tape measure with them and came empty-handed. They went through the motions of having a good look around as if measuring up for a decorating job and then left. That evening, when I finished work, I loaded up the car with a few packs of glazed tiles and set off to drop them off at Arnaud's place.

The police tailed me and had seen me entering Arnaud's apartment, so they figured he had some hand in the kidnapping. Those were the conditions we were working under. Arnaud's apartment was littered with lots of building materials and when they asked Arnaud said that I had given them to him. The police leapt to conclusions. Unable to comprehend how I, a mere workman, might have anything to give a wealthy man, they concluded that we had both been in on the abduction. Anne and I, as well as Arnaud and his wife, wound up in jail over a gift I had given a friend; but then that's what life was like in the building trade back then. There was a plentiful supply of everything, and we helped ourselves, and I used to give my friends whatever they needed, something in which I took a real delight.

I don't mean to suggest that I am the cleverest man alive, and I have always had a healthy respect for, and fear of, the police. In this instance, they got it wrong, but they are allowed to get things wrong, several times over, if need be, or even to fail. Whereas we are not; if we make a mistake or miss out just once, it is curtains for us.

Victor Dojlida

On September 26, 1989, the newspaper *Libération* devoted its entire front page to a man who had just regained his freedom after forty-three years behind bars, something that just defies belief. It was my friend Victor Dojlida, whom I met through Didier Richard's wife Irène, who was keen to make a documentary about his life. Victor was living in Aubervilliers near our firm and the Richards knew me because I had recently taken on the job of refurbishing the headquarters of the Ligue des Droits de l'Homme (Human Rights League).

Victor was excited that I wanted to meet him. I called to see him with a friend from Bilbao and we had some trouble finding the tiny apartment where he was living, an apartment allocated to him by the Aubervilliers city council.

Irène started shooting the documentary she had in mind, but Victor was one of those nonviolent types who are nonviolent in theory only, as I am wont to point out; everything went swimmingly with him if you didn't get on his bad side. Irène and Didier put a lot of work into their documentary and showed great patience, but in the end the inevitable happened and Victor pulled the plug on it.

Since he was living very close to Atelier 71, Victor would drop in to see me whenever he had a spare minute. We'd share a good bottle of wine and a bit of food. He was already in his seventies and still driving, even though he had no license, so he was eager for me to get him one at any cost, because driving without a license was as much an annoyance to him as it was for any of us. He was the worst driver, with a childish mindset. He had several brand-new cars, but they took so many knocks every day that they lasted only a very short time. He was not used to driving and his reflexes were shot, but there was no way you could tell him that. Whenever he turned into the entrance to our firm, all us pedestrians were seized by panic, but he was never afraid and always did what he wanted.

On one occasion, an accident left his car quite badly dented and in order to pay for the repairs, he looked up a friend and told him, "I'll be leaving such-and-such a place, you'll be bringing up the rear, you tail-end me and we'll make a claim as if the car was new, and they'll pay for everything." It all went off as anticipated, but instead of his friend running into the car, it was a truck that made a mess of it and Victor, leaving him with a broken leg and several broken ribs.

Under the German Occupation, Victor—seventeen at the time—started out, like many others, doing whatever he could against the occupiers and had ties to what was, historically, the most significant band of resisters in the Paris region, the so-called Manouchian Gang. Louis Aragon wrote a poem about them, *L'affiche rouge*, and it was put to music by Léo Ferré. Every time we heard it, it would send a chill down our spines. The gang was made up of twenty-three foreigners—Polish, Jews, Italians, and Spaniards, and Manouchian was one of its leaders. All twenty-three were captured and executed. Their story is very well known, a real legend.

Victor Dojlida was of Polish extraction and had been very close to the Manouchian Gang. They were all very young and Victor told me, "We were such kids that whenever we mounted an operation, it took three of us just to throw a Molotov cocktail." Obviously, this was an exaggeration, his way of relating to me what the Resistance was like and who its stalwarts were. France has not given these people the credit they deserve. If arrested, the Spaniards were handed over to Spain where they were imprisoned or executed; the Jews were deported to the death camps. Those who fought in such conditions displayed a courage and valor that France has yet to give adequate recognition.

Victor himself was deported to Mauthausen and there became friendly with people who went on to make careers in politics and became government ministers. After the Liberation he set off for Africa to track down the judge who had passed sentence on him during the Occupation, and he killed him. Not that that was the only crime he committed, but of the rest I shall say nothing: he was a friend of mine and no angel. He was just seventeen when he was captured, sentenced, and deported under the Occupation, and he never grew up. He was still a boy even after the Liberation and throughout the years he served in a range of prisons. He claimed to know every single prison in France and all the jailers, but they never broke him or put one over on him.

Victor was frequently sent to the isolation cells for punishment, several times for trying to escape. One of these escape attempts took place in Clairvaux prison, a very old but top security prison from which no one had ever managed to escape. Victor and another comrade tried to break out by crawling through the sewers, but the guards discovered them crawling and turned on the taps. Victor and his friend had to scramble out, half drowned, and failure was followed up by a beating and a period in the isolation cells.

One Sunday I was sorting through a few things at the office when Victor called me. I hadn't heard from him for several days, and he was very curt, as he always was when talking on the phone, "Hi, Lucio," he said. "I'm in hospital. I have cancer and I don't think I'll last much longer." I pressed him to tell me where he was, to which he replied, "I'm about to be discharged. I'll give you a call." He hung up. A few days later he showed up at my office with some friends. He was living in a commune of young people, all or almost all of them anarchists, sound people whom I got to know quite well over time and who looked out for him as if he was their own father. On several occasions he offered me money and I always gave him the same answer, "There's nothing I need. Help these youngsters who are looking after you and doing a bloody good job of it, given how hard you are to deal with."

One morning I had a very early appointment at the doctor's and when I arrived at the office, he told me to call my secretary. I did just that and Madame Belloy told me, "Victor rang you. He says he's going to take his own life tonight and wants to see you before he dies." I postponed my visit to the doctor and scurried off to see Victor. He told me straight out, "I'm going to die tonight, Lucio. I'd like you to drop in on the mayor of Auber-villiers and tell him to come and see me."

I made my way to the town hall and said that I was there to see Mon-sieur Rallitte, the mayor, only to be told by the staff there that without an appointment he couldn't see me. I insisted and started up the stairs, the secretaries raising their voices and I doing likewise. Suddenly, the mayor emerged to see what the shouting was all about. I filled him in on the sit-uation, that Victor—who he knew—meant to commit suicide and wanted to see him first, and that I had come to get him to Victor. He told me that it wasn't an option, that he had appointments scheduled and people expect-ing him, but be that as it may, mayor though he was, and minister though he was to become, Monsieur Rallitte dropped everything and went to see Victor. Since then I have had a respect for him that I have never felt for people who hold offices such as his.

Victor and the mayor got to see each other and said whatever they had to say to each other. I called back to see Victor again at six o'clock and he said,

"Lucio, I want to die tonight in the presence of my four best friends. You are one of them; go home, put on a suit and tie, and get a bottle of champagne. I want to die having a drink with the four of you." I went home, donned my best suit and a tie, then rejoined Victor and those other friends to uncork a bottle. The four of us were overawed by the situation. Out of the blue he told us, "To your health, and now the urge to die has left me." I left and by the time I got home, the phone was ringing, and they told me he was dead.

Victor had wanted his funeral to be a party in the Père Lachaise cemetery. I can think of nothing ghastlier than watching a friend disappear into the flames, cremated in front of your eyes. The undertaker told us to go on up to the hall to get some rest and he would hand over the ashes an hour later. About forty of us took his advice and went upstairs; some went off to get champagne to hold a party in Victor's honor, just as he had wished, but I kept to myself, half asleep. Suddenly, I heard "Bella ciao," "Los Hijos del pueblo," "A las barricadas," and "Arroja la bomba" and a host of other revolutionary anthems. They startled me awake; Victor's party had begun.

The official came upstairs to hand over Victor's ashes, and told us that, if we wanted, we could scatter them nearby. We followed him to the spot, and he asked who was in charge. I responded that it was Olivier, and then I said to Olivier, "Pull the chain." He raised up the urn, but at that moment our friends began to set off firecrackers and raised one hell of a racket. Olivier lost his grip and the ashes spilled onto his head. Victor would have laughed long and hearty at that.

In 2001, the novelist Michèle Lesbre wrote a biography of Victor entitled *Victor Dojlida, une vie dans l'ombre* (Victor Dojlida: A Life in the Shadows) published by the Noésis publishing house.

In the Matignon and Elysée Palaces

The Hôtel Matignon and the Elysée Palace are two unique places that many people dream of getting to know. I have been invited to both.

One day, my dear friend Louis Joinet, legal advisor to all the socialist prime ministers and subsequently to President Mitterrand, called me at work to ask me if I'd like to have dinner with him at the house of the prime minister, Michel Rocard, "Come dine with me and you'll get to see the Hôtel

Matignon. You'll really love it." I was not sure whether or not to take him up on this invitation, because, then as now, there was nothing about the place for me to miss out on. Then again, Louis Joinet is a man of immense prestige, standing head and shoulders above most politicians, and is respected even by his opponents for the great work he has accomplished and for his proven talents in a variety of negotiations but above all for his integrity. So it wasn't easy for me to turn him down because it seemed rather uncouth, so after having a bit of a think I called him back and said I'd join him. My friend had also told me, "Bring along one of the old hands from your firm," so I told him I'd bring Benito Ferreiro, a Galician from Vilagarcía de Arousa.

My friend told me what procedures we were to follow and said that "The gendarmes on duty will be in the know." Benito and I spruced ourselves up a bit, I picked him up in a van, and off we went to the Hôtel Matignon, a historic building that is currently the residence of the prime minister and hosts ministerial meetings. When we got there the gendarmes opened the gates and pointed us toward our allocated place. They said, "The advisor will be down to get you shortly," and in fact my friend came downstairs within a minute and asked us to follow him.

We climbed to one of the upstairs apartments and Joinet took us into his own quarters, the premises he used while on call or on duty. We sat in the kitchen for a glass of champagne and then we began our round of the offices and bureau. At that hour there was next to no one working. My friend filled us in on the use and purpose of each of the apartments we were passing through, and his briefing was very interesting and the building itself luxurious. Next, we entered the prime ministerial office; it is a sight to behold, a true wonder that left us stunned.

Suddenly, someone showed up looking for Joinet in an urgent matter. As he stepped out to attend to it, he told me, "There's no problem with you having a look around. Only thing is, I would ask you, above all, not to sit in the prime minister's chair."

As soon as he was out the door I went and sat in that chair and launched into a sort of a speech, addressing myself to Benito, "Here you have it, Lucio Urtubia, newest tenant of the Matignon palace, has seized the prime minister's chair without any violence."

The last word was still on my lips when my friend reappeared. The first thing he said to me was: "Even as I was warning you not to, I knew you would. I just knew you'd sit in that chair." He was disgusted with what I'd done. The fact is that we found all this luxury overpowering. Our tour continued through the gardens, which are magnificent, but I'm used to gardens and I was not all that impressed. Then we were shown the room where weekly cabinet meetings are held; it was a real gem. The flooring was unique and a very demanding piece of workmanship and the whole décor screamed craftsmanship and profound expertise. It's a pity that everyone doesn't get to see this, and that something like this is set aside for only a minority. Astounded, I was also thinking how, in the event of an uprising or revolution, we should avoid the burning and destruction of all these treasures. Why destroy them? I came away impressed and thinking that this was something that should be shared because everything is unique.

Next, we were seated for dinner in the event hall. My friend explained that when he is on duty, standing in for the prime minister, all reports of what is happening around the world cross his desk. He then briefs the prime minister who carries the news to the president of the Republic.

Dinner was superb: a fine vegetable soup, lamb cutlets, cheese board, coffee, and a few other things. We talked about a thousand things, and our friend was soon asking us about how a firm as small as ours operated. I told him that we faced a great number of difficulties: lack of professionalism in our workforce, problems finding jobs, enormously burdensome taxes, and that nobody in the civil service would give a contract to a small firm like ours. And there was another big gripe: revenue, because sometimes clients may owe but don't pay; and you then must wait and work twice as hard until payment comes in.

"Right at this moment," I told him, "Elf Aquitaine owes us something like two million francs. I know they will pay up eventually. . ."

Before I could complete my sentence my friend, who was really taken aback, said, "Elf Aquitaine owes you all that money? How can I help? Monday, bring me all the invoices and you'll see just how quick they will pay up."

He was as good as his word. Early on the Monday morning I gave all of the invoices and paperwork to one of his staff. That night, after I got home from the firm, our secretary, Madame Belloy, received a call from Elf Aquitaine saying they'd be paying all of our invoices. How could that have happened so quickly? It turns out our friend Louis had called one of the motorcycle gendarmes who performs such errands and sent him with all the Atelier 71 invoices on a prime ministerial collection round. Elf Aquitaine or not, they were shaking in their boots and hurriedly paid up. We were out in Rueil working on some buildings for Elf Aquitaine's engineers and no one said a single word to us. But the story of the invoices quickly spread and many Elf managers who had never even bothered to glance at us began to ask us about our company. I told some of them that Michel Rocard was a personal friend of mine and that he would come to our *sanfermines* party every year, and I told others that my sister the prime minister's chef. They quickly concluded that we were VIPs and that our firm must have at least one or two thousand workers on the payroll. They looked at us with different eyes, having no idea that there were only ten of us that were Spanish and Portuguese, ten Arabs, and eight or nine Basque refugees working without papers or permits. And also a boss that was frequently in and out of jail, but who was a worker and sound and who, as such, was not ready to let antifascist friends be forced into stealing just to feed themselves.

The other dinner at the Elysée was also down to my friend Louis who was advisor to President François Mitterrand at the time. Louis is a fellow that likes to treat people and that's how I was invited. The meal was even better than at the Matignon, but the president was away, so we didn't get to drop in on him. As I say the drink and the food were better than at the Matignon and I grabbed the chance to "liberate" a few Cuban cigars, but I was suddenly overcome with regret. There I was in those surroundings, and I could just see my passage through the jails of Cascante and Tudela, Pamplona, Vera de Bidasoa, Nanterre, Bois d'Arcy, and La Santé. I remembered the friend who had had to answer the call of nature every day just as we were sitting down to eat and the noises issuing from his guts, ruined by malnutrition . . . and the stench! I could see the sink we had used for washing and for doing the dishes and I thought about my father's time in prison. Was I letting them all down? At some effort I rose from my chair and returned to the table. Lighting up a Montecristo cigar—I have never been a smoker—my thoughts turned to Camilo Cienfuegos, and I broke out into an anarchist song: "You would build ideal cities, but first you must destroy the ugliness, the regiments, and the cathedrals, and we libertarians must join forces once and for all."

I doubt that anybody had ever sung that song there before. And at three o'clock in the morning, my cigar and I climbed into the car bringing us home to Aubervilliers and I imagined being stopped by the gendarmes, breathalyzed and arrested. And had I, with my cigar aglow, told them at that point that I had just come from the Elysée Palace, they would have arrested me for being drunk and crazy. They'd never have believed me.

Let me say, in conclusion, that I was not so keen on the Matignon, the prime ministerial residence, and the Elysée, the presidential residence, but I did enjoy the honest pleasure that my friend Louis Joinet derived from sharing the privileges of office with me. This man, whom few can match for integrity and who is highly placed in politics, worked tirelessly for the good of his country, France, for other countries in need and also on behalf of his friends, including me. I can say with pride that, if it weren't for him, for his assistance, I would have lived my whole life behind bars.

Belle Île

October 1975, 5:00 a.m., one hour before I am due to set off for work. Someone is knocking at the door. It worries me because of the early hour, as you can never be sure who may come knocking at the door. But they had never come for me this early before, not even on the many occasions when they'd come to collect me. It's a few minutes before I open the door because the answers and explanations coming from the other side of the door are not too consistent and because, that night, a very well-renowned Spanish journalist, still a great friend of mine at the time, was spending the night with us. He's hiding under the bed when I open the door. Several police officers come inside, and I breathe a momentary sigh of relief because they don't ask me outright to accompany them, like they have on previous occasions, and they don't search the house (leaving the place topsy turvy as they do).

They get typewriters and conduct themselves well enough with Anne and Juliette and, after a few minutes, two of them ask my permission to sit down and take some notes, while others step out into the street or remain outside on the landing.

They fill me in: this is an arrest without cause, or a suggestion of offence committed and they apologize for the fact, but it is being made—they say— in the interests of the Republic. The authorities have decided to banish me from Paris for the duration of Prince Juan Carlos of Spain's official visit.

They inform me that they are to bring me to Belle Île in Brittany, an island I know nothing about, and that I will be put up at a four-star hotel at absolutely no cost to myself. All the costs are to be borne by the French Republic.

To set us at our ease, they ask if we might make them a coffee, so we do. Whereupon they inform me that they are taking me to Nanterre where the prefect awaits my arrival. In a three-car cavalcade with myself in the middle car, we arrive at the police station. The prefect is there to greet me and escorts me to his office. We spend a few hours chatting about libertarian ideas and, to while away the time, he offers me several cups of coffee. As officials arrive, the prefect introduces me to them and issues them with the requisite orders for my transfer to the island. None of them is happy about this and they give this away by continually rehearsing it to me that in this instance I am not being accused of anything. They make a phone call to my current employer and fill him in about my situation.

The prefect orders the police to take me to Montparnasse station to catch the train in which they have reserved me a compartment. He also stresses to them that I am to get whatever I ask for and that they are to treat me to a meal at a good restaurant. The seven of us—six police officers and I—say our goodbyes and the three-car cavalcade moves off, lights flashing and sirens wailing, heading directly to the station, without stopping at intersections or traffic lights. Life can be so unfathomable at times.

When we arrive at Montparnasse, I tell them that I am hungry and want a good meal as we have a long trip ahead of us and the prefect's advice and instructions must be heeded. We grab a table in La Coupole, a swanky restaurant, and after a splendid meal and a drink I am much more at ease and getting used to the odd position in which I find myself. Up until now I was worried and was assailed by all manner of misgivings; you can never tell when a policeman is telling you the truth and you always have something to hide. But there is a consistency to all the explanations they have been handing me since five o'clock this morning and I see nothing untoward and, as I say, I am feeling more at ease.

The reserved compartment, when we get to it, is under lock and key. The porter opens it, and hands the keys to the expedition leader who, once we are inside, locks the door behind him and unfolds a small table for a hand of cards. We play "*tarreau,*" a game familiar to me, and throughout the trip they ask me a thousand questions about life in Spain and I answer them in my humble way as best I can. They tell me that, should I get up to any escape nonsense, they are under strict orders not to use their weapons. When we arrive in Vanves, a gendarmerie coach is waiting for us and ferries us to a barracks where I dine alone and where they find me a place to sleep.

The next morning, I run into several comrades who have also been placed under arrest and together they take us to the ferry that will carry us out to the island. Once all we friends are reunited, everything changes. There are eleven of us in all and we are kept under very close surveillance throughout the trip. The guards watching us are armed with automatic rifles and bulging ammunition pouches, all very showy. When we reach Belle Île, another company of the CRS with several scout cars await us. In a coach and several cars and army trucks we are ferried to a huge four-star hotel cordoned off on four sides by police trucks and scout cars. We step inside and the gendarmerie commander gathers us in the great hall and informs us that we are here on account of Juan Carlos of Spain's visit and that our stay will last from eight to ten days, for the duration of the king's visit to France.

The hotel is very plush; it has everything, and we just have to ask for whatever we want. We are completely free to go anywhere on the island, as long as we have a CRS or gendarme escort. The news has been full of our arrests and banishment to Belle Île, so the hotel is full because people have flooded in to have a look at us. The radio has been describing us as fantastic, almost legendary characters, and children sidle up to us, eager to be photographed with the "terrorists," and we pick them up in our arms for the photos to be taken.

I ask to visit the Palais, the docks area with its shops and cafés, and a woman going that direction gives me a ride in her car. I step into a bar and order a beer the moment we arrive and am still waiting to be served when a man in his forties accosts me, introducing himself as a fisherman. He is a tall, sturdy fellow who must stand a good two meters tall and weigh upwards of a hundred kilos—a real bruiser. He keeps me company for a long time, and we talk a great deal about the civil war in Spain and the Spaniards in the Resistance in France. We have been chatting for a good half hour when he tells me he is disgusted by the French government's treatment of us; he knows his politics and his politicians and if we have been taken to the island, it has nothing to do with violence or terrorism, no. This farce is because the French government is in negotiations with its Spanish counterpart over a very important economic matter, and we are merely the pawns making their dealings that much easier. This is eye-opening to me and gives me an insight into our weakness and poverty. My friend proposes that, if I like, he can get me off the island tonight on his boat and take me wherever I would like; he is on our side and at our disposal if he can be of any assistance. I don't take him up on it, but I have fond memories of his words.

I leave the bar and go for a stroll, passing a bicycle garage on my way to the hotel. When I get to the hotel, I suggest to the others that we each rent out a bike. All eleven of us make for the Palais to rent our bikes; the police and CRS who granted us permission to go wherever we pleased are left standing, baffled outside the garage, absurdly waiting. One hour later, a gendarmerie helicopter lands with twenty bicycles for the policemen. Later, we hand in our rented bicycles and go for dinner, each of us choosing whatever he likes, and I remember I chose hot oysters, never having tasted them before, and champagne.

I am wakened from a deep sleep by the clatter of stones on glass. The young people of the island have come to show their solidarity with us, and we are all delighted. Over the ensuing days whenever we step out for a stroll anywhere, people show great solidarity and invite us in, taking issue with the government.

Throughout this time, the press and radio and TV give us "anarchist terrorists" a lot of coverage; we are just a bunch of libertarian working men and not one of us is a terrorist. The authorities have slandered us by labelling us as what we are not, which has resulted in people being afraid of some act of sabotage or arson, so they treat us like royalty. We play the odd prank on the owners. The hotel is for fat cats; some movies have been shot here and, on occasion, it's played host to the president of the Republic.

After a few days they bring us home again and our families are at Montparnasse station to welcome us: Anne, Juliette, and my sisters meet me. It has all turned out fine.

Sometime later, the movie-maker Gabriel Auer contacted the entire group of deportees because he was eager to make a film about our Belle Île experience, which he does. Called *Vacances royales* (Royal Vacation), the film won a prize at the 1980 Cannes Festival. All our friends are up for the movie, except me. I am more wary and only my voice and silhouette appear in the movie.

The Story of a blank

I have been lucky enough to have been able to help many VIPs, for the sake of our ideal. One of these was Albert Boadella, whom I consider a friend. In his memoirs there is a very nice sentence where he says, "If I had to wage a guerrilla war, Lucio would be my choice as leader." It was a pleasure getting him everything he needed while he was a wanted man in Spain and we were ready to sacrifice our own freedom for his sake, if necessary.

One day a friend who was very dear to me at the time but who no longer is that, an Aragonese journalist with a full resume, called to ask me to get some papers ready to help Eliseo Bayo. He supplied me with photographs, and I asked no more questions. I did him the complete set: passport, ID documents, and driver's license. After three or four days he called back and asked if I had finished. I answered, "Yes, I've read the books and I'll bring them to you wherever you say." He gave me the address and it proved to be one of the finest hotels in the Opéra district, which struck me as odd because friends in need of assistance are usually anarchists, Basques, or Italians and are always to be found living in rooms and bedsits rather than in the elegant surroundings of a hotel. The upshot was that I met my friend there with another gentleman who was all agog: I never asked him a thing, nor did I wish to know his name. I had him sign the papers, affixed the plastic covers, and handed them over. He threw his arms around me. "What's your name?" he asked, and I told him "Fermín." I took it for granted that the guy must be some wealthy socialist or republican, or factory owner perhaps. When Eliseo Bayo walked with me into the street, he asked me, "Did you recognize him? Well, he's the money behind Barcelona Football Club. His photograph is all over the newspapers and Interpol is after him."

As it happens, a few days later I had a call from Eliseo Bayo and his friend inviting me to dinner. I told them that Anne would have to come too, and we both went. We arranged to meet at Le Drugstore in the Champs Elsyées and from there we were taken to Le Fouquet, the most renowned luxury restaurant in the area, much patronized by Sarkozy recently. Splendid dinner. As we were chatting about forgeries and repression and Francoism and the like, the gentleman unknown to me abruptly produced a check and slipped it across to me. I held it up to the light looking for the metal thread and finding that it had none and was drawn on the Banco de España, I told him,

"Piece of cake. We can do it whenever you like." I thought he was showing it to me as what was to be copied, maybe ten or twelve kilos' worth, but he said to me, "It's for you." He was Pere Baret, manager of the Barcelona soccer squad. He absconded to Brazil and the blank check bearing his signature, as given to me, I keep between the pages of a book.

Some years later, in the process of arresting me, the police searched the house and found Baret's signed check in the pages of that book, and they handed it over to the authorities in Barcelona. I could have stuck as many zeroes as I chose on the check and cashed it. Somebody with an interest in seeing my actions misrepresented lied and said that I had handed the police a blank check hoping to buy immunity for myself rather than converting it into cash. This was the origin of the "Lucio's treasure" canard put about by the police and tacked on to the forgery and other affairs to which I had previously been linked. It was beyond their comprehension how a man like me, who could have cashed in a fortune, hadn't done so. As I have recounted elsewhere, that "treasure" never existed.

Now, who knew about the story of the check? Three or four friends only. And of those in the know, I reckon, by a simple process of elimination, the one who told the police was that journalist from Aragon because he is a money grubber, and it is money that he is out for. This is the same fellow who traveled to Miami and became friendly with Bush's brother, the governor of Florida. And the very same man who married the niece of Lázaro Cárdenas, and who plays dirty tricks just to make money.

My first lawful journey

It was the early 1980s and a few of us were working on the Paco Rabanne project, all under very close police surveillance, but nobody bothered us. A delegation from Bilbao visited Paris and dropped by to see us. Mario Onaindia was among them, and I mentioned to him the threats made against me by certain maverick organizations, which were just beginning to operate on both sides of the border around that time. My friend Mario brought my situation to the attention of the Spanish Interior Minister, the socialist José Barrionuevo, and he gave his word that we would have protection when entering and leaving the country. I then approached several agencies, starting with the consulate, to regularize my position, vis à vis the Spanish authorities, and then I bought a couple of plane tickets to Barcelona for Juliette and myself. I couldn't believe that I was traveling on legit documents, since my entire life up until then had been spent roaming the world as an undocumented immigrant.

I was reassured but I still had misgivings; you never can tell if something more is going on under the surface and this was especially true where I was concerned. At Orly, Juliette and I managed to pass unnoticed but then we bumped into Luis Fernández from Cascante who was working out at the airport and he, delighted to see me and in an effort to please, the first thing he did was introduce us to the flight crew. I was exasperated because I trusted nothing and nobody at the time, and I sometimes saw things that were not there.

My friend Luis escorted us on to the plane and into first class, no less, and no sooner had I sat down than I spotted people and uniforms I certainly had no urge to lay eyes on. So I drew up a list of several names and phone numbers and very discreetly slipped it to Juliette, telling her, "If anything happens to me in Barcelona, call one of these numbers and let them know."

Juliette must have been about ten or twelve at the time. She took charge of my list and very stealthily slipped it inside her shoe. I gave her a little nudge and said, "Not there. That's the first place they'll look." Embarrassed, she asked, "Where shall I put it, Papa?" To which I replied, "In your backside. Go to the toilet and sort it out." At which the girl did precisely that.

But nothing untoward happened in Barcelona. We rented a car and headed for Cascante, crazy with happiness. By the time we got there, evening was falling and that was the first day in decades that I felt free. I had been in the town before but without papers and had been elsewhere on phony documents or in France on refugee documents. That first day, a meeting had been arranged in the Nuestra Señora de la Asunción church and the speakers were people I didn't know at all: there was the mayor of Pamplona, Señor Caballero; a very well-known figure, Señor Urmeneta; and Victor Manuel Arbeloa. All the youth of Cascante were in the vestry, and two Civil Guards in tricorn hats and armed to the teeth were posted at either end of the huge speakers' table. It struck me as surreal, like something out of a Buñuel movie. Why the brazen display of weapons? The three speakers talked of democracy and, when they finished, the floor was thrown open to the folks in the vestry. The first to speak was Román who asked, "How can you talk about democracy when several people lost their lives in San Esteban just the other day?" The initial response from one of the public speakers was, "That is not something to be spoken of here. Next question." Whereupon Román's brother put the very same question and got the very same answer. People were intimidated by the responses and by the Civil Guards' guns. I have never been fussy about asking questions, but I asked to speak.

"Our two friends here have asked something," I said. "You have said your piece, but our friends' words carry just as much weight as yours do, so be kind enough to answer them."

Before I could even finish, Señor Arbeloa cut in with:

"Listen, you anarchist!"

I was stunned for I had never dreamed that there were so many libertarians in Cascante. As he was leaving the meeting, one of the speakers, Señor Urmeneta, very much the *euskaldun* (Basque speaker) mentioned the castle of Urtubia to me, and all three of the speakers invited me to come to Pamplona for dinner. I made my apologies, telling them, "If word were to get out to my friends that I had taken you up on your invitation, I would be an outcast." The whole day passed off very well. Later I corresponded with Urmeneta, the director of the Savings Bank, and on the same occasion I met several people who are still friends of mine today, Tuñón, Lezana, Uruñuela, García, and others.

Héliette

Where there is a will, there is always a way to help others and for solidarity work. These days there is so much more money around but the will is sorely lacking, or that's what I believe anyway. I remember that in the past our elders would be up to date with their trade union dues because they were or had been workers and remained affiliated to the CNT, as well as belonging to other organizations and associations to which they also paid dues and participated in. Keeping up to date was necessary for the making of decisions or putting suggestions forward at assemblies. Older people with not much money might choose to go without a coffee at Le Point du Jour, but they paid for the stamp in their union card month in and month out. And then there was also the prisoners' solidarity fund and the stamp for that. These days we have more money, but people prefer their coffee or their beer, and solidarity funds are crying out for subscribers.

As I see it, wealth makes us lose ourselves and distances us from one another. I cannot understand how or why people have changed, but it is a fact that they have. Money used to be in short supply but it was used better and shared more. And language has changed as well, but I sometimes wonder if that change has had less of an impact on us than economic change. These days, if three of us get together for a chat, we promptly argue and fall out with one another; it is as if nobody is willing to listen to differing opinions.

My life is an open book, and everybody knows my background; I was no angel, but I am not trying to excuse what I did. I am trying to tell everybody what I know and what I have lived through and carry on doing. I want to keep championing all the active groups and organizations that operate outside the law, even though I think they may be wrong on certain matters.

But let me take as my example not myself but my friend Héliette. I have mentioned her elsewhere: she is a woman known throughout libertarian circles and in every jail in France. She lives very modestly, and it isn't every day that she would have a hot meal. From where and how does she gain the strength to sort things out, and find whatever is needed to carry on her support of her Action Directe friends and comrades who are serving massive sentences in the prison system? Let me say again that it is not every day that she would have a hot meal, but she visits them week in and week out and brings them whatever they need. Every week, when she gets home from some jail at night, I am privileged to have her visit and tell me about the meeting she has had. And I say to her, "With the sort of wealth you possess, you cannot live *and* have a bank account as well." Single-handedly, Héliette works miracles and occasionally her adversaries have questioned this. She is how she is by choice, and the same can be said of her friends from Action Directe and kindred groups. They opted for a way of life and activity based on the funding available to them. They cannot be accused of living like bourgeois gentlemen; they dressed like ordinary working people, and I happen to know that one of them felt guilty for once having worn a fresh, very stylish shirt, which somebody took him to task for.

There was a time when I was extremely short of money, living hand to mouth, and then—how or from where I have no idea—an envelope arrived with quite a bit of money inside. I never found out who had sent it to me. Everything that people like Héliette have is shared with all their comrades. Lots of them had cars, lived in neat apartments, occasionally ate out in fancy restaurants, but that was as far as it went; They didn't live like rich people and didn't spend months holidaying in Nice or places like that. Many of their bills were run up on printed matter, basic materials, or machinery; all of it cost and cost dearly and there was just the one infrastructure serving everybody: Italians, Americans, everybody. Nobody who came knocking was sent away empty-handed; it all belonged to and was for everyone's use: those who could pay paid, those who could not could pay later. Very few people in those groups were full-time militants and virtually everybody had a job to go to.

My Basque friends

I made the acquaintance of my Basque friends in Le Clôtre, a place in the Latin Quarter that was run by Pedro Meca from Pamplona, a kindly priest. People who had fallen on hard times used to end up there and that was where I met my Basque friends for the first time. Somebody introduced me to them. They were all living on badly done phony papers, so we made them better ones and they started working with me. There were about ten of them, all living together, under the radar. None of them had a trade but they had plenty of aplenty. They were all refugees and were wanted by the courts in Spain, and among them were *milis*, *polimilis*, and *autónomos*. Eventually they all found work in Paris or elsewhere in France or across Europe or the Americas. Some of them carried on with their studies and made great careers for themselves. I feel proud of them all and I am also proud of the Basques imprisoned in French jails. Compared with the rest of the prison population they have conducted themselves in exemplary fashion. They are far from their families so I do whatever I can, when I can, to encourage them and help them through talks and all sorts of meetings that arise.

One day, April 23, 1981, to be precise, on the eve of the presidential election of François Mitterrand, at the crack of dawn, someone turned up at the house where they were living, knocking and asking for Xabier Agirre, a lad from Vergara. "Is Javier in?" All the Basque refugees were in an outer room and there were masses of people there. From within, somebody called out, "Yes, but he's in the bath." They thought it might be a friend of Agirre's and had no idea what would be going through his head. At this point, this person made for the bathroom, Xabier opened the door, and the visitor gunned him down in a hail of fire. Fortunately, Xabier had recoiled instinctively and survived.

I read the reports in the press the following day and broke down crying because it said that Xabier had been killed. But no, luckily, he had managed to survive and was in hospital. His friends were afraid to visit him, and I sent an Argentinean friend, a surgeon, cofounder with Bernard Kouchner of Médecins Sans Frontières—I mean Dr. Mario Durán. He went to the hospital and found the police posted at the entrance as security and to prevent anyone from visiting Xabier. Mario waited around for a while and soon glimpsed Xabier popping out to go to the washroom for a shave. He followed. Mario entered the bathroom and asked if he was Xabier Agirre. Xabier thought that a second attempt was about to me made on his life. Once he had recovered and been discharged from hospital, I introduced him to Roland Dumas who became his defense counsel and who smoothed out his situation. This was one of the last attacks mounted by the Spanish parapolice groups, in this instance the Spanish Basque Battalion, that were so active back then and which, from 1982 onward, were to adopt the initials GAL (*Grupos Antiterroristas de Liberación*).

I never saw Xabier again. He was a young man who loved painting. I got news about him from time to time from mutual friends and I know that he has kept up the painting.

Another refugee whose acquaintance I made and who is now a great friend of mine is Txaber Gómez. He did a lot of bricklaying work with me. Later, he left for Nicaragua and was expelled from that country for being an anarchist. Those Nicaraguan Catholics. From Nicaragua he moved on to Mexico, only to be expelled from there as well. At that point, he decided to move to Uruguay and there he was captured with his Tupamaro printer friends, all of them close friends and most of them in power down there these days. They all spent some time with us here in Paris and I got to meet them but they must have become suspicious for they were keen to discover more about Txaber. They started off referring to him as my "nephew" and suggesting that he had not gone to Uruguay just to make a living but on some mission from France. They started out very distrustful, but later they became friends. Txaber later came back here, only to be arrested at the airport, but once they became aware of his extraordinary credentials as a doctor, they let him go. He was here for a couple of years working at his profession at the hospital in Tudela and is currently working at the Cruces hospital in Baracaldo.

Josemari Larretxea, who died in Cuba, was a really outstanding individual. He had amazing arms which were of great service to him in escaping the GAL when they grappled with him. One time I traveled down to Marseilles with Larretxea in search of weapons. Every trip to Marseilles had its own story. Prior to this I had gone there with my friend Floreal. When we arrived at the rendezvous point, the place was full of firefighters and police; some guy had just been killed in a café . . . the guy we were meeting.

On another occasion, Larretxea and I went to Marseilles with the same purpose. The contacts were Romani and they looked high and low for the gear we needed. By the time Josemari and I reached the city, it turned out that there had been a bit of argument between them. Not that we gave a damn for we were there strictly as buyers; we didn't care if there was bad blood between them or if this one or that one hijacked the other's customers. The fact is that, by the time we arrived, they had exchanged shots and so we weren't able to buy anything other than one solitary piece of junk.

Later we were both deep in thought on the train. "At best they'll arrest us when we reach the Gare de Lyon, and they'll find only the one 'rod.' And people, I mean our friends, are going to say to themselves: 'What a pair of nitwits. Two of them, all the way to Marseilles to buy one lousy gun!'" The fact of the matter was very different, but of course, we alone knew that. Many times, all we know of an incident is what we learn from the media, and it turns out the facts are very different. Anyway, despite our worries, we made our way back to Paris without mishap.

Josemari Larretxea Goñi was born in Hernani on March 17, 1943, and died in Havana on February 29, 1996. He was living in Cuba as a refugee and must have fallen ill and died there far from his native land.

There was another refugee, too, who was a real whizz in his day—Mikel Azurmendi—who has changed greatly and is very far to the right these days. They tell me he is now a teacher in the United States. He has made some very lousy statements, very racist statements against emigrants, from the post assigned to him by Señor Aznar, the People's Party leader. I cannot understand how people can change that much. Switching from one side to the other, from black to white, just like that. I imagine it all has to do with self-serving, maybe improving one's financial prospects. It's a shame that such things happen.

As for our own side, we have always had a number of Basques in the libertarian ranks, be it Chiapuso or Likiniano. We have always been friendly and solicitous toward one another, being brothers. And I must say that among the Basque refugees we have had our Stalinists, but we have also had some very good people too; I have some friends who are extraordinary. And of course, I've been an exile myself and, for all their shortcomings, they have been revolutionaries.

So, what is the revolution? The revolution is not a Carlist father who backed independence for Navarra, as mine did, nor is it what we nowadays would call independence. But in administrative terms, at any rate, if only we had it in us to bring to society the harmony that it deserves, as we should do, then I have no problem with small countries such as the Basque Country making their own way in the world.

I told Julen Madariaga, one of the historic founders of ETA, that, at best, our homeland might set the benchmark for something that does not exist, the benchmark for genuine socialism. I have given them whatever help I have been able to give, regardless of whether they have been *milis*, *polimilis*, or *autónomos*, although I have not been secretive of my own libertarian beliefs. Make no mistake about that.

Cipriano Mera

Earlier, I mentioned in passing Cipriano Mera, colonel of the Spanish republican army, who was under sentence of death, a survivor of the French concentration camps, still plying his bricklayer's trade in his seventies.

At the outbreak of the civil war, Mera was in prison for his part in the campaigns and strikes of the CNT. As soon as he was freed, he joined the confederal ranks, by which I mean, became a militiaman, but the vagaries of war turned him into one of the most effective officers in the army of the Republic.

He had been a working man and a highly regarded trade unionist; on one occasion when the employers were refusing to give him work, his comrades forced them to hire him. He was a real construction pro and when militarization was introduced, he embraced it and all that it implied and handled himself better than his career officer colleagues. Except for Negrín, the government and the socialists held him in high regard because of his courage and intelligence. Mera was eventually put in charge of the Republic's IV Army Corps and made lieutenant colonel and he saw off the Italians in Alcalá de Henares, Guadalajara, and Cuenca, taking thousands of prisoners of war. He also oversaw the republican government's relocation from Madrid to Valencia and played a unique role on Casado's so-called Defense Junta: he supported a negotiated peace, given that the Republic was doomed, and he proposed the creation of guerrilla bands and uncovered and thwarted the treachery of the communists whom he referred to as "*chinos.*"

He always spoke very well to me about Largo Caballero and Indalecio Prieto, whereas he had hair-raising stories to tell about the communists and their scandalous part in the arrests of IV Army Corps and POUM personnel. For instance, one of his own advisers, Verardini by name, went missing one day and Mera managed to find out that he was being held by a sort of *checa*. At that point, he issued the communists with an ultimatum and Verardini was freed inside the two-hour period of grace allowed.

It was also my good fortune to know Mika Etchebehere, whose Argentinean army officer and POUM member husband, perished in battle. Mika stepped into his shoes and performed very well indeed: Cipriano frequently praised the courage and intelligence she displayed in the field, and Mika had nothing but praise for Mera. I met them both on the CNT's premises in Paris and had the sad privilege of escorting them both to their final resting place.

Korda the photographer

There is another anecdote I need to put on record: my meeting with the man who had the good fortune to take the most celebrated photo of Che Guevara, one of the most intense, beautiful, and penetrating portraits we know of. That man, Korda, was not a great photographer prior to or after taking that picture and can scarcely be compared to the likes of Cartier-Bresson or Willi Ronis.

In November 2001, I had a call from Jean Cormier: "Lucio, are you doing anything tonight? Can we have dinner?" We decided that I would pick him up in my car, and when I arrived, he said, "We're going for dinner at the home of my friend Muriel who lives on a boat on the Seine, in Boulogne." So, we made for the Porte de St Cloud and a fair bit before you come to the bridge on the Avenue de la Reine, we stopped off to buy a few things to take to Muriel's houseboat. We parked down by the dockside, and there were other boats in front of and behind our friend's houseboat. We climbed the gangplank, rang a bell at the door, and out came our hostess to greet us. She was an elegant woman who knew what life is all about. She poured us champagne and told me, in particular, that she had been making arrangements to meet me, having read the book *Lucio l'irréductible*. Muriel then introduced me to the remainder of her guests, at which point the bell rang and we watched as two men of around my own age came downstairs, with two young women in tow. Muriel did the introductions, and I could tell from the way he talked that one of the men was Cuban. We stepped slightly off to one side and blithely starting chatting in Spanish. He was smoking a Montecristo cigar and the first thing he did was regale me with a Pablo Neruda poem with which I was unfamiliar. I replied with the opening verses of García Lorca's "Romance de la guardia civil" and, seeing that he was very pleased with this, I recited the whole thing, albeit falteringly. He sang me songs about war and Melilla, and I responded with one from Bilbao, "Virgen de Begoña traéme otro marido." He was tickled by this and chuckling; it was as if we had known each other for years and were great pals so that, none too politely, as we say in these parts, but in a friendly way, I asked him, "Where are you from?" "I'm Cuban," he replied, and I told him I came from Pamplona. "The city of Hemingway and San Fermín," he interjected immediately. We carried on chatting, and I told him that Cuba had me under its spell and that I had once been an enthusiastic admirer of the Cuban revolution; he told me he had known Hemingway very well and that the latter had talked to him many times about Pamplona and the pleasantest, friendliest festivities in the entire world.

It was a very friendly, agreeable exchange. I pretended to be very knowledgeable about Hemingway, which was far from true, although I have read *For Whom the Bell Tolls* and *The Old Man and the Sea* and I referred to his having had a reputation as a sloppy drunk. My new friend replied that he did drink a lot. Then, in a very unaffected way, he said, "So these days you do not like and are not too appreciative of the Cuban revolution, eh? Why?" And I told him, full of all the confidence I had built up during our brief acquaintance, "Because Fidel has betrayed the revolution. It's all up there now." He told me that this was the line of argument of the US capitalists, and I retorted that Fidel had liquidated the revolution's finest men and *comandantes*.

Then he became edgy. "Yankee slanders," he said, "designed to besmirch our revolution because we are the enemies of capitalism." Without thinking, I blurted out, "Benigno is a friend of mine." This was too much for the man, of whom I knew nothing other than that he had told me he was Cuban; he blanched, started to stutter, and suddenly left me standing there on my own. Off he went to his friends, the two women and the other man who had arrived with him, and I was left somewhat startled and with a guilty conscience.

But soon I could hear him saying to his friends: "This *maricón* (queer) here is criticizing Cuba and the Cuban revolution. . ." On hearing it, I shrugged off the hypocrisy, which I have never taken kindly to, and leaned into the education I had learned the hard way. I strode up to him and shouted at him, "Listen, you doddering old fool, I'm no *maricón*, but you are a Stalinist." An icy silence descended on all present. Nobody spoke, and I was feeling a bit embarrassed but still had no idea of the identity of the fellow in question. Quickly, by way of relieving the tension, our most elegant and intelligent hostess called out, "Right, dinner is served. The table awaits." We sat around the table, but no one spoke, and the atmosphere was gloomy. Some of us got stuck into the hors d'oeuvres, but the quartet who had arrived together, the two women and the two men, touched nothing and soon stood up, dropped their napkins to the table, bade our host farewell, climbed the stairs, and disappeared. I felt sorry and embarrassed about the turn that things had taken in such distinguished surroundings and in the company of strangers. Muriel came right up to me and, in a voice loud enough for all to hear, said, "Thank you, Lucio, for what has just happened.

Can I ask you to drop by frequently and rid me of all the trash that Cormier brings in his wake?"

I was delighted to hear this, but I still didn't know with whom I'd been talking. It was then that I was told that the fellow was the celebrated photographer Korda, and I began to feel more content with myself and with the rest of the guests.

All the other guests knew Korda and were big fans of his historic portrait of Che, but, being unfamiliar with him, there had been no affectation in how I had behaved toward him, and I had been completely honest. But Korda wasn't used to talking to people who were not solidly behind everything that was happening in Cuba. From what I was told, Dorticós (the president of revolutionary Cuba and a very influential figure) was in the custom of going for a coffee close to the tiny little shop of Korda, an unknown photographer at the time. Dorticós was on the lookout for someone to cover official meetings and ceremonies and offered Korda the job. And then a miracle happened: out of nowhere Korda produced that snapshot of Che and became an overnight sensation. I was enthralled by that photograph, and it had my respect; Fidel picked it out as an icon of the revolution and it spread around the world, doing more for Cuba than all their propaganda and printed words.

Which confirms my theory that one should believe in nothing yet believe in everything. An insignificant photographer's name was made with one snapshot that, over time, has become an icon of Cuba, symbolizing freedom and guerrilla struggle.

Henri Cartier-Bresson

One day in March 2000, I got a call from Gérard Mélinat, the owner of a big libertarian publishing house. Because of his great height, Mélinat is known to all his friends (of which I have been one for the past thirty years) as Big Gégé. We went to my favorite restaurant, the Terminus Nord, opposite the Gare du Nord, for dinner and he recounted how, a few days earlier, in a program broadcast by the ARTE television channel, the great photographer Cartier-Bresson had been interviewed by reporters over the course of two hours. After extensively covering his very varied lifetime and *oeuvre*, to wind things up, the presenter asked, "Monsieur Cartier-Bresson, you have traveled the world and met all sorts of personalities of global standing . . . in the arts and literature and politics. Could you, would you tell us now, now that you are ninety-two years of age, where you yourself stand? Are you a republican, a socialist, a communist, a monarchist? What are you? Who are you?" And with that elegance that seems to be a feature of great men, Cartier answered, "Monsieur, I am an anarchist. I follow Bakunin and his ideas." This came as a bombshell as none of those present had anticipated his answer. When the broadcast finished, the station received a call from a group of young libertarians, itching to talk to Cartier. By all accounts, it was harder to get to talk to this man than to the president of the Republic, but both his secretary María Teresa and his wife, Martine, were kind enough and patient enough to accommodate them and schedule a meeting. Out of that meeting came the idea of holding a libertarian exhibition in some like-minded venue. Which is where Mélinat believed that the Espace Louise Michel and I came in. Naturally I agreed with alacrity.

Three days later, Cartier and three friends turned up at the Espace, to inspect the premises and make ready for the exhibition. I had brought in a few bottles of Cascante wine, Manchego cheese, and such, but he didn't taste the wine and cold meats, except for a sliver of *pata negra* ham. It all went off well; he told us that he would drop off twenty pieces, which he would arrange to suit himself, and so he did.

We advertised the exhibit on several radio and TV stations, and I took out a special insurance policy in case any of the priceless exhibits were damaged or went missing. We printed up several thousand catalogues and fifty thousand posters measuring 60 x 80 cms, with the photograph of a man cycling through the countryside with a huge and priceless violin slung over his shoulder. These all but sold out.

But what about a title for the exhibition? Cartier-Bresson, the greatest photographer of the age, the man whose work was hanging in the Louvre, here in the home of Lucio the anarchist; I could not take it in. In the end what we came up with was: "Cartier-Bresson, A Libertarian Gaze. In the Direction of a Different Future. A Photographic Exhibition. Texts by Mikhail Bakunin. At the Espace Louise Michel, ground floor, 42 Rue des Cascades. Paris 75020, from April 25 to May 25, 2000, from 2 to 7 p.m."

The exhibition was a success, visited by thousands upon thousands, and Cartier himself visited several times with his wife Martine and his secretary Maria Teresa Dumas. We chatted about the Spanish anarchists and the CNT, and he told me that it had been a great pleasure to meet so many anarchists at the Espace. We sang to him, and he joined in as we sang songs from the Commune. One night, several players from the French rugby squad dropped by and we all had dinner together at the little Cascador restaurant at 49, Rue des Cascades. The street was teeming with people craning to catch sight of Cartier and the sportsmen.

Henri Cartier-Bresson died on August 2, 2004, in his summer home in L'Isle-sur-la-Sorgue, near the Spanish border. I had long chats with him about the history of France and especially about the Paris Commune, and he talked to me of Elisée Reclus and Buenaventura Durruti, with whose life he was familiar. He was kind enough to allow us to be photographed together, even though he did not like being photographed. He talked to me about his travels around the globe and of some of the VIPs whose portraits he had taken. Much of his work, he told me, was meant for galleries and advertising and he placed no great store by it; but what motivated him above all else and what he regarded as more precious was capturing life as it was lived in the slums and remoter hamlets of the countries he had visited.

Cartier's exhibition and visits boosted the reputation and standing of the Espace Louise Michel, and since then, it has been included in a few tourist guidebooks and its address is listed on nearby bus services. Many still believe that the Espace is part of the Ministry of Culture's facilities, but it is not.

Abbé Pierre

I want to tell you how I came to make the acquaintance of the Abbé Pierre and tell you a little about this priest. People who were involved or lived with him have been lavish in their praises of the man, a real character, a Franciscan who died a few months back at the age of ninety, on January 22, 2007, to be precise. The Abbé Pierre first came to prominence after the Second World War during which he had done his bit for the resistance in the Maquis. Deeply religious, he had never had any time for Marshal Pétain's collaborationist government and was a decent person even then, unlike many self-styled leftists and socialists, or indeed communists like Doriot who became advisors to the German occupiers. The Abbé Pierre was not one of those who jumped the wrong way when he reached those crossroads. He defended his homeland and his resistance comrades, stood for election, and was returned to the National Assembly in the 1950s. He used his seat in parliament to work on behalf of the poor and when he had served out his term, he did not seek re-election. Then along came 1956 and its notoriously freezing winter, with temperatures plunging to 20 degrees below freezing; the homeless poor sought shelter under the Seine aqueduct in the sixth arrondissement, the plushest, wealthiest district of Paris, and people were wretched and dying. At which point this decent man went on the radio and issued an appeal for aid, stating that the doors of listeners' homes should be thrown open and those who were perishing of hunger and cold welcomed in. This man who sought nothing for himself nor for his church breached the conspiracy of silence.

People got up and trooped to the locations where the Abbé Pierre told them they could drop off aid—clothing, footwear, blankets, and money. The appeal for solidarity was a success. The Abbé Pierre has been caring for the homeless for many years. He was also very well known also as the founder of the "Ragpickers of Emmaus" organization, which has branches in several countries these days and which finds work for huge numbers of people in the collection and recycling of used clothing. Most of the employees have no chance of finding work elsewhere.

The Abbé Pierre was highly regarded by all French politicians and could move the public with appeals through the press, radio, television, political parties, and trade unions. In the eyes of the public, he was the most highly respected man in France after his decades of campaigning.

When he felt himself getting too old, he was accompanied in his work by an Italian doctor devoted to humanitarian activity. This doctor had lost a brother during the "years of lead" in Italy and, for reasons unknown to me, this physician had to use his dead brother's identity papers.

Our friend's name is Micael Auria, and for years he worked in a range of African countries with Médecins Sans Frontières. When he came to France he worked as the Abbe Pierre's personal physician, traveling wherever he went. Their association lasted for twelve years and there was a real rapport and profound affection between them. All Auria ever did was work and eat and it had never occurred to him that he might get himself a small apartment where he could live as he pleased. For that he would have needed to have all his papers in order. As far as the police were concerned, that side of things had been sorted out, but when the time came for him to apply for a license to practice as a doctor, the medical authorities turned him down despite his background of several years' work with Médecins Sans Frontières, as well as his twelve years of service with the Abbé Pierre. The medical authorities focused on the fact that he'd used papers belonging to his dead brother, so the hospitals and clinics where he could have been working would not accept him because he had no license issued by the Medical Council. After a while, he made up his mind to go on an indefinite hunger strike, but before he started the strike my friend Louis Joinet called to my home and asked me if I would be prepared to welcome Auria into my home at the Espace Louise Michel. Obviously, even though I barely knew Auria, I agreed, since this request was coming from Joinet, and I saw no problem. At the same time, another friend, a fellow Italian refugee, wanted to mount a hunger strike at the Espace. In the end he was taken into the St Antoine hospital and Auria was advised to mount his strike on the premises of the DAL (Housing Rights), of which the Abbé Pierre was the president. So he did. Auria embarked upon a hunger strike on the aforesaid premises and there was a lot of press coverage given to the affair as well as support demonstrations and, after very many days, a compromise was agreed between the Medical Council and the hunger striker who promptly called off his strike.

However, the Council failed to issue him with the license required for him to practice his profession, so he resumed his hunger strike. Once again there was the press coverage, especially in *Libération*, where the reporter Dominique Simon became the spirit behind the campaign, paying him many visits. I took part in all the demonstrations mounted outside the Medical Council and after forty days of his strike the medical services and authorities decided that Auria would be admitted to the Saint Louis hospital where our friend, albeit greatly weakened, carried on with his strike. The press coverage and the ever-larger demonstrations as well as hospital visits, by the Abbé Pierre in particular, sounded the alarm bells over Auria's condition.

By his forty-fourth day on strike, he was no longer getting out of bed and was having difficulty talking. On that very day I called to see him at the hospital, as I did every day, and once the Abbé Pierre left the room, I went in and greeted him, and we exchanged a few words. Then I said to him, "Micael, the Abbé Pierre is your friend, and he comes to see you every day, so why not suggest to him, if he really is your friend and loves you, that, even at ninety-two years old, he should show his solidarity and go on hunger strike with you. I am sure that if he were to do so your problem could be over within twenty-four hours, including your quarrel with the Medical Council."

Even before I could finish, he said to me, "Hey! That's an inspired idea!" I would suggest it to the Abbé the following day. It would only take a minute. Micael said, "Put it to him tomorrow. I shall see to it that you are the only two in my room."

The next day I went to the hospital as we had agreed. The Abbé was already there, as were others. Also, as ever, there were several radio and TV reporters. Micael was expecting me; he had not slept all night or the remainder of the day. And it was Micael that put the suggestion to the Abbé who immediately agreed. He promptly summoned the reporters and told them, "I regard what is happening to my physician friend Micael Auria as a scandal and I am beginning a hunger strike in solidarity with him until such time as he receives justice. I am prepared even to see it through to the end." Within half an hour, the whole of France had learned of the Abbé's stance and the president of the Republic wasted no time in contacting him by phone to tell him that he was making it his business to do whatever was needed to bring the two strikes to an end. And so, by day forty-five, everything was sorted out. As seems apt in these cases, I believe in nothing, but I believe in everything. Of such stuff was the Abbé Pierre made.

The Bobadilla Clan

It is a very small world. One day I was told by my Catalan friends Carmen and Paco that they had a friend who knew me, that I had worked on his house and that my son-in-law José Luis had worked on his daughter's house. I eventually worked out who he was and was delighted. They also referred to a scion of Cascante and of the Bobadilla family who was a friend of theirs. At the mention of the name Bobadilla, I jokingly replied with a quote from the poet Atahualpa Yupanqui: "No such important Lord has visited my household." I had known that wealthy family since I was a boy. An ancient, very wealthy Catholic family. Not that I had had much to do with them; they were a family that had not done much in the way of mingling with the common folks. They were one of the last remaining moneyed families left in our village, in their very splendid house in Cascante. They even had a chapel on their estate—or so one of the locals told us—which must have been used for family prayers and weddings.

In short, my childhood came flooding back and with it the name of this clan of "saviors of Spain" who had no dealings with the common village people. They must have owned huge estates in Aragon and Catalonia, and they were descended from one of the oldest families who had played a part in the "discovery" of the Americas. All of this was part of the folklore and chatter of hard-working people who had nothing in common with such a family other than that they worked as gamekeepers on its estates, protecting its holdings. That was how it had been centuries ago and how it remains to this day in my beloved village. And this brings to mind those grand families that, to the detriment of us all, still cling to their country estates in certain villages in Andalusia.

When he got home, my friend Paco had turned on his computer to check something about the Bobadilla family and we discovered that it was a Bobadilla who had arrested Christopher Columbus in America, had him bound and chained and shipped back to Spain for imprisonment. I cannot be certain if those Bobadillas were from Cascante or from Andalusia, but we know for sure that, according to the history books, the first question that Christopher Columbus and all those who went with him asked the natives was whether they knew of or knew of anywhere where there was gold. On all their expeditions, it was gold that our fortune-seeking countrymen were after. Some say that gold was the ruination of Spain, but not everyone agrees. We now know that many people made fortunes from those expeditions and not in a very catholic way, that's for sure. The Bobadillas from Cascante and Aragon were dispossessed by anarchists in 1936; their estates were turned into collectives. People worked in accordance with their abilities and consumed in accordance with their needs. I was lucky enough to find this out from speaking to somebody who had lived alongside and worked for those families prior to the anarchists' collectivization.

It must have been happy memories for those who lived through that and who sought to build a fairer and more humane society.

Louis Joinet

There was a time when several judges were on my trail and had issued search and arrest warrants for me. Those were the days when I had every police agency out searching for me by land, sea, and air. I realized that I was "most wanted" and felt really under pressure. One of the few people I saw back then was Liber Forti and one of my safe houses was the home of Mari Patrik and Sonia. Liber Forti knew Régis Debray and Louis Joinet, who had always had an interest in the Americas and served alongside Arianne Musquine and several intellectuals on a solidarity committee that had ferried the injured Liber Forti over from Boston. Forti was still on friendly terms with all these celebrities.

I didn't know where to turn. Joinet was legal advisor to the socialist prime minister, Michel Rocard, and later served all the prime ministers in the same capacity and then the president of the Republic himself, François Mitterrand. At one point, Liber told me, "Joinet is the only person who can save us. Let's go see him." I called him up and he asked if we really urgently had to see him. I answered was that I was very ill and under pressure, so he agreed to meet me in a grand café, now gone, in the Boulevard Saint Germain. We arranged to meet on the ground floor; the first one to get there would be reading a copy of *Le Canard enchaîné*. I was the first there; I unfolded the newspaper and within ten minutes I was feeling edgy and friendless. Nothing there inspired me with confidence; the place was frequented by ministers and was always swarming with police.

I left with my nerves shot and the next day, since our meeting had not taken place, I called him again to set up a fresh rendezvous. He told me that he had kept his side of the arrangement but had missed me. Once again, I spelled out my worries, after which he gave me his home phone number and address, and we arranged to meet on Sunday at his home, at eleven o'clock in the morning. It went ahead. At eleven o'clock I rang his doorbell and his tiny wife, Germaine, opened the door. She may have lacked height but in terms of her life and courage she stood very tall. I say that because we have socialized since. She opened the door, and I asked her if this was the home of Louis Joinet. She said that it was but went on to say that he was not home just then. I told her we had arranged a meeting for eleven o'clock, but it turns out that Louis had forgotten about it. The advisor must have reckoned that I wanted to see him to sort out some problem with a fine or such like. Then Germaine picked up the phone and rang him at the Matignon palace which is where she told me he was and, with me standing there, she told him, "Louis, there's a gentleman here with whom you have an appointment." Within seconds she was hanging up and said to me, "Look, pick up a few things that he forgot to bring with him. He's with the prime minister at the Matignon. Go there and he'll meet you at the gate." Clearly, neither Germaine nor Louis knew anything about me or my life. I answered, "Madame, I am a wanted man and quite ill and I cannot go where you are sending me. I am very, very ill." No sooner had I uttered those last two words than Germaine dialed the Matignon again and bluntly she let her husband have it straight: "Louis, the gentleman cannot travel. He is very ill." At which she hung up. Five minutes later Louis arrived home in a ministerial car. Solicitous and amiable, he showed me through to the library and music room (for he plays several instruments as he has proven to me at parties we have attended with friends and other lawyers). We seated ourselves as best we could, the whole place being a mess of books, stacked pamphlets, and a small space where he could set down a bottle of champagne and three glasses, one for each of us.

He began by asking after Liber, whether he had recovered from the attempt on his life, in that he had been seriously injured and moved from Boston to Paris, a transfer in which Régis Debray had brought some influence to bear. Liber and Régis had met in Bolivia during Che's guerrilla venture, which proved a disaster. Fidel washed his hands of Che and tricked him, as Benigno has told me time and time again. Before Che's death, Régis Debray had been taken prisoner and sentenced to death (it was later commuted to a thirty-year prison term, of which he served only three). The acquaintanceship between Liber and Régis dated from that time.

While we sipped champagne, Louis asked me who I was and the reason for all the urgency. I opened by telling him of my fear that I might be arrested, that I was living on the run, that there were a number of search and arrest warrants out for me, issued by different judges. As I was filling in the picture, Louis was astounded, and the champagne was no longer so chilled or so good and soon I was telling him that my wife and I, and another ten comrades had an appointment with the High Court to stand trial over some weeks. We faced charges of involvement in the abduction of the Banco de Bilbao's director in Paris. I explained how "the lads," the comrades who had carried out the kidnapping, had behaved very correctly in every respect and had been pressing the Spanish government, in the wake of the execution of Salvador Puig Antich, to ensure that no further death sentences would be carried out and that ailing prisoners would be released. All of which was very reasonable and, as one might expect, having set their demands, the friends who had orchestrated the abduction superbly and cared well for the bank director throughout had asked the bank for a sum of money. That money was not for use on a summer holiday fund but was to fund the struggles being waged at that very moment.

As I said, the champagne had lost something of its crispness and I carried on putting him in the picture, as if we had known each other for twenty or thirty years. Then I added that there was yet another judge by whom I was wanted because several arrests had been made in various countries and the record claimed that I had fabricated their documents. Whereupon Joinet asked me if this was the case, whether or not I had forged the documents. When I told him that I had, he grew edgy, for he would never have guessed that the person facing him, a working man dressed like one and talking like a builder's laborer, could be so badly wanted for forging fake civil documents and for kidnapping a banker. The empathy that had been building between us a few moments before was suddenly banished and the feeling grew that I had told him nothing of my previous life; nor had I finished telling him everything regarding the purpose of my visit. We talked for a time about the two cases and the two heaviest charges I was facing. In the case of the first, my trial was fast approaching as he well knew. The press would soon be describing it as "The last Francoist trial."

Suddenly I told him very humbly that they were also accusing me of counterfeiting First National City Bank traveler's checks in US dollars. No sooner had I told him that than, as if spring-loaded, he jumped from his seat and said very nervously, "Governments and all that just don't exist as far as you are concerned, do they? You just do whatever you feel like." Uneasy, he suddenly asked, "Who are your lawyers?" I replied that I had a few of them, and I counted them off. "Christine Martineau." "Good," he told me. "And Thierry Fagart." "Very good." "And Roland Dumas." "Top notch." "And Antoine Compte is a great friend of mine." "Very good," he stared and then he added, "Go away, I don't want to see you again, but I will be seeing all of them who are friends of mine, and we shall meet again." Off I went and Louis told his wife, Germaine, "Have a careful look through the window to see if that guy is being watched. Because, with everything he's just told me, there's no way there isn't a whole regiment on his tail." Louis Joinet contacted the lawyers I had named and everything I am today I owe to them.

Louis is an honest politician, a very rare creature these days. If it hadn't been for his help I might be rotting behind bars.

The MIL and Action Directe

I would not like to forget to set something down in writing about my friends from the MIL and from Action Directe. What I can tell you is that, back then, I didn't know them, and we went our separate ways. There was no connection between us, but after the operation mounted in solidarity with them at the time of the Salvador Puig Antich affair, well, clearly, we were all the same, them and us. Besides, the world is such a small place that we had bumped into each other in the fray and not a week passed without some news of his having been captured, his belonging to the MIL, and then going over to Action Directe—my friend Jean-Marc Rouillan, I mean. There was a mutual fellowship between us, and I still stand behind them all, especially Jean-Marc. The methods he used and the way he conducted himself were very different from mine. I have always been a working man, always on site. They have not. These fellows, like Régis Schleicher and Rouillan are doing a twenty-two year stretch in prison, which strikes me as complete nonsense. When I was in Iparralde last year I told the friends there, and I say it again now, that people like us have been treated well and treated badly, but as I see things it is nonsensical to keep people like us, political activists like us, in prison. I was fortunate in that they gave me a helping hand and I managed to avoid going to prison. I have set up two firms and a little arts center, the Espace Louise Michel. What would have become of me had I spent all this time in prison? I could not have achieved a damned thing there. The bottom line is that I don't see eye to eye with them and the things they did, but that is the way society is, and it seems silly to me to keep somebody in jail year after year the way they are doing with our Action Directe friends.

Jean-Marc Rouillan, it should be said, was in the MIL, the Movimiento Ibérico de Liberación (Iberian Liberation Movement). When Salvador Puig Antich was caught, they were together and both youngsters, in short, novices with lots of complexes. They were people who had never been in any anarcho-syndicalist movement, trade union, or any other sort of organization, but who were up for action and itching to do something, even though they had no roots in the workplace, the way we did. They were something else, something new and different and they went their own way.

A little while ago they granted Jean-Marc Rouillan release on conditional release, he and his partner Nathalie. By day he now works at Éditions Agone in Marseilles, but at night he must return to the prison to sleep. Another Action Directe member, one who these days wants nothing more to do with it, is Régis Schleicher who was in prison with me, my cellmate. Régis has now served twenty-four years behind bars. Nathalie Ménigon has been freed on probation, meaning that she too must spend her nights in prison. Another member of the group was Joëlle Aubron who fell very ill and died. It's ghastly; people with a record of struggle like theirs now reduced to this.

Last November, an exhibition of paintings and drawings was staged at the Espace Louise Michel to raise some money in solidarity with these Action Directe people and their friends.

I think too of the Italian comrades from Prima Linea and other groups who are still living in exile in Paris and who regularly meet up at our center. Several of them have been extradited after all these years and now, just in December past, a court granted an order for the extradition to Italy of fifty-three-year-old ex-Red Brigader Marina Petrella, who was arrested in the summer of 2007 after spending upwards of fifteen years as a refugee in Paris. She has a young daughter aged between ten and twelve. . . I don't see eye to eye with some of the things they did but take Nathalie for example: she was sent to prison when she was twenty-something years old, and she has served as much time in prison. What does fifty-three-year-old Nathalie have in common with the Nathalie who became an activist in her twenties? Not a damned thing.

Mouesca and the Basque Prisoners

I may be laboring the point somewhat but let me stress again the nonsensicality of the justice system. Last year when I was invited down to Iparralde, traveling there was my biggest headache. Why can these people not be sent home, given that their parents and relatives must make journeys of between one and two thousand kilometers just to see their children or siblings? What sort of a world is this that we are living in when situations that unfair exist? I don't think anybody gains anything from it. I find the treatment meted out to these people horrifying because the punishment is being visited not just on the imprisoned offspring but also upon the entire family and all their friends.

Take the case of Gabi Mouesca who has been behind bars for no less than seventeen years. Antoine Comte, a friend of ours, was his lawyer. Antoine Comte's wife is seriously ill, and my wife Anne tends to her a lot. She had a bookshop and I refurbished it for her. Ttotte Etxebeste, Mouesca, and Philippe Bidart all have the same lawyer, the aforementioned Antoine Comte.

Nowadays, happily, Gabi lives in Bayonne. He is a very kind person, and he too has dropped in to the Espace on several occasions. These days he has an important civil service job in the inspectorate of prisons with which he is, of course, very familiar. He took over the position from Thierry Levi who was a friend of Arnaud Chastel's. You never know what's around the next corner in this life.

My home hosts a group of people who put together a newspaper called *L'envolent*, meaning *The Vanisher*. The paper is written by prisoners behind bars, and publishing it is an attempt to encourage solidarity with those in prison because they do not get as much as they should. Some of the contributors to the paper are ex-cons and they all have good things to say about the Basques in prison and how they show solidarity with the other inmates.

Many times, I have wondered if the world can be changed because it is such a small place so I don't think it would require all that much effort. Here we have the example of Herri Batasuna, who may be few but have triggered an extraordinary movement. If there was more solidarity around, it would be fantastic and so much could be achieved. If we pause and think for a moment: who are the groups actually rebelling these days? I see the squatters' movement, the migrants; these are the people stirring things up and moving things along. And in the land of our birth, we have Herri Batasuna, who are the driving force.

Francisco Sánchez Ruano

Let me tell you an anecdote about a Madrid intellectual, Francisco Sánchez Ruano, who is a writer that also lectures at the Society for International Relations in Madrid. It transpires that he has a case pending against the government, but in his younger day, as a student, he was a tour guide and once upon a time he went to this place called Cuelgamuros. On that day, August 12, 1962, Antonio Martin, a libertarian activist, together with Paul Desnais, had planted a bomb as anti-Francoist propaganda. The bomb went off and Ruano's shoes were blown off and his clothing shredded but no one was killed. Antonio and Paul successfully returned to France and a month later this fellow Ruano was arrested. But Ruano had had nothing to do with the planting of the bomb, and just happened to be there at the wrong time, a fatal coincidence. They gave him a twenty-six-year prison sentence, of which he served eleven.

Antonio Martin, someone I see and speak to fairly regularly—he often drops in to see me— was also involved in the bombings behind the Granados and Delgado affair, and he issued statements declaring that Ruano had had no hand, act, or part in the bombing. This was just for the record and in the hope that the Spanish government might compensate Ruano for all those years he was unjustly imprisoned. In November 2004, Ruano traveled to Paris to meet Antonio Martin while clarifying a few things to screw more money out of the government for those eleven awful years he spent behind bars.

Ruano came to my home with Antonio, and we went out for a meal. Every time I went to speak—and talking is, as everybody knows, not my forte—he would correct me, saying, "No, no, that's not how we say it."

What I said was, "Francisco, you are annoying me. I understand I do not know how to talk, but can you see those two houses over there? One belongs to an architect and one to a scientific commission, and I built them both. When we are leaving, I'll point out a few more houses that I built and when we get to my neighborhood, you'll see my house. And I have done whatsoever took my fancy and nobody jailed me for it. Whereas you are only a mouthpiece." I was pissed off with this intellectual because he spent all his time correcting me.

Albert Boadella

Albert Boadella has always treated me very well.

Once upon a time, people visited me, hoping to get some documents for Albert since there was a chance of his breaking out of prison during the uproar about his having been arrested over his play *La Torna*. I did the documents up and we took them down to Barcelona, which is where Eliseo Bayo comes in. Eliseo is a friend of Albert's, having met him through some Barcelona lawyer, a Valencian Falangist. I found out subsequently that it was a French diplomat that helped them attempt Boadella's escape.

Anyway, all the paperwork was handed over and no sooner was I over the border than they called me. I said to them, "You can come home whenever you please." The following day I had a call from Boadella. The message was "Hurry up because the *cunill* (rabbit) is cooked. Get a move on!" The moment he showed up, we had dinner and since the house was under constant surveillance I brought him to the home of a girl friend who worked for *Interviú* magazine, Evelyn Mesquida. He stayed there.

Two days later, there was a press conference in defense of Boadella held at the Bouffes du Nord theater. It was attended by Jack Lang, Jean Paul Sartre, and some other the intellectuals, and though I had some misgivings, I went along too with a number of friends. Out of friendship, we simply had to do whatever we could to rescue him. Since then, we have seen each other thousands of times and I have respect and affection for him because of the very proper way in which he has always conducted himself.

Pierre de la Dupienne

When I obtained a steel-plated door for the lads at Edit 71, I asked Jack, one of the guys working there, "Why don't you run me off some ID documents?" He burst out laughing. I didn't realize, but he thought that the offset press could be used for all sorts of purposes, but it turned out it could not. He explained that there was a printer with the finest color workshop, who was a photoengraver and a libertarian comrade and a close friend of Denis, a retired doctor living in the 20th arrondissement. "You can get the address from him." Denis did come up with the address and he called the photoengraver and made me an appointment to meet him. It was summer and I turned up at his offices, which occupied a single and none too spacious premises, all of it taken up by presses. I asked for Dupienne and was told that he wasn't there, that he was out at the restaurant. I asked what he was wearing and was told he was wearing all white, and I was making my way downstairs when I bumped into him. He confirmed that he was indeed Pierre, and I said, "Well, I'm here to see you about a certain matter." "Yes, yes, I've had the phone call already," he replied. I told him that there were a thousand things we could be doing in Spain but that we were short of materials, color printing materials that is, to which he replied that that was no problem and that he would have a little think about how to tackle the job. When you set eyes on someone for the very first time, you need to bear in mind that what they tell you is one thing and what they actually get around to doing quite another.

He told me, "Bring me whatever you need doing tomorrow and I'll help you out. There'll be no problem. When the target is Francoism, you can count on us." We arranged to meet the following day at the café next door. When I arrived for this new appointment, I showed him a passport and ID card and surprised, he said, "You never mentioned that this was what you were after. I thought it had to do with pamphlets, posters, propaganda materials that needed printing. How am I supposed to handle this stuff? If they scoop me, I'll get thirty years in jail or else I'll be shot or who knows what they'll do. I can't do it." The fact is that—and I cannot explain it—somehow, in my halting French, a ragamuffin like me managed to convince him. I told him that this job could save the lives of thousands who were fighting Franco and then his said, "Come back at one or two o'clock on Friday morning and I'll have it all batched up for you."

I did and they were, all the photomontages. I should explain that the passport and ID cards were ten pellicles with ten layers on each and they all had to be run through the machine; this was precision work and very complicated, delicate work. Everything had to be flawless; otherwise, it would not pass inspection and the document would be utterly useless. When he handed me the papers, I was overwhelmed because, well, who would have thought that somebody with his own important business, who does not know you from Adam, could do you such a huge favor and expose himself to the risk of jail? It was magnificent and such things make life worth the living.

Octavio Alberola

Alberola is a lot more decent than many others these days, in that he at least opens his home to people from the Americas and helps them. The man himself came from Mexico where his father, an exile, met his death in strange circumstances. He is one of those people who pass for intellectuals.

Let me dredge up an anecdote about Octavio. At the time of the banker Suárez affair, there were several teams of us youngsters that had come together for the operation, at which point Octavio was contacted. He had quite a record already, and was quite well known, so we thought we couldn't achieve anything with his participation. We got together and agreed that he would play no part in the operation. If we needed somebody to pick up the ransom money, he could maybe suggest someone, but he himself would not get involved because, even before the kidnapping was carried out, he would be the number one suspect. And indeed, shortly after the kidnap took place, Alberola's name cropped up in all the papers. It was astounding. This is the sort of thing that happens in every group and every movement—the ones I have ever encountered anyway. The pick-up was made, and everything went well and Octavio, who thinks of himself as the old hand, the know-all, the only one who *should not* have been involved and whose name should never have come up, well, he worked around us and took a direct hand in the collection of the ransom. We grabbed him and told him, "From now on you can write and you can talk and do what you please, but if you ever think about getting involved in an operation again, we'll break your legs."

I had a call one day from Evelyn Mesquida who asked me to come over, she had something to tell me. I dropped over to her house and she introduced me to a lad from Bilbao with GRAPO connections. In Bilbao, this young man was in charge of collecting the money from foosball machines and such like. They introduced him to me and said, "Look, he comes from Bilbao, from your part of the country, and needs help." He told me he was waiting for the money and that the organization needed it. His comrades had said he was to get the money and it was handed over to him, but he had had to make himself scarce and ended up at the Porte de Saint Claude. His friends had said that they couldn't join him as they had records. And now here I was meeting him with Evelyn.

It turned out that back home the lad from Bilbao had been given Octavio's address. I told him, "Look, whatever else you do, do not go and see Octavio because you'll wind up in prison immediately." A few days after our meeting, Evelyn rang me: "Have you heard what happened? The police sent for Cristino and questioned him at headquarters about a thousand matters and then finally questioned him about Octavio Alberola. He told them that he had no idea who he was, but the police then produced photos because they had been tailing him." "I told you so," was my reaction.

One day several friends and I had a little get together, among them Octavio, who is tall and well-built, and I confronted him, "Octavio, how much longer are you going to act like a child? You were told to keep out of everything. Now you know what has happened to that lad Cristino. The police picked him up and asked him about you and they have photographs." Octavio replied, in front of all the others, "You have that from the police, do you?" I gave him a slap and sent him spinning to the floor.

PART SIX

FROM THE ESPACE LOUISE MICHEL

Toward a shared understanding

There is a human and societal imbalance with very different and opposing (and I would contend, irreconcilable) social classes and ways of life, because one class is dominant and on top, and the other lorded over and cowed. For all our sakes, we need to stride forward unhindered, demolishing any obstacles in our path. Some will have to try to achieve understanding and solidarity and a shared outlook; others are going to have to learn to accept a discipline, which I find an enhancement.

I have welcomed all sorts of people to the Espace Louise Michel, even the most complicated types: homeless friends, friends with lots of homes, the unemployed, industrialists great and small, people without documents, the marginalized, artists, magistrates, ministers, journalists, bandits, and anarchists like me. It is my belief that the Espace Louise Michel, for some reason that escapes me, although I am sure of it, attracts the intelligentsia and, thanks to this small space filled with riches, I have come the conclusion (which I have spelled out elsewhere) that we possess great potential that we are not harnessing and we ought to put this potential to work and do the exact opposite of what we have been doing so far. Let us leave the assets of the mighty to doze on and put our own wisdom, knowledge, education, culture, and urge to share to work. How can we require from others effort and behavior that we ourselves feel powerless to deliver? How do you expect people to follow you in a fractured, broken-down society without certainty and without dreams? How are we to inculcate into people an education so very different from the one we ourselves received? There is no other option, no alternative to the stark imbalance we are suffering. The price is going to be high, because some individuals, some nations are going to have to agree to be brought low while others are going to have to make a very onerous effort to rise up until everybody's options balance out, until we make a reality of the equality that these days exists only in the form of inscriptions etched into the stone of our public monuments.

Durruti and Che Guevara

In March 2002 I got a call from a libertarian trade union group, the León CGT, "Lucio, as you know, our friend and comrade Buenaventura Durruti hailed from these parts and the León city council, which is socialist-controlled, is about to name a street after him. We've been asked to find some comrade to represent our libertarian friends on inauguration day and deliver a talk on Durruti, and your name was mentioned. Would you be willing to come?"

I was caught off guard by the proposition. I am neither speaker nor am I accustomed to public speaking, and I am not sufficiently conversant with Durruti's life to launch into a talk about the man and the greatest comrade our homeland has ever given to the international revolutionary movement. I told them that I didn't feel that I was equal to the task, but I did know somebody living very close to them, in Gijón, who has done a lot of reading and writing and who had been in prison with Durruti. That person is Ramón Álvarez and he and I have spoken many times and promised to keep in communication.

This was a historic occasion: a street being named in memory of Durruti when, for decades, the mere mention of his name by itself had constituted a dangerous act. He was looked upon as a criminal, a gangster, an armed robber, a terrorist, a murderer of priests, and there was an entire litany of charges concocted by fascists. Durruti had been quite the opposite, and we'll need a lot more Durrutis to make this world a better place. He died seventy years ago, and when people talk about him it's as if he still walked among us.

I went to bed but was unable to sleep as I was thinking about this invitation to speak about Durruti in public, quite possibly the most extraordinary and unimaginable proposition ever put to me. There is nothing logical about my life; that much is true, but you can't compare risking one's life and liberty in rash actions or smuggling oneself across borders or forging official documents with what Buenaventura Durruti did in his forty-year lifetime of toil, moral example, and selflessness. To compare us and to invite someone as unimportant as I am in the dedication of a street for Durruti floored me.

The friends from León called back a week later, "Lucio, we've approached Ramón Álvarez as you suggested, but the Council has requested a modern anarchist, and it seems to us that you fit the bill best." I demurred again, arguing that I did not have the expertise and was no public speaker, but this got me nowhere. They wanted me, so in the end I did it. We settled on a date, and I flew Iberia Airlines to Madrid, where a comrade met me and escorted me as far as León. There I was welcomed by some CGT comrades who brought me to a top-notch hotel, which was booked at the Council's expense.

I didn't get much sleep that night. What was I getting myself into, giving a public talk about an extraordinary individual in the Council arts center with the press, radio, and television there? I decided to tell what I knew and speak my mind: that there is no one anywhere to compare to this comrade in terms of his shrewdness of achievement, his instinct for operations, and his long life, because, as is generally appreciated, activists and idealists are usually short-lived. I also decided to mention Che Guevara: I like talking about him because he is in fashion these days, but he doesn't look good in comparison to our own Durruti. I don't say that to start a sort of a competition between them because no one is any better than anyone else and every person's history is what it is. Che was shrewd enough to switch tack before corruption could set in and opted for death rather than become a bureaucrat. He committed his life to liberation but, for all that I respect and am fond of him, it must be said that he was mistaken and that he followed a different path from Durruti's.

Durruti's life was very intense. Che's eyes were opened to poverty while on a trip as a tourist, at the age of twenty-five, whereas Durruti had been working from the age of fifteen, knew the value of work, and was always "of the workers." In all his operations, it was workers who opened doors for him, and he had nothing to do with dropout types, ministers, or military. The latter are what they are and understand nothing of the poor or about those who create the wealth; self-management is something for the workers to achieve for themselves, without intermediaries or capitalist bosses.

Sometimes I make a game out of looking for similarities between Louise Michel and Durruti and I have only come up with one other person with whom to compare them—Blanqui. But he spent thirty years behind bars, and he was never able to put his ideas into practice. It is my belief that no other authentic revolutionary shared the luck, fate, or *je ne sais quoi* of Buenaventura Durruti. That is why I find there is something very sad about swallowing the portrayals of other people who purport to be revolutionaries but who are the very opposite of that, even though the media would have us swallow whatever they choose to feed us.

If I decided to write, it is primarily because I think we need libertarian ideas and because Durruti's example, like Louise Michel, has to be publicized before it can be imitated. The course they plotted for us—the life of a revolutionary worker believing in a fraternal world of social harmony, where there is no army, state, religion, or anything that pits us against one another and forces us to live in a world of lacking understanding and with human alienation—is the only course open to us. Nobody holds a patent on humane values. They are the result of the direct or indirect participation of very many people, and if placing on record the empathy and love those two friends have inspired in me prompts anybody to turn to some religious or personal cult, that can be blamed entirely on my having failed to get my point across properly or because I've unwittingly misrepresented their stories. It has nothing to do with manufacturing heroes. Neither Che nor Durruti fits that bill. Every day, we all perform simple acts that are filled with understanding or kindness but sometimes we fail or get it wrong. Acts of heroism go hand in hand with grave errors, and when a myth is woven around a person there is a tendency to sanctify even his mistakes.

I sometimes wonder why the world always has to backfire; Durruti and Che are two men who committed their lives to liberate the peoples of Europe and the Americas; they have a thousand things in common, the same mother tongue, the same Basque extraction. But their lives were very different and unless we have a reversal of the verdict passed on them by certain official historians determined to get us to believe in something unreal, a Stalinism that has brought us ruination, the world will carry on making a god of one and a criminal of the other. Durruti stands alone as an example that can lead us in the direction of liberation.

I was willing to push myself by giving a presentation on Buenaventura Durruti because of his ability to move people with his straightforwardness as well as because of the empathy and respect he can inspire even today in very many people who are not anarchists. I keep him very much in mind and his example has been a great help to me in my life. Knowing him and being so close to him must gave been a real blessing. No other life can stand comparison with our friend's.

The Lucio Group

There is more to life than work and burdensome activities that we engage in without any real enthusiasm; life should have its pleasures too. A group of youngsters from Saint Claude, a gem of a village in the Jura region and a place I had never even heard tell of, called to tell me that they had launched a libertarian arts group and that, having read *Lucio l'irréductible* and having seen a number of reports in the press and on TV about me, they were thinking of calling their group after me: the Groupe Lucio. This was a real bolt from the blue for me and I was left stunned and amazed by their initiative. I told them that I saw it as an extraordinary and underserved honor they were doing me. After that, I traveled down to meet them a few times and to talk about what little I know; they advertise talks and debates in whatever premises they can get access to, halls or bookshops, and then there are al fresco events in the mountains and I address a different topic each time. Last year, 2006, I gave my first talk in Saint Claude's most prestigious bookshop, and posters and the local and Lyon newspapers advertised a lecture-cum-debate and press conference organized by the Anarchist Federation's Groupe Lucio, with the backing of the newspaper *Jura Libertaire*. There was a pretty good turnout, with lots of young people especially and the Lyon press was in attendance. As usual, somebody made a few introductory remarks and, again as usual, there was a hail of questions and people were greatly taken aback that the streets should have been filled with posters and newspapers advertising an event featuring somebody from outside the region and a different country.

It was my third trip to Saint Claude, which boasts a rather shabby Maison du Peuple (People's House) that must have been quite something in its day. It accommodates the House of Culture where talks, lectures, and plays are staged, and there is a cinema as well and a sort of a beerhall/restaurant. The town was a center of industry once upon a time: pipes were made for the use of smokers and diamonds were finished for top-class shops and traders. I have been in most of France's major cities, but I have never found as much tradition and history as exists in the Jura region. In terms of social and political life, the region has produced more personalities than any other and it has had an extraordinary impact on French and world history. For instance, 150 years ago, the Jura played a very significant role when, before any socialist club existed, it established a cooperative arrangement for the artisan watchmakers' shops. Mikhail Bakunin was intrigued by the venture and visited the area and, indeed, lived there for a time. At the time of the First International, the Jura Federation opposed Marxism and, as far as we Spaniards are concerned, this was a crucial factor in the inception and advancement of libertarian ideas in Madrid, Andalusia, and Barcelona. And we should not forget the experiment in which the Lipp plant was self-managed in the 1970s after the workers occupied the factory and restructured it along libertarian lines.

I have tried to find out why the Jura region has spawned such experiments in cooperation and self-management. Some have cited the role played by armies and invasions that tramped through the area; Napoleon devastated and brutally torched whole counties and the German and Italian armies have each looted the area at some point. The destruction gave way to reconstruction at various times and a range of materials and architectural styles were utilized. Many districts of Besançon boast an unmistakably Spanish inspiration and style married with the typical Empire style. To explain this, people have told me about the two waves of immigration into the area, a wave of armies and a wave of workers, and the climatic factor: the landscape is stunning but hard going due to the rugged terrain, which poses as much of a problem to agriculture as it does to communications: snow falls for three months of the year and temperatures plummet very low. With people housebound for long periods of time, they eked out a living as best they could; the main earner, livestock, was run along very collective, communal lines and locals were obliged to share their lives and needs and developed a very pronounced solidarity in every facet of their lives. This mutual aid arrangement probably gave birth to the cooperatives, and maybe the thinking that grew up around this experience triggered experiments in human and social reorganization, such as the theories of Charles Fourier, the first of the utopian socialists and a native of the region. Voltaire, the leading philosopher of the Age of Enlightenment who tackled the tyranny of religion, was also born in the Jura mountains. Pierre-Joseph Proudhon, also from the Jura, is regarded as the founding father of anarchism, a great pioneer of cooperativism, and an ideological opponent of Karl Marx whom he openly opposed in talks, lectures, and books. Painter Gustave Courbet, a friend of Proudhon's, was not merely a great artist but also a revolutionary who took part in the Commune, for which he was convicted, had his assets impounded, and was forced into exile in Belgium. And finally, another illustrious son of the region was Louis Pasteur, the biologist and chemist whose many very significant contributions include discovery of the rabies vaccine.

Such is the region where the young people have chosen my name as a way of making themselves—and me—known.

Radio invitations

One of the finest radio reporters, Luis Del Olmo, invited me to chat with him on his popular early morning breakfast radio show. With enormous delicacy and professionalism, he bombarded me with questions about my life, my past, and above all, my family. It was all done respectfully—the questions intelligent and put in a language intelligible to me. Soon somebody was asking me about the Basque Country or the Basque movement, but my answer was not at all to his liking. There was a change of mood and attitude, and things took a rather blunt turn; I felt the same way and came within a hair of storming out of the studio, but we were both intelligent enough to calm ourselves and our interview proceeded.

Later it was said that Señor Del Olmo had received threats from the Basque movement. The interview was just about over when he asked me if I would be prepared to do an interview with King Juan Carlos; I was startled by the question and almost terrified by it. I could never have dreamed that I would be asked such a question. Floundering, I replied that yes, I would take up the invitation, but the interview would have to be public rather than private. I think that was the right answer and it was all I could come up with. Luckily that seemed to be what they were looking for and got me out of that pickle.

In the wake of the publication of *Lucio l'irréductible*, the France Inter radio station also invited me on to a program called "When I Grow Up." The reporter, out of the blue as far as I was concerned, asked me, "How would you account for the fact that you who are depicted in the book as a peaceable, nonviolent type, but champion the Action Directe terrorists and the Basque terrorists?" My answer was that I came from a very Catholic and highly conservative region, Navarra. I have nothing to do with its politics, but I love and hold the land in great affection. The Action Directe activists and Basques are friends of mine and I cherish them, but I do not share their politics. Once again, I had come up with a lucky answer!

Another equally unexpected question alluded to why I spoke so slightingly of Cuba, to which I replied, "Because I cherish the Cuban people, but not their politicians nor the policies they enforce." I was then informed that, just the day before, on TV, President Mitterrand's wife had had quite a different opinion about Cuba, to which I replied, "When Madame Mitterrand goes to Cuba, Monsieur Fidel, or 'Infidel,' indulges her unimaginably, with several carloads of companions lest she become bored; she is a guest in unbelievable, high-security locations reserved for people like her or Fidel, who believes he is the lord of Cuba and behaves accordingly. This woman knows nothing of Cuba, and, on that score, she is an ignoramus, and I should love to have a chat with her to educate her." My answer drew a lot of attention.

In other radio interviews, the questions and answers were friendly throughout. I particularly remember one interview at peak listening times when we finished up singing anarchist revolutionary songs the way they do in schools, universities, arts centers, and cafés.

I have given around sixty talks, but my time spent with Del Olmo and France Inter were the most uncomfortable. Everywhere else I was listened to very attentively and indeed with affection, in France and in Spain alike. But I cannot forget how dangerous professional journalists can be when they use their experience and professionalism on us who have led a danger-fraught, clandestine existence and how they can catch us off guard and get us to say something we neither want to say or believe.

My last trip to Iparralde

I visited Iparralde on the last day of October 2006, having been invited to address the prisoners. I said what I always say: that it strikes me as a waste of humanity to keep people locked up who have served twenty-three years already and that I might easily have found myself in the very same position, and that it is my profound belief that very many inmates, if they were to be given back their freedom, would perform as I have, because I am no better than anybody else.

I've spoken in bookshops, cafés, restaurants, and one *frontón* (handball) court and I found the audiences very receptive.

In June I had a phone call from Julen de Madariaga's daughter and comrade Urmeneta, asking me if Julen might come and live with me at the Espace for a while, in that judge Laurence Levert, who on one occasion had Anne and me arrested, had granted him bail. Julen was one of the founders of ETA and was taught by the Jesuits. It is a great honor for me to welcome people like him and I told him that I kept an open house. And then I threw the door open, turned on all the lights, and waited for him. I didn't know him in the flesh, and it was around one o'clock in the morning when he climbed out of a taxi and hailed us. I said, "Friend, comrade, welcome to the Espace Louise Michel—named after the great anarchist, as you know. I whole-heartedly hope that once we in the Basque Country, our homeland, have our independence, the first thing we do will be to do away with the courts and the police in accordance with the principles of the Spanish anarchists and the CNT."

Friend Julen was pleased by this and told me that he would take heed of it.

Jacques's story

What to do? How to go about it? It is December 22, 2006, six o'clock in the morning, and I am sipping coffee with my friend Javier Cruz at the Espace Louise Michel when the doorbell rings. I open up to the father of one of the local youngsters, a man I see day in and day out. The first question out of his mouth is, "Have you see my son Jacques today?" I tell him I haven't.

He goes on that, "The idiot will be the death of his mother and me. We can do nothing with him. Won't go to school and won't go to work. The headmaster wants to expel him and cannot put up with him any longer. He definitely won't be able to find any other school to take him in. And as to work, the boss had agreed to take him on at the firm because he was a friend of mine and this was my son, but now he won't even speak to me. He has had it up to here with that son of mine and I am paying the price. I'll kill him if I get my hands on him."

Such is the plight of working-class fathers of seventeen-year-old sons who are members of the local gang. There are about twenty such youngsters, all with the same habits and the same problems. I am on very good terms with them all, but I think I am the only one. They often drop by my home, I hear them out, and share my time and lots of other things with these boys whom I find have gone astray and are a real handful. Their families grapple, on a daily basis, with awful situations, but I have no idea what solution I can offer.

Jacques, a tall, good-looking, mixed-race youngster came to see me one day with his hair dyed yellow. I was startled to see him that way, so I asked him if he was gay. I did this to provoke him, because he and the whole gang think they are macho men because they carry out petty thievery on a daily basis. Jacques asked me if I would come with him to see the judge, because he had received a summons. I asked what he was being accused of and he explained, "I smashed a car window and snatched a little radio from inside."

"Why do you so this nonsense, such idiotic nonsense?" I asked him.

And he told me he intended to sell the radio and use the money to buy himself a pair of the latest multicolored trainers with a metallic mudguard.

"You are a nitwit. Why didn't just grab and make off with a pair from the shop, instead of smashing the car window?"

"Because I thought that in the case of the car nobody would see me whereas they are distrustful of us in the shops and know us and watch us from the moment we walk in."

We chatted for a while and I told him that, yes, I would go with him. So, I accompanied him to the courthouse, but the judge said that, since the boy was not a relative, there was no need to hear from me. I waited in the bar opposite so that we could go home together. On the journey home, he told me how he had no sooner entered the office than the judge asked him why he had dyed his hair during the last three days, to which he answered that it had been dyed for quite some time now. This got him nowhere: the judge was very aware that there are lots of petty offenders who dye their hair to confuse witnesses. Sometimes they go dark and sometimes brassy blond, or sometimes wear their hair long and curly one day and become skinheads the next.

"Lest we waste any more time on questions," the judge said, "and since there was no violence against the person, off you go right now. Before the month is out, bring me back the radio and payment for the broken glass. That way we can avoid something much more complicated, because you have a previous conviction, and if we follow this through, you'll be getting two convictions instead of one, and that will make you a repeat offender."

Since I was on good terms with the youngsters on the streets and at the Epace, when *Lucio l'irréductible* came out, I handed out a few copies as an excuse to be able to strike up a different sort of a conversation with them. Many times, they dropped in to ask me a lot of questions, but the only thing they were really interested was learning how to rob banks. I cut them short: put that idea out of your heads, it's a very difficult business these days. It's not like it used to be. The security systems inside and outside the banks have been greatly improved and the police and the courts have completely changed their approaches.

These lads call in at the Espace every single day. In summer it is because they are thirsty and overheated and in winter because it is cold out on the streets, and sometimes they want to use the phone and I never argue or ask about the whys and wherefores of their being there. After several years now, I cannot see them making any progress, but I am mindful of my own past back when we had nothing at home to eat, wear, or put on our feet. My greatest asset back then was my craving for knowledge, working hard to learn a trade and help everybody out, my father, mother, and siblings. These days things are very different. Mothers get some sort of assistance, fathers could not care less, and youngsters go their own way. There is a price on everything, family life included. I find the youngsters I know are profoundly ignorant of the facts of life, not merely educationally but also in terms of affection and solidarity. Bad though schools may be and as difficult as it may be to acquire a trade, they are always going to be an improvement on such a neglected life and pointless company.

On several occasions my radios, cash, and cameras have gone missing. One night a gang dropped by to see me and while I was making them coffee, one of them pretended to go to the toilet, popped upstairs, and made off with what little cash I had, plus my car keys. One of the "main men" sorted things out the next day and brought everything back to me, telling his friends that Lucio was not to be robbed. I was delighted but the problem remains, and I can see no solution. Life does not change, and we have no alternative to offer: the world these days contains more and more wealth, but that wealth is leaving more and more poor behind. The solution doesn't lie in more prisons or in more welfare money; work is the only medicine, and everyone has to get whatever he needs, because I don't believe in doping oneself or that self-destruction is a part of human need.

Those who have nothing may be a minority, but they are a minority around which everything revolves everywhere: and since this minority has nothing, it also has nothing to lose. Lots of youngsters waste their days on the streets, leaning up against the walls as if they were holding them up. The ground at their feet is usually spattered with spit, because not a minute passes that they aren't spitting. The fashion in France these days is to set fire to cars or to garbage bins. How does that benefit anybody? Yes, there is danger in it, due to the closeness of power installations or gas mains capable of doing great damage and hurting innocent people. This is meaningless violence with no political purpose; it merely underpins the arguments of those who rule us and of our adversaries, and leaves those who resort to it that much poorer off. I tell them, the district is your home, you live here, and here you are dirtying what is your own; go and spit at the feet of the prime minister or the people who live in Neuilly. Their districts are better protected than ours and a hell of a lot cleaner. That comes as news to nobody, and everybody knows it.

Not that everything boils down to funding. Only a few days ago, the wife of one of France's best theatrical performers told me about a robbery endured by a young female employee of her husband's and a male friend of hers. They were coming home from work and were attacked by a gang on the steps in the Rue Fernand Renault. Jacques was one of their assailants and he, who hears me out on a one-to-one basis, who is well turned out and looks like he wouldn't harm a fly, was the main aggressor and the one who stuck his boot into the heads of the two young people who had not done him any harm. A gratuitous, cretinous violence that has nothing to do with economics, wealth, or poverty.

We all carry some of the blame for this catastrophic situation. We have all had a hand in creating it, and failing to respond is criminal and silence spells complicity. There was a time when books and entire libraries were put to the torch, and our adversaries' preference was for us to carry on with our eyes closed. More police and more courts are not going to bring a solution; we need more light. I set up the Espace Louise Michel with that hope in mind. We have put on hundreds of events here and held up the revolutionary example of Louise Michel, Elisée Reclus, and Buenaventura Durruti: The Age of Enlightenment, the Black population and how we have treated them so badly, antiwar debates, trade unionism, and neighborhood issues. The premises are packed, but not with our friends from the neighborhood.

Let me end this painful section where I began it. Jacques's father showed up, I was sipping coffee with Javier Cruz, he told us of his fight, distraught and sick, and swore that he was going to kill his son. Suddenly he slumped to the floor. Javier and I helped him up until he was able to stand and walk unassisted. The following day, the lad popped into the Espace, I told him, "You'll be the death of your father and mother. You bad-mouth the police, the courts, and everything. But you are worse."

The libertarian prize

Some time ago I set out to record what I thought and what I had lived through, and this is what I am trying to do again now in fuller detail in what you, dear reader, are now reading. I drafted 320 pages, but I am what I am, and there is very little or nothing of the writer in me. I called in a libertarian friend, and it was she who put things in order and proofread them for me. Claire Aunias, for that is her name, did the necessary edits and passed the text on to Éditions Libertaires who undertook to publish it. Claire was delighted at this and brought me the news. I was very happy myself that it was libertarians that would be publishing my experiences, which was only natural after all. The title they came up with was *Ma morale anarchiste* and the manager and publisher, a comrade, came to see me. We talked about the thing, the manuscript he had received, which he had very much enjoyed, or so he said, and so we agreed to go to print.

Then came the day when a copy of the book arrived. As to the quality of the publishing I can offer no opinion, not being an expert, but I did spot a few mistakes. As far as I could see they had failed to print and proofread about two-hundred pages from the manuscript I had passed on to them. I can say it now, with no rancor of any sort toward anybody, because every-thing we do, he and I, we do in service of our ideals, without thought of gain. The profits from *Ma morale anarchiste* were to go toward the purchase of premises for libertarians as we have agreed in advance. The last straw with this edition was that two hundred of my pages were missing, but as I always say, the media are useless unless you know how to handle them or if we mishandle them. The outcome is always going to be the same.

Shortly after that I received an invitation to attend a libertarian get-together at which the so-called *Ni dieu ni maître* (No God, No Master) prizes would be handed out; my book was among that year's nominations. The ceremony was taking place in a town called Merlieu where there was to be a libertarian festival held over a weekend. I went with my friends Olivier Perrier, his partner, and Marc Tomsen. I arrived at the meeting to find there were many there who knew me and came up to welcome me and congrat-ulate me on the award. We had a meal and some drinks and within hours, prior to the ceremony and the actual tribute, my libertarian friends handed me a copy of the book.

I had done radio and TV interviews but made no reference to the pages missing from the book. After several hours chatting with all those pres-ent, we moved on to the enormous premises where about a hundred tables and chairs had been arranged. Everything was ready for the dinner and for the play, a parody of one of my court cases. The play featured a judge, a prosecution lawyer, my defense counsels, and some others. It was very well done. The prosecution said all that he had to say about my life, about the operations and robberies carried out and there was an army general who also pointed the finger. After the case for the defense had been put by my lawyers, I was offered the chance to say a few words in case I had something to say about all these charges. Whereupon I merely stated, "Ladies and gen-tlemen, I have nothing to say. I am what you have made me."

That was my defense, and it went down a storm with everybody. It was nothing more than the truth and a complete reflection of the fact that I owe what I am, my life, my education, and my life to libertarians. Today, though, allow me a word of complaint. Not by way of a settling of scores, and not prompted by rancor towards the imprint that published the prize-winning book. I simply must criticize them for their childish, and anything but libertarian behavior. I ought to say that I never asked for any explanation. The damage was done, and the unacceptable behavior was in the past.

Diligence: that is what we need, what we lack. Or so I reckon, at least. Which is not to say that we are all the same and all behave alike, but in this specific instance either the comrade publisher is flighty and irresponsible, or he is an ignoramus who has no idea what it is to work. And there I end my grievance against Éditions Libertaires, hoping for a better performance in the future. Which is what is expected of us all.

Allow me to take this opportunity to talk about the libertarian movement, about us, for I hold and grow more convinced every day, that our ideas can light our way but, for them to do that, we must put them into practice. They represent our ideal and stand for the notions of necessary progress, ideas that, throughout history, have raised our consciousness, the practical part of them as much as the utopian part. We should cling to these ideas as tools and put them to use. It is pointless to pride oneself on being against the state, against elections, against religion, and against authority, if this is all merely for show. I am not trying to say that I am any better than anyone else. I do something we could all be doing, and I'm convinced that we are doing very little compared to what we have it within our power to do. It's not merely a question of economics; there are other forms of solidarity. We can all help because it is all there is to do.

These days the libertarian movement has more economic resources than its militants had in times gone by when the *bourses du travail*, CGT in France, and CNT in Spain were set up. Back in those days people cared more about paying their dues than drinking a beer and they would bring out newspapers at a time when there was not universal literacy. Walls could talk and people used to give talks and lectures. These days we are free to put up notices and give talks, unless we play it safe by saying that we have no freedom, as a justification for our own uselessness. It is all within our capability, as long as we have the required strength and gumption needed to help others who are in greater need. This too is part of the revolution and part of the task facing revolutionaries and it falls to those who practice it.

I would direct these reproaches at anything that purports to stand for or hark back to the ideas underlying the history of contestation, with occasional recourse to violence, not always well advised. But, for all that, libertarian utopian ideas are still the ones that have kept us moving forward.

To conclude, allow me to say that human beings are what they are because of what they do, and this is why we must work hard and work smart if we are to have any credibility.

If somebody doesn't know how to work, it's because he never has, and without some understanding of it, all his efforts will come to nothing and will never have any credibility. Remember too that the libertarian movements always belonged to the workers, and we can include the great artists and poets in there, as they were always good bedfellows. For all the headaches and hours upon hours of sleepless nights, we mustn't forget how to behave and should strive for improvement, without arguing the case for the poverty of the past, which spelled death, however creative it may have been. Once and for all let me say that every human being is entitled to have his say and have a try but just because he has all his rights does not make them sufficient because having all one's rights and reasons is one thing, and one's being, handiwork and, above all, capability, quite another.

Neither hate nor forgetting, Monsignor Sebastián

May 4, 2007. I leave home at 8 in the morning to catch the 9:30 a.m. high-speed train from Montparnasse station and arrive in Hendaye at 3:30p.m. This is my schedule, more or less, for my trips back to Spain or to Navarra. Once in Hendaye, I decide to catch the little train they call *Topo* (Mole), the very same train I took on my first trip away from home at the age of eighteen, when I was arrested and sent back home again. I get down from the *Topo* and ask about the bus that will bring me to Tudela where my sisters Ángeles and Pili are waiting for me. We drop my luggage off at home and all three of us head for Ángeles's house where there is a huge casserole of artichokes and ham waiting for us. Cascante artichokes are not the same as the ones as we are used to in France; the Cascante version are tiny artichoke hearts diced up with slivers of ham and garlic, mixed with flour, and then fried. Here in France, artichokes are eaten with vinaigrette when very ripe. Completely different dishes.

I eat until I can eat no more and, at about midnight, I head home. Point number one. I left Paris at eight o'clock that morning and by eight o'clock that evening I am back home in Cascante, without having rested but perfectly safe and sound. Meaning that I can afford to stay with my sisters until about midnight. Years ago, the trip would have been fraught with danger, exhausting, and made in the direst conditions.

On May 25, I go with my sister to Tarazona to buy some shoes, as the ones I was wearing let in water. I've only just arrived when my sisters say what Mercedes has told me: that I look like a bum. I put on a pair of shoes and never take them off. One month later and I still haven't taken them off. I wanted to pick up another pair, but they didn't have another pair the same.

We find Tarazona, which is more modern, though poorer, and more to our taste than Tudela. It is also more forgotten and stricken, especially by Francoism. Like Cascante, like Pamplona, like San Sebastián, like Irún and districts, Tarazona is filled with cranes. The whole place is a building site. It must be seen to be believed. I wonder about the source of all the money needed for the construction work and all these people.

In Cascante, my hometown, where the days I spend there bring me great pleasure, the first thing I spot is the absent friends and relatives who are not around anymore but who live on in my memory as my mother and father do and others such as Martina, whose brother was shot and who lost everything. Her children had to go to the front "for the salvation of Spain." Year in and year out, Martina would curse the people who had destroyed her family, referring to them as "criminals, cowards who murdered men with balls to spare."

I remember one of the trips I made when I was very young, along with that girlfriend and another girl, Patro "la Maña," whose husband they also shot. When Federico García Lorca's *Romancero gitano* was published, I used to listen to it with them and others, and it had us all in tears. We'd listen to the recording by Antonio el Camborio and could spend hours chatting about it, but there were stacks of dramas like this in Cascante and throughout the Ribera de Navarra. I start to speak but then I stop and fall silent, for I have said enough.

While I was in Cascante in May 2007, the paper there carried statements made by the archbishop of Pamplona and Tudela, Monsignor Fernando Sebastián. He was calling on people to vote for the Falange as the party that stood for Christian values. I didn't believe it initially and had to verify it against some other newspapers before I could. It seems to me that the archbishop is the same as anybody ese and, no matter how clever he may be, he has this one wrong. He lacks maturity, but I don't think he is a Falangist. Far from it; I believe he is a very kindly person, but mistaken. I suggest that he make a fact-finding trip to Cascante so that I can fill him in on the crimes carried out by Falangists and Carlists with the connivance of the Church I will escort him to places where, when I was just a boy, my father and others told me what had happened. I can remember Aspra, Urzante, Las Bardenas, and the local cemetery. I will volunteer my services to the monsignor to help him shake out of his error in covering up the crimes committed then, which amounts to a further crime.

I should say, as I have said elsewhere, that I feel no hatred for anyone, however I do despise many sons and grandsons who lost their fathers and grandfathers but cling to no morsel of their memory, the memory of all those who were shot simply for caring about and loving their fellow human beings. They are no friends of mine, though their fathers, uncles, and brothers may have been. Life holds many surprises. I can tell you that, in Cascante, many of the sons of those who were once upon a time the enemy have caught on and changed, and are now dear friends. I continue to think for myself and love life and detest crime. Which is why, when I return to Cascante this July or September, and since there are welcoming restaurants in the town, I would love to invite Archbishop Sebastián to share a working lunch of fellowship and love with me and I could take him into the barrios and other places that live in my memory. Places where, after they had mown down our brothers, they dumped their corpses.

To be specific, our most beloved and respected archbishop of our beloved homeland and city, our beloved Pamplona, I did not have the good fortune to attend certain choice educational establishments, but I have, on account of my life as an idealist, had occasion to associate with some magistrate friends. And those friends have always said that one is never 100 percent right, and this is what has prompted me to think about what I went through as a child. I have come across many examples that should never be called into question. They are so obvious, so strikingly obvious that there is no reason to doubt them, but if anybody wants to question them, go ahead. We already know about the instances of Basque clerics, clerics from our own homeland, being executed; we all lived through it and there is no misrepresentation at work there and nothing and no one can dispute that. The same goes for the many thousands shot in the Ribera de Navarra, our own Ribera. If we believe in saints and if we insist on canonizing saints, these priests and peasants should be placed upon the altar—although I, myself, do not believe in all that. What I do believe in is doing good and shunning evil, which is why, Lord Archbishop, I am a believer in dialogue and in freedom; I believe that our tolerance should be deployed and brought to bear in certain encounters and books. That we should take to heart what my magistrate friends have taught me: that no one is ever 100 percent correct.

You are perfectly within your rights, Lord Archbishop, to consider everything that is known about me, a fair amount has been written about me. I am a miscreant, I am a terrorist—or have been, depending on who was doing the writing—a bandit, a smuggler, a forger, in short, a highly dangerous individual and a disreputable one. On the other hand, to my nearest and dearest, I am the very opposite of that, and my mother used to think of me as a saint. My friends still offer me their respect, affection, and solidarity, and if you, Lord Archbishop, were to ask them about the charges leveled against me and then multiply those a thousand-fold, my friends might say the very same of you. I am all for dialogue and mutual freedom, so I am alarmed when I see in the press that you are appealing for people to vote for the Falange. It horrifies me, for my life and everything I have experienced first-hand in this land flies in the face of what the Falange stands for. No matter how much evil they did, if they were to return, they would do the same. If people like that are around, fear and violence will persist, and we will not have enjoyed the freedom and tolerance required for dialogue in harmony and free of all hatred.

To conclude, Lord Archbishop, with all due respect to you, should you wish to come to Cascante some day, I invite you to break bread in one of the restaurants in town or in my own home, whichever you prefer. We should meet each other and move beyond certain poisonous and perverse places. Age doesn't matter where there is a will and love of one's neighbor. That is the burden that I carry on my shoulders and that I cannot lay down, and if I were to do so, I would be like that great sage, a member of one of the last guerrilla bands to perish in the Pyrenees and to whom I am so heavily indebted. I told him, let's go via Valcarlos, let's go via Navarra. Where I come from, what we call the left, were beyond reproach. The left here did no harm, and none could accuse them of any. The horrors, Lord Archbishop, were committed by those for whom you canvass votes, particularly the Falange.

As I have told you, my desire for peace, love, solidarity, and respect, and without hatred, but clinging to my memories, I send you every best wish, Lord Archbishop of Pamplona and Tudela.

Your countryman, Lucio Urtubia from Cascante.

A short letter to Señor Rodríguez Zapatero

Señor Don José Luis Rodríguez Zapatero
Monclova Palace
Madrid (Spain)

Paris May 21, 2007

Esteemed Prime Minister,
This comes with all humility and respect, not just for yourself but for everyone. Life has taught me that nobody is better than anybody else, although we are all different. In a very limited sense, I have also learned how vast our world is and how unfathomable it is, in certain respects, and, indeed, how tiny it is in other regards.

Allow me to say that although I personally don't know you, I do regard you as somewhat of a friend. I have reached an advanced age and the only thing I am interested in is respect and love for one's neighbor.

I was born in the so-called Ribera de Navarra, into a poor, hard-working socialist family. I followed the path of libertarian ideas, for which I have struggled and continue to struggle. Each of us according to we think is right, we all have our inspirations. I believe in everything and in nothing, and the only thing I am certain of is the limited recollection that I struggle to preserve and retain, without any hatred.

Here in my home, Señor Prime Minister, and with my very own hands, I have built a little arts center known as the Espace Louise Michel. This place is frequented by the most neglected people, the poorest of the poor, as well as by what we might describe as some of France's leading personalities, whether socialists or rightwingers, persons of your own rank, highly discreet in that these people are acquainted with me, and I believe they respect and cherish me but not my anarchist beliefs. Which is why so very many of our meetings are held in confidence.

Everybody worships Louise Michel, the person, but her beliefs are, unfortunately, another matter. Even though I have been poor, my life has been blessed with riches. I am one of that breed of whom it might be said that, if I had it to do all over again, I would choose the very same life I've had, though it was not always very Catholic. I regret not a minute of it.

Señor Rodríguez Zapatero, I have been a working man all my life and these days am aged seventy-six. I worked up until I was seventy-two, and now I find myself in a privileged position because my bricklayer's pension enables me not only to live but to help others. I ask nothing from no one; my wife oversees humanitarian action in the Americas, with a particular emphasis on Haiti, where there are people who survive by eating dirt. Thirty-five years ago, my wife committed her life to the Médecins du Monde, formerly the Médecins Sans Frontières.

Man is what he is because of what he does. Certain reporters asked Monsieur François Mitterrand during the election campaign if he was still inclined to abolish the death penalty, since 75 percent of the French population supported keeping it. Monsieur Mitterrand's response was, "Whether they like it or not, I am elected president of the Republic, I will do away with the death penalty." That was an act of courage, and the death penalty was abolished. Like most people, I acknowledge his courage.

Monsieur Prime Minister, there are prisoners in the jails who should, under the law, be walking the streets as free men. I am merely a humble working man, and that is my belief. And the Basque prisoners, should they remain held, should be closer to the Basque Country. Those are my thoughts and beliefs. You can do it. Do it and your standing will rise in the eyes of very many. It would be an achievement very much akin to Monsieur Mitterrand's. You must be prime minister for some reason. Let us lay down a marker for how a prime minister serves and can serve. This is what

I propose. It was put to your counterpart on the French side and now I am proposing it again.

Without further ado, please accept the respect and humble courage that have accompanied me all my life as the only means of living in peace.

Lucio Urtubia, Cascante (Navarra)

Biopic

I received a call one day from Donostia (San Sebastián) who said, "Lucio, I have some good news for you. But before we get to that, do you have a nice tie to wear?" I replied, "I have a number of ties, from years ago, not very pretty or modern but there is one I have been holding on to for a long, long time." From the other end, Gaby retorted, "Run the iron over it cause you're going to have to come down to San Sebastián where the documentary *Lucio* is screening at the film festival. We'd like to have you here for it, since most of the people we've spoken to or who are in the know have their doubts about the whole story and think it's a complete concoction, that you don't exist. A lot of interest has been generated. And I'd like to meet the man in the flesh myself!" Wasting no time, I went off to the barbershop for a haircut, butterflies in my stomach. This was in May and the film festival is held in late September; by which I mean I was overwhelmed by this unexpected news, and that's what led me to the barber. I felt rejuvenated by the haircut and as I left the shop, and since there was nothing wrong with my legs, I skipped down the escalator at the Pyrénées metro station and headed up the Avenue des Termes to the shops, looking for something presentable, something stylish to wear. I was there to window shop, looking for something for the day or days ahead, and at the first store I told the helpful assistant, "I'd welcome your advice, as there are some areas where I'm a novice. I've been invited to a very important event and am looking for something really snazzy to wear." The girl produced a blue striped shirt and a red tie with blue stripes. I told her that I liked both! I was looking at my reflection and chuckling to myself, for the haircut had made me look younger and I was thinking that I was going to walk out of there like a boy. I was feeling good, and the assistant started to select trousers and modern jackets for me to have a look at. This was the first time in my life that I had spent fifteen minutes in a store trying on and looking at some very fashionable brands: waistcoat, jacket, and pants. To me I looked like an Argentinean dandy from the Pampas or Patagonia; the only thing missing was the old-fashioned button boots, all black and tightly fitting. I settled up with the assistant and it was only when I left the shop that I realized that I had spent four hours there! I sat down on a bench to wait for the next metro and the morning's frivolity sank in. I said to myself that a change of outfit will bring a change of behavior, and I will change and no longer be what I am or what I have been to date, a modern fool. I got on the metro and became so worried about my behavior that, when I got off, I left my parcel behind and headed for home, worn out.

After the news about the screening of the documentary about me—anything but a work of imagination—I must have said to myself thousands of times: "Who has seen me and who sees me now?" Right up until September 22, and the screening in Donostia (San Sebastián), I slept badly. Looking for a change of surroundings in the hope of getting some rest, I headed for Cascante a few days before of the screening. My sister had rented a small car for me, and I was able to get away from it all and from everybody for a few days. I took the car from Tudela to San Sebastián where the friends of mine who had shot the documentary were waiting for me. I must have been eleven o'clock in the morning by the time I got off the local bus in Donostia, and Jabi was waiting at the stop with a gentleman all done up in a naval officer's uniform complete with gold buttons. We shook hands and they told me I should get into the car that was waiting. I was startled and at something of a loss, but the gentleman in the gold-buttoned blue uniform relayed that he was there to collect me and get me to my hotel. Really surprised by this and in a bit of a panic, I made them promise me that nobody would ever find out, and would they ever tell or talk about such a performance. "Lucio, who has seen you and who is seeing you?"

Over the years I have come across some unbelievably strange situations, but this one was one of the oddest. A friend of mine, Joxerra Bustillo, who was with me after we had spent a few days together in Cascante, was also very surprised when he found a few people waiting to pick him up in the largest, most luxurious car he'd ever seen. From there, wisecracking or not wisecracking, we made our way to the film screening, where they signed me in and gave me a pass that entitled me to eat and drink free of charge anywhere. Having little in the way of education but a healthy appetite, I tasted the finest *tapas* I have ever had in my life. I munched my way through heaps of them and I thought it was because of the pass I was wearing around my neck, but I discovered that the waiters hadn't realized how many skewers I had worked my way through. I popped outside for a walk with a few friends only to find my face staring down at me from posters on the walls: "Lucio—anarchist, hold-up man, forger, but first and foremost, bricklayer." And, as in the case in most of the important, unexpected, or telling experiences of my life, tears welled in my eyes and images of my father and mother, the Chicago Martyrs, the Paris Commune, Louise Michel, Pancho Villa, Emiliano Zapata, Durruti, and El Quico flashed through my mind. All of this while several photographers got on with their work and drove me crazy. And after the *tapas* and the dinner, it was off to bed in a luxuriously comfortable hotel room. The next day started with a breakfast of churros, which transported me, although lots of people told me they are not the best and are very greasy. I hear them and I let them have their say but I am so captivated by them that I leave not even one. After breakfast, a big car came to pick me up, and Jabi and I headed off to pick Anne up in Hendaye. Then it was back to Donostia where I had lots of interviews to do; all craziness with as many people around—or more than—during the San Fermín festival.

And then it came to the presentation of *Lucio*, with our producer friends, Anne, my sisters, and a squad of friends from a variety of places. The theater had been sold out for days and was jam-packed and, as ever, I was a bit jittery. The thought that "some have seen you before and some are seeing you for the first time" was ever present in my mind. Then it was time for us to exit into the hall, climbing twenty steps that seemed more like a hundred. The applause was never-ending, and I was deeply moved and highly emotional, and then the movie started. Even as I was replaying in my mind scenes from my past and present life. Everything was well relayed, but it could equally have gone the other way. When the screening was over there was a tidal wave of raised voices and applause that lingered for a long time. The filmmakers had their say and when I was told that now it was my turn, I uttered a few words that I had been waiting many years to say. First there was Picasso's reply to the German officer: "It isn't me, it's you."

Then there was Fraga Iribarne's answer regarding remembrance: "I have not forgotten. I am still here, and my conscience is at ease. Anyone eager to forget must have a reason for that." Thirdly there was that appeal by the Archbishop of Pamplona, Monsignor Sebastián for people to cast their votes for the Falange: something that defied belief and was scandalous.

We spent the entire morning of September 24 acceding to TV broadcasters and reporters and afterward, at the Hotel María Cristina, with masses of newspapermen from all corners of the globe, the shapers of the future, each of them having his say in turn. When my turn came, my answer was somewhat abashed. First of all, I said that I was overwhelmed and was thinking of the day when I had gone to the Elysée for dinner, when I had suddenly been assailed by memories of my father and of my own boyhood; the jail time when we had sat down to eat even as our cellmate was answering a call of nature. I remember being in the Elysée palace and settling on a chair away from the table and thinking to myself that this was no place for the likes of me, and now, here in this topnotch hotel surrounded by all these present and future movie VIPs, I was feeling out of place on account of my past, which had nothing to do with all this spectacle. The audience clapped for me and the next day we gave a talk at the Koldo Mitxelena Centre in Donostia, which was filled to overflowing, and then it was off to Eibar to take up an invitation issued by the young people from the *gaztexte* (youth center). Delightful people. I was privileged to be welcomed into the home of my friend Olaia who lives with another five or six young people. Later we went for dinner at the Txurruka restaurant. As we made our way back toward town, I said to myself that Eibar is a backwater but full of life. It was the first town to proclaim the Second Republic. I asked Olaia if something phenomenal, something inexplicable had passed through. A town nestling in the mountains, where nothing grows other than a few cows and oxen and that's it, and yet, once you see it and gaze upon this backwater, the effect is entirely inexplicable and even magical.

The following day it was on to the *gaztexte* in Irún with massive crowds and interesting exchanges. The only flaw was dinner, which was vegetarian, and this with all the good food available in the Basque Country. The day after that I gave a talk in Beasain in a huge *gaztexte* filled with youngsters before going for dinner at the cycling club. I just hope these foods have something more to them and help spread culture like the libertarian *ateneos* in the past.

I had a couple of days' rest in Cascante and then it was back to Paris, for there was an exhibition scheduled at the Espace. But the calm was short-lived because I had another call from my filmmaker friends asking me to give a series of interviews in Pamplona. I caught the night train and woke up the next morning in Hendaye. Then it was on to Iruñea and a round of appointments with reporters, which bore fruit the following day in the shape of articles about the documentary. Then it was back to Paris to the opening of an exhibition about remembrance, all very professional covering the period from the first stirrings of the workers' movement, the First Republic, the Primo de Rivera dictatorship, the Second Republic, and the Civil War—in short, the entire series of afflictions visited upon poor people—and the struggles waged by the anarchists and other upright folks.

Later there were further interviews and reports in *El País*, *Telecinco*, and *Gara*, and the documentary was shown in many Basque villages and at the Amsterdam Film Festival. That February we were off to Uruguay, the land of publishing, and to Brazil, with our filmmaker friends.

Now, today, November 26, 2007, I think and am increasingly convinced that what we do is who we are. Nobody knows what tomorrow holds and nobody knows why things happen. As I am forever saying, there are those that have a lot but do little, and those with nothing, or next to nothing, who do a lot. Nobody has the solution, but that is hardly news. We can make change by fighting and working, without having illusions. What we do know is that, in the absence of struggle and hard work, the outlook is bleak, nothing can be achieved, there is no manna from heaven, and everything has a price. Not only is struggle necessary, but it is more than that: it is a duty; it is and should be an obligation. We need to eat and sleep as well, but if there is no struggle the enemy just gets stronger.

We poor folks—the workers—are rich, we have always been the ones that created everything. The rich man and his wealth are poor, and their means generate poverty. The United States, the world's wealthiest country, is a pauper; Spain these days is rich because the world's poor, the unloved, create the wealth and send us their children and even then, we would not have those but for them.

Have you changed, Lucio?

As with most things that are out of the ordinary, the question posed by many people, especially journalists in every one of Spain's newspapers (or most at any rate), some of them very favorable and others less so, is whether there is a continuity to my behavior. The usual comment is: "Everything they say about him is all well and good, but what is our Lucio up to these days? For we should never forget how revolutionaries finish up: some in power and the rest surrounded by wealth and the easy life."

I very much agree with this widely held view. They are entirely correct, as history has shown, and I shall attempt to defend myself by assuring people that I have not lapsed into the nonsensical and highly dangerous craziness into which political revolutionaries frequently descend. The practicalities of my lifestyle are there for all to see. I continue to think and believe that real wealth is the life that is an open book, earning one's living by the sweat of one's brow. And I can tell you that my door is open to all and sundry, all day long, and that this is the secret of my wealth: I give but also receive.

Not everything comes down to economics; there is some wealth that does not destroy the human being. I believe that I have no reason to feel envious of those who have amassed great economic wealth because, in very many cases, they have paid very dearly for it. As I see it, the real wealth is what we have been bequeathed by Louise Michel and Buenaventura Durruti, a wealth for which they paid the bill in terms of jail time, deportation, and lack of liberty, all to help the poor in particular and to deliver more human justice to them. Day in and day out my eyes are opened to the high esteem in which both are held, even by our adversaries on the right or on the left who carry on showing them the respect they earned. Both Durruti and Michel died paupers, which I see as very logical. They were both blessed with riches even though they had no wealth and they both died in a simple bed. Yet they live on inside us. What a pity we are such small creatures and can never come close to their moral stature.

I can tell you that here in France, here in Paris, I own one house in Belleville on the same premises shared by the Espace Louise Michel. When I first arrived in this district, there were several houses or buildings being squatted. Now squatting is something that people do not find gratifying and for that reason the district was very poorly regarded. Around here, I have seen people behaving atrociously and courts that were simply not up to the mark. Having witnessed and tried out certain lifestyles, I was confirmed in my belief that poverty does not excuse everything. Being poor is no excuse for raising one's hand against one's wife and children, being poor is no excuse for getting drunk day in and day out, and no excuse for living like nobody's child. And it is as if the courts suffered from a bad conscience. But there is not justice, and what passes for it is a sham, yet I stand by it because I still believe that, if it did not exist, things would be even worse.

I believe having a home is very important; most people who have no house in Paris today can think of themselves as aggrieved. I had the chance to buy mine at a time when nobody was willing to invest in that district, it being very poor and with a very bad reputation. The old saying is that property is theft and an injury to the individual, but I built my home with my own labor, most of the materials I used were "liberated," and it wasn't that great an effort, because when doing this sort of thing for yourself, it's easier to bear than when you are working for a boss and trying to make a living.

I have another home in Navarra, which my siblings let me have for nothing, or next to nothing, several years ago, since I had nothing there of my own. In this respect I genuinely do see myself as blessed and I acknowledge that, but I feel like I earned it and deserved it. True, there are millions upon millions every bit as deserving as me who have nothing, and that goes for here and abroad.

I think I have, in part, answered those people who believe that I have changed or may yet change. In my eyes, real wealth has always been the education of labor, the education I picked up from my family, especially my parents, and the education received from the movement, the only movement I have ever been active in, the libertarian movement, membership of which is contingent upon being a laborer and a hard worker. That's the moral code I picked up and in which I still believe, the code of self-management and accountability. I have been a worker my whole life and I have virtually always been against the bosses. I despise them, but I have also despised workers who were worse than the bosses themselves and, indeed, as people, less interesting. Let me say the same thing as I said when I wanted to set up that cooperative with the comrades from prison: before one can build, one must have knowledge, and whatever we possess we had to work for and sweat for and no manna fell from heaven. Since we are economically better off than other countries who work for us, in certain trades we are being impoverished and losing the most elementary skills. I should say you don't need to have a fortune before you can do much, and that things can be done by lots of people who have the wherewithal at their disposal—people, indeed, with more resources than me.

I am content with my little Espace, just as I am with my home; I ask nothing of anybody and see myself as a free man. Having worked all my life for precisely that. The mayor of Paris sent me two or three thousand francs once with a proposal that the Espace be run jointly with the city council. I thanked him but said that it was called the Espace Louise Michel for a reason.

Money I neither burn nor tear up because it is vital if a whole host of things are to get done and made. How delightful it would be if we could set up one or several sites as libertarian ateneos or restore some pretty little church as an arts center and name it after Durruti or Louis Michel, or a place open to all, a house of understanding! For the moment I live my life as a free man. My life now has nothing to do with the life I lived as a child, though that is not the reason I think of myself as being wholly free.

IN CONCLUSION

To finish, allow me to say yet again what I always say: my life is unfathomable, sheer luck, sheer coincidence, sheer happenstance, sheer fluke. My life does not belong to me. Nothing belongs to me. And the people who have had a hand in it and who have helped me along have been many. I have done a lot with courage and stamina, driven on by my libertarian self-managerial ideals, as well as with a modicum of intelligence, albeit that I am no academic.

I relish the life I lead these days, but I have not forgotten my starveling past. There are men with a lot who are impoverished and men with very little who should be counted among the wealthy. Our means are no good to us unless we put them to use.

The wheel just keeps on turning and to everything there is a season: utopia included. For the sake of progress, all must be free; this may entail enormous drawbacks because freedom is never easy, but such is life, and it will eventually deliver our emancipation.

AK PRESS is small, in terms of staff and resources, but we also manage to be one of the world's most productive anarchist publishing houses. We publish close to twenty books every year, and distribute thousands of other titles published by like-minded independent presses and projects from around the globe. We're entirely worker-run and democratically managed. We operate without a corporate structure—no boss, no managers, no bullshit.

The **FRIENDS OF AK PRESS** program is a way you can directly contribute to the continued existence of AK Press, and ensure that we're able to keep publishing books like this one! Friends pay $25 a month directly into our publishing account ($30 for Canada, $35 for international), and receive a copy of every book AK PRESS publishes for the duration of their membership! Friends also receive a discount on anything they order from our website or buy at a table: 50% on AK titles, and 30% on everything else. We have a Friends of AK ebook program as well: $15 a month gets you an electronic copy of every book we publish for the duration of your membership. *You can even sponsor a very discounted membership for someone in prison.*

Email **friendsofak@akpress.org** for more info, or visit the website: **https://www.akpress.org/friends.html**.

There are always great book projects in the works—so sign up now to become a Friend of AK Press, and let the presses roll!